The What, Where, When, How & Why
Of Gardening In Louisiana

Louisiana GARDENER'S GUIDE

DAN GILL
JOE WHITE

COOL SPRINGS PRESS

Gill, Dan and White, Joe
Louisiana Gardener's Guide: the what, where, when, how & why of gardenin in Louisiana / Dan Gill and Joe White

p. cm.
Includes bibliographical references (p.) and index.
ISBN 1-888608-33-1
1. Landscape plants -- Louisiana 2. Landscape gardening -- Louisiana
3. Gardening -- Louisiana I. Title
635.9--dc20
Gil/Whi

Cool Springs Press, Inc.
206 Bridge Street
Franklin, Tennessee 37064

First printing 1997
Printed in the United States of America
10 9 8 7 6 5 4 3 2 1

On the cover (clockwise from top left): Camellia, Louisiana Iris, Pineapple Guava, Yellow Floribunda Rose

Map (p. 8) provided by Agricultural Research Service, USDA

Visit the Cool Springs Press website at: www.coolspringspress.com

DEDICATION

Gardens of joy, fragrant flowers.
Sunlight shining through the trees,
A parent's love, there are no words
To thank for treasures such as these.

TO MY PARENTS, LUTHER AND BILLYE, whose love of gardening is a constant inspiration to me.

—Dan Gill

THIS BOOK IS DEDICATED TO THE RESIDENTS of Louisiana who are first-time gardeners and to those who have moved to Louisiana from other states or countries with different climates and who find adjusting to the gardening techniques and the vast array of plant materials that grow here a bit overwhelming.

—Joe White

ACKNOWLEDGMENTS

THE ASSISTANCE AND ADVICE of friends, family, and horticulturists is hereby recognized:

Tommy Smith	Shreveport horticulturist who made suggestions for plants to include.
Mark Woodall	Barnwell greenhouse staff, for assistance with plant selection.
Michael Kromer	Executive Director, American Rose Society, for review of rose chapter text.
Leonard Veazey	Grounds Supervisor at American Rose Center, for review of rose chapter text.
Preston Friedley	Executive Director, Shreveport-Bossier Convention and Tourist Bureau, for assistance in securing list of state's public gardens and arboreta.
My family	Including my wife, Barbara White, daughter, Barzanna White, and father-in-law Charles F. "Buck" Williams, all of whom were supportive of my efforts and did extra household, garden, and yard duties to give me more time for the writing.

—Joe White

Dr. Severn Doughty	For his input on palms and for showing me what it means to be an outstanding horticultural educator.
The New Orleans Botanical Garden Volunteers	Whose friendship and dedication have taught me much about the love of gardening.

—Dan Gill

CONTENTS

INTRODUCTION

Gardening in Louisiana

GREAT! YOU MUST HAVE AN INTEREST IN GARDENING, or you wouldn't be thinking about buying this book . . . or if it was a gift, you wouldn't be thumbing through it now. It appears that you are serious about gardening and want your garden to at least turn out "nice." "Better-than-average" would be even more desirable, right? Want to shoot for "outstanding" or "spectacular"? We think you're on the right track by consulting this book, because successful Louisiana gardeners commonly begin by accumulating information on their subject.

Louisiana is a state of varied and wonderful gardening worlds. From the humid south to the cooler north . . . from the clay-like soils of the Red River to the acid soils of the coastal plains . . . from the formal gardens that are a legacy of the French to the more naturalistic gardens that are a contribution of the English . . . gardeners in Louisiana face different and challenging styles and environments.

Gardening in Louisiana can certainly be a challenge, but it is not without its rewards. For one thing, it is good for your health. Consider the wonderful physical exercise it provides. There is also a direct benefit to mental health. We all feel better when at home busying ourselves with gardens and all of their needs. Plant therapy is recognized as one of the most effective means by which a person under stress can "unwind."

Gardening also provides an opportunity to be creative, using a variety of plants to create a colorful three-dimensional picture that changes with the seasons. Gardening has also long been recognized as a wonderful way to expand friendships. All over Louisiana are garden clubs, and plant societies that offer opportunities to share interests with other gardeners.

Gardening Considerations

Several major factors should be evaluated when determining the type and size of gardens that you will tend. The temperatures you receive in the area in which you live, the amount of sunlight available to your property, the types of soils in your potential planting sites, and your own resources—of time, energy and money will affect your gardening decisions. We will discuss these constraints and how to best use them to determine the garden that is right for you.

Climate Affects Gardening

The hardiness of a plant refers to how much cold it will endure; hardy plants can tolerate temperatures below freezing without significant injury. There are degrees of hardiness. A plant that can tolerate temperatures down to 15 degrees Fahrenheit is not as hardy as a plant that will tolerate a temperature of 0 degrees. "Tender" is the term used for those plants that cannot survive temperatures below freezing without significant injury or even death. The United States Department of Agriculture (USDA) has divided the nation into various zones (Zone 3, coldest, to Zone 10, warmest) based on the minimum temperatures areas usually experience in winter. Knowing the zones a plant is hardy in helps gardeners avoid planting species that will not survive their winters. In this book, the southernmost zone in Louisiana a plant is likely to be successful in is indicated. This is of particular concern to us, as many plants cannot tolerate the hot summers and mild winters of the South.

Louisiana has only two zones, 8 and 9. Since this book is written exclusively for Louisiana gardeners, only these zones are indicated in the plant information, although many of the plants can be grown successfully further north. Virtually all of the plants included in this book will thrive throughout the state. A few, such as bearded irises, will generally do better in northern Louisiana. Others, such as some of the palms and tropicals, are better suited to the southern part of the state.

Northern Louisiana (Zone 8) has about 50 inches of annual rainfall and a growing season that stretches from late March until nearly mid-November. Typically, the spring and late-fall periods have better "growing" temperatures for plants; in summer, temperatures may soar into the 90s (Fahrenheit) for days on end. And unlike the spring and fall seasons during which rainfall is generally

USDA HARDINESS ZONE MAP

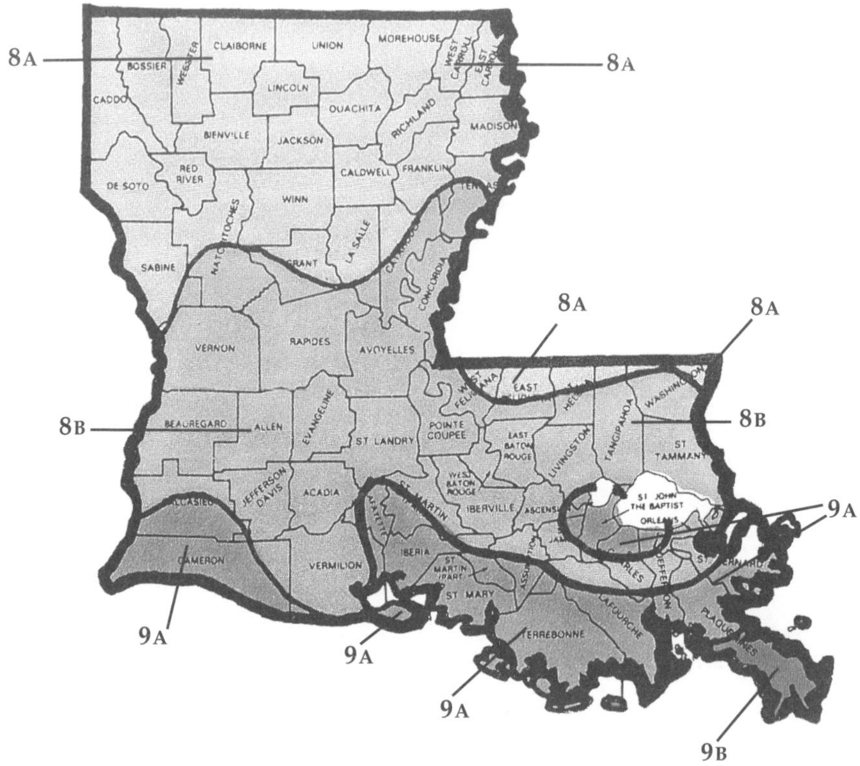

AVERAGE ANNUAL MINIMUM TEMPERATURE

8A	15° F TO 10° F
8B	20° F TO 15° F
9A	25° F TO 20° F
9B	30° F TO 25° F

adequate, extremely dry conditions can predominate in the summer months, particularly in the late summer months of August and September. The winter season is marked by many cloudy or overcast days and considerable rain that is triggered by weather systems or fronts moving out of the Midwest. Temperatures at this time of year are mildly cold, usually in the 40s and 50s, with only brief periods of freezing and sub-freezing temperatures. Rarely do these freezes last more than two or three days at a time, and temperatures in the teens usually occur only a few times throughout the entire winter season.

Those who garden in the warmer zone (9) in south and central Louisiana will experience more of the subtropical-type weather that makes it possible to grow several plants that would not survive winters further north. This zone may receive 15 to 20 inches more rainfall per year than north Louisiana. In addition, the rainfall tends to be more widely distributed over the entire 12 months of the year, so drought conditions are less common. Southern Louisiana gardeners enjoy a year-round growing season. Winter temperatures of the southern parishes are milder than in the northern part of the state and will generally range from the 40s through the 60s, with a few days of even warmer temperatures. Although temperatures have on occasion been recorded in the mid- and low teens in the southern areas, these are relatively rare and seldom last very long. Summer temperatures in south Louisiana, consistently in the 90s, seem less intense due to the high humidity, but the sultry, muggy atmosphere is not exactly pleasant.

Gardeners are invariably an adventurous lot and enjoy trying to grow plants that are unfamiliar to them, or plants they have been told will not grow in their areas. By taking advantage of microclimates in their landscapes and providing special care when necessary, gardeners can sometimes be successful in these adventures. Do limit your experiments (and you should experiment to your heart's content) to small plantings, and use reliable, proven plants for major plantings.

Introduction

Sunlight Affects Gardening

In this guide you will find important information on light requirements for individual plants. If a plant is recommended for a shade or semi-shade location, it is important that the plant be given such a situation. Plants that require full sun rarely do well, almost never bloom, and generally do not last too long if placed in heavy shade. While some plants can partially adjust in time to less-than-ideal light conditions, most will be lost.

Let's look at this light requirement in a more detailed way, for it is one of the most important factors in growing plants successfully. Plants are literally "solar-powered organisms"—they use the energy in light to manufacture the food they need to grow. Light is as important to them as the food you eat is to you. It is essential to locate plants in areas that provide sufficient light for them to do their best.

Some plants evolved in shady, low-light environments under the canopies of trees, and they need only moderate amounts of light to be healthy. Others evolved in the full sun of meadows or deserts and must have abundant light to grow properly. In this book, we have used the terms full sun, part sun, part shade, and shade to describe the amount of light that various plants need. If you're a bit unsure of what these terms mean, these guidelines should help.

Full sun: 8 hours or more of direct sun

Part sun: about 6 hours of direct sun
Part shade: about 4 hours of direct sun

Shade: about 2 hours of direct sun

Full-shade areas, which receive no direct sun at any time during the day, are not especially common in most landscapes. When present, they require careful selection of plants that will tolerate such limited light.

Soil Type Affects Gardening

The kind of soil used by a gardener often determines how the gardening is done and what kind of plants can be successfully grown. The part of the state you live in determines the kind of soil you have to use. Due to differences of origin and other properties of the environment, the soils of Louisiana have been divided into seven groups or areas. These are (1) the gently sloping to hilly coastal plains soils, (2) the southern Mississippi Valley loessial uplands soils, (3) the flatwoods soils, (4) the coastal prairies soils, (5) the Mississippi River alluvial soils, (6) the Red and Ouachita Rivers alluvial soils, and (7) the coastal marshlands soils. In general, the coastal plains soils will contain more of the acid-type soils with moderate to low fertility levels. This soil area accounts for around 50 to 60 percent of northern Louisiana, primarily the western two-thirds of that area. The soils found here are usually quite responsive to fertilizers and other amendments and can become quite acceptable for gardening purposes.

The alluvial soils that border the Red River as it courses through the state from northwest to southeast are generally very fertile but quite alkaline and often contain substantial amounts of clay, making them difficult to cultivate or work. Properly handled, you can grow just about anything in them except acid-soil plants. The loessial soils and the alluvial soils that border or are close to the Mississippi River are usually of moderate to high fertility, but their pH can range from moderately acid to moderately alkaline. These also are great for gardening.

Alluvial soils that border the Ouachita River tend to be dependable for productive gardening; other soil areas have many soil types that are suitable for gardening as well. But for specific information on soils anywhere in the state, it's best to consult with the local agricultural agencies for advice about how to use or improve them.

In order to make the best use of what you have in the way of native soil, beds must be thoroughly prepared and amended with a variety of materials to improve their physical and chemical properties. In some instances, it may even be necessary to "import" some soil of a better quality and grow your plants on a raised bed made of it.

SOIL TESTS ARE IMPORTANT

It is in the best interest of the gardener to monitor his or her garden soil by testing it every two or three years. It is virtually impossible to look at a soil and tell very much about its chemistry, but we can feel the soil and get some idea of its texture. Numerous firms across the nation test soils for whatever information is needed, but the cost is usually less when the testing is done by your state university. The LSU Agricultural Center operates a soil-testing laboratory and currently processes samples in a routine analysis for a four-dollar fee; add a dollar to get a reading on the content of organic matter.

If you are using this service, first collect soil samples from several spots in the area to be tested. These samples should represent the top 6 or 8 inches of soil in the area of interest. All the sub-samples collected from the test area should be mixed together into a homogenous blend, and one pint of that blend should be taken to your nearest or most convenient Louisiana Cooperative Extension Service office. Remember, there's one in each parish.

When you receive the soil-test report, usually in about three weeks, you will know what's in the soil and will have instructions for correcting any element deficiencies. Any time you have a question or difficulty in interpreting the report, just call your county agent. He or she will have a copy of your report and will be able to assist you in determining the steps you must take to increase the productivity of your soil to obtain peak plant performance.

AMENDMENTS ENHANCE SOILS

Amendments are those materials we add to soils to improve them, not including regular fertilizers. Often a soil is too acidic and we must incorporate lime to reduce its acidity; in other cases, an alkaline soil may require sulfur to reduce its alkalinity. Compost is frequently mixed in garden soils and beds to increase the amount of organic matter that eventually becomes humus. Also used are less-decomposed forms of organic materials such as dried lawn clippings, old hay, grain straw, gin trash, and bagasse. These forms that have a way to go before reaching a full state of decomposition may be incorporated with small amounts of fertilizer to speed decomposition along and to prevent stunting and off-colors in the plants.

WHY USE MULCHES?

Gardeners who have not discovered mulches are wasting a lot of unnecessary time and energy that could be devoted to other, more productive, chores. Mulches come in both organic and inorganic forms, but we advocate use of the organic type since these can eventually be incorporated into the soil of the bed as an amendment. Materials commonly used include bagasse, rice hulls, pine bark in various-sized chips, old hay, pine straw, shredded cypress bark, shredded paper, pea gravel, marble chips, volcanic nuggets, black plastic, and landscape fabric—and we're quite sure there are others. While black plastic is extensively used in vegetable gardens, we believe it's a poor choice for landscape use. To be effective, organic mulches must be of sufficient depth to exclude all or practically all sunlight. For most materials, a three- to four-inch depth is required.

What exactly are the benefits of using a mulch? There are several. Mulches suppress weeds that would compete with your flowers and other plants, they insulate the soil (and your plants' root systems) against temperature extremes, they conserve moisture, they give a dressier appearance to the bed, and they keep the featured plants clean. On sloping sites they deter soil erosion from between the plants. Check out the mulches that are available to you in your locale.

We have been told that the use of bagasse (sugar cane residues) as a mulch helps keep cats out of flower beds. You may want to investigate this for yourself if you have a problem of that kind.

UNDERSTANDING FERTILIZERS

Plants are just like any other living organism: they require some basic substances in order to maintain life. Botanists, horticulturists, and other scientists have learned that most higher plants need rather hefty quantities of carbon, hydrogen, and oxygen, which are primarily supplied by air and water, along with nitrogen, phosphorus, and potassium, which are available in the soil (until they run out, for whatever reason). These last three are referred to as major elements or macro-elements. They are, by law, listed on any container of fertilizer, whatever its shape or size.

The percentage figures (for example, 10-10-10) are known as the analysis of a fertilizer. As we read from left to right, nitrogen (N) is the left-hand figure, phosphorus (P) is the middle number, and potassium (K) is on the right. These numbers are percentage figures, not actual amounts of material. Thus, if nitrogen is given as 10, the amount is 10 pounds if the container holds 100 pounds of material, but only 5 pounds if the container is a 50-pound sack, and only 2 pounds if it is packaged in a 20-pound box. Sulfur, magnesium, and calcium are considered secondary elements; though important, they are not needed in such large amounts. Although sulfur may be included in some containers of complete fertilizers, it and the other secondary materials are usually purchased separately.

There is a host of minor or "trace" elements that most plants require in very minute amounts. These elements may only occasionally have to be added to the garden soil. There are trace-element mixes commercially available.

While granular-type fertilizers are generally the most common form, soluble plant foods (usually, but not always dry powders designed for mixing with water) are popular with many gardeners and slow-release (also called "timed release" and "controlled release") fertilizers are rapidly increasing in favor among gardeners despite their slightly higher cost.

Whatever type you use, make sure it suits the plant you are growing. When foliage is the dominant feature of the plant, choose a product that has a relatively high amount of nitrogen, preferably of two types—one that will be immediately available to the plant while the other gradually becomes available. If your plants are grown for their pretty blossoms or fruits, choose a fertilizer that has intermediate to low nitrogen content, but moderate to heavy amounts of phosphorus and potassium unless a soil test reveals that these are already present in adequate quantities.

BASIC BED PREPARATION

A bed is a designated area used to grow plants other than turfgrass (areas of turfgrass are called lawns). Most annuals, perennials, bulbs, groundcovers, and shrubs are planted in beds. Some plants, such as trees and specimen shrubs, are generally planted into individual planting holes in lawns rather than into beds. The soil of beds is usually improved in some way to enhance the growth of the plants planted into them. Whenever there is any question about the sufficiency of drainage, construct a raised planting surface. Even a six- to eight-inch rise above the surrounding ground can work wonders. Use seed catalogs or other sources to check mature plant height. Plant the taller-growing plants at the rear of border beds and at the center of island beds; place those expected to be the shortest in the front of such beds. Lay out curved bed edges with a warm piece of garden hose—if your first design is unacceptable, it's much easier to move a hose than to re-dig an area. Beds with deep curves are often more satisfying since it takes your eyes longer to explore their contents. Use flowers of pastel colors in small areas to make the space appear larger; intense reds, oranges, and yellows have the opposite effect. There are several steps to basic bed preparation.

1. Remove unwanted vegetation. This might mean taking up existing turf to create a new bed, or just cleaning out weeds that have grown in an existing bed. Do a thorough job. If you

are removing weeds by hand, get the roots and all. It is often helpful to use a systemic herbicide such as glyphosate or Finale®, especially on difficult-to-control weeds such as nut grass, Bermudagrass, oxalis, and others. Follow label directions carefully.

2. Turn the soil to a depth of 8 to 10 inches with a shovel, spade, or turning fork.
3. Add amendments to improve the soil. Always add a two- to three-inch layer of organic matter. Compost is best, but other suitable materials include peat moss and rotted manure. If the soil is heavy, finely ground pine bark is excellent for improving drainage. One to two inches of coarse sand may also be applied to heavy clay soils to improve water penetration and drainage. If the pH is too low, lime may be added at this stage. To lower a pH that is too high, sulfur, copperas, or aluminum sulfate may be applied. Finally, improve the fertility of the soil with the addition of a fertilizer, generally one with a 1:1:1 ratio, such as 8-8-8 at 1 cup per 30 square feet of bed area. In some areas of the state, soil phosphorus is naturally very high and fertilizers with a 3:1:2 ratio (such as 15-5-10 at 1/2 cup per 30 square feet of bed area) would be more appropriate. A soil test is tremendously helpful in determining the types of amendments that would benefit your soil.
4. Thoroughly incorporate and blend the amendments into the existing soil.
5. Rake the bed and shape the sides. You will find the bed is slightly raised above the surrounding soil level; this will improve drainage and is desirable. Now you're ready to plant.

Bed preparation is one of the most arduous parts of gardening, and gardeners are often tempted to skip it or to minimize their efforts. Remember, how well plants grow depends directly on the effort you put into preparing a bed for them. If you do a good job, you can in good conscience tell your plants, "I made your bed, now grow in it."

Water Supply Affects Gardening

You can look out over the state's surface from an airplane and see that presently there is no shortage of water. You will see lake after lake, several rivers, many bayous, ponds, and a good many swamps as well. All this surface water means high water tables that can lead to problems when trying to grow certain plants. Water quality can be a problem. Both wells and municipal water supplies are very alkaline in much of north Louisiana, and the Red River is salty. The salty river water is not suitable for most plants and the alkaline well and municipal water can adversely affect sensitive acid-soil plants such as azaleas, camellias, gardenias, and dogwoods.

Fortunately, a moisture-laden stream of air moves up across the state from the Gulf of Mexico for much of the year and keeps most surface bodies of water charged with water of acceptable quality. Water from these sources is great for garden use. If a surface water source is not convenient, you will have to use whatever water is available. Catching rainwater in barrels or buckets for use with sensitive plants is a practice used by a few gardeners who have small gardens and who have water that is unsuitable for the plants they grow.

There are a number of variables to consider when determining water needs: soil type and slope, humidity, density and type of plants grown, weather, season, light intensity, wind, temperature, and mulches. These factors determine how much and how often plantings need to be irrigated. Gardeners know that there are many times every year when extra water is needed to keep the garden plants vigorous, healthy, and attractive. Irrigation water can be provided to supplement inadequate rainfall during the growing season. In our climate, this is an occasional rather than a constant need.

The ideal garden soil absorbs nearly all the water that falls on it, holds a large quantity in its fine pores, and allows any excess to drain away, leaving ample air-filled spaces. Light-textured or sandy soils allow excellent water penetration and drainage but hold and store less water, so frequent watering is required. Heavy-textured or clay soils have poorer water penetration, drain slowly, and hold more water. Water management is more difficult with these soils. Watering too much can drown roots, and allowing clay soil to become too dry inhibits water penetration.

Soil textures can be determined with soil testing. Adding organic matter to either type of soil improves the situation: it increases the water-holding capacity of sandy soils and the porosity of clay soils, allowing more air and water to enter.

When you water, water thoroughly; then allow the soil to dry out a little before the next watering. Learn to evaluate the condition of your soil and plants so you will know when you need to water again. Timing depends primarily on temperature, rainfall, humidity, season, and plant material. If you water thoroughly and too frequently, you will reduce oxygen's availability to the root system. This impairs the function of the roots and may lead to fungal diseases such as root rot. Frequent wetting of the foliage with a sprinkler system may increase foliar diseases. If you water too lightly and frequently, the water never penetrates deeply into the soil. The plants may do well as long as you water often, but since roots only grow where there is adequate moisture, they will have a shallow root system, preventing the plants from tapping reserves of water deeper in the soil and making them prone to drought stress in even brief periods of drought and high temperatures.

The amount of water needed to thoroughly irrigate an area depends on soil type. When irrigating, enough water should be applied to penetrate at least 6 inches into the soil. Applying an inch of water to medium-textured soils will generally accomplish this. The water needs to be applied slowly over a period of time to allow the water to soak into the soil. *Watering by hand is not effective for irrigating plants growing in the ground.* When hand-watering, the water is applied too fast over too short a period of time for it to penetrate deeply into the soil. Sprinklers are an option.

To calibrate a sprinkler system, place several empty coffee cans in the spray pattern of the sprinkler system. Turn on the sprinklers and check the time. When at least an inch of water has accumulated in all of the cans, check the time again. That's how long it takes your sprinkler system to apply an inch of water, and how long the system should be left on to thoroughly irrigate the area. The best check of how thoroughly an area has been watered is to go back about 20 minutes after watering and dig into the soil. Use a trowel or soil probe to look at the soil 6 to 8 inches down. Did the water penetrate that deep? Check in several places.

Morning is the best time to irrigate. This provides the plants with adequate moisture as they go into the hottest time of the day when they need it most. Watering early in the day also allows the foliage to dry thoroughly before nightfall, reducing the possibility of foliar disease problems. You should, however, water whenever plants are drought-stressed regardless of the time of day. Watering plants while the sun is shining on them will not injure them.

METHODS OF APPLYING WATER

Flooding: This is not generally practical in most landscapes or home gardens. It is an effective method for irrigating newly planted trees when they are ringed by a levee; the basin is periodically filled with water to thoroughly water the root area.

Soaker Hoses: Soaker hoses are made of a material that oozes or seeps water slowly. They apply water economically, are easy to use, and can be left in place or easily moved.

Drip/Trickle: Several drip/trickle systems are available to the home gardener. They provide small, steady, precise amounts of water exactly where needed. They are generally easy to install, though clogging of the emitters may be a problem and a filter system will be needed. These systems tend to be more useful in dryer areas where plants rely on irrigation for most or all of their water needs during certain times of the year.

Hose-end Nozzles: Many types are available. They are good for watering plants in containers and newly seeded beds, and for rinsing off foliage and other uses. Remember, hand watering is not an effective way to irrigate plants growing in the ground. When watering plants in containers, always add enough water so that some runs out of the drainage holes.

Sprinklers: This is the most common and popular method of irrigation. There are two basic types, underground systems and hose-end sprinklers. Underground systems are effective but expensive, and they must be installed professionally. They are more common in commercial landscapes than in residential landscapes. They often include automatic timers for convenience, but they are frequently set to come on too often for too short a time. Most home gardeners use hose-end sprinklers. They are less expensive and do not require professional installation, but they are more inconvenient to use since they must be moved around to cover large areas and generally can't be left in place. There are many types of sprinkler heads and styles to cover areas of different sizes and shapes. Watch spray patterns and include sufficient overlap to ensure even watering of an area.

Resources Affect Gardening

Cost can be a consideration when you decide to garden. As you might expect, expenses are quite variable. For example, a recently developed plant can cost as much as several hundred dollars or more for a single specimen . . . or a friend or plant society member may give you a good-quality plant at no cost at all. An expensive trellis you see at the garden center and want for a climbing vine may be passed up in favor of a homemade one which costs only a small amount of money for a few pieces of lumber and a little paint or preservative.

Some costs are basic. Equipment and tools for preparing beds and a good inventory of basic garden tools, fertilizers, and pesticides are all essential for keeping a garden well groomed and attractive.

Think of the cost factor as making an investment. Well-manicured landscapes, which usually include attractive gardens, can raise the total value of a property by several thousand dollars. Sometimes values in the range of 10 to 20 percent are quoted as the percentage-value increase attributed to a landscape and its gardens—and the gardener had the fun of developing and maintaining the garden!

TOOLS AND EQUIPMENT

You may by now have reached a point where you can't wait to get a little dirt (pardon us, soil) under your fingernails and get that garden started. But wait. Do you have the basic tools and equipment? You need a good garden spade. This is a long-handled spade that has a blade in a line almost straight with the handle. The average homeowner will have a contractor's or construction spade with a blade at a 30-degree angle from the handle. After you've used both to dig a hole for a plant, you're not likely to pick up the construction spade again. And how about a rake? You may need two kinds. For leveling the soil and removing clods and debris, you need a good stiff garden rake; for removing leaves from your lawn, a flexible leaf rake works best. Every gardener must have a hoe; in fact, having two or three types is nice. The broad-bladed hoe has special uses like chopping weeds in large areas, while the narrow-bladed hoe is great for working around your plants in close places. Garden trowels are needed for planting and a pitchfork is handy for moving or applying mulches and for handling the prunings from thorn-laden shrubs or trees.

A bonafide pruning saw along with some lopping shears and high-quality hand pruners are essential for gardening. All but dwarf plants will need to have size, density, or form altered in time. There will nearly always be damaged parts to remove, and training a plant from an early age requires this type of equipment.

If you live in Louisiana, you can count on having to deal with a variety of pests, including insects, diseases, and weeds. This calls for spray equipment of some type; hose-end units may be all you need, but we lean toward having a tank-type apparatus as well.

There are several tools we haven't mentioned that you may want to add to your tool inventory such as a posthole digger, a small tiller, an edger, a weed-whacker, a pH meter for monitoring the acidity level of individual beds, and a moisture meter to help you decide when to water. If you have a lawn tractor, a small trailer pulled behind it will make it easier to get your tools, plants, and other "stuff" from place to place.

If a gardener has enough space and funds, a small hobby-type greenhouse will bring many hours of joy. You can start your tender flowers well ahead of their season, you can take pieces of your woody plants and root them to share with friends, neighbors, and relatives, you will have a place to store plants during the winter season, and there will be times when what you want to plant is available only as a seed which has to be started under controlled conditions. A greenhouse is a great addition as long as you remain an active gardener.

Pests Affect Gardening

A variety of factors combine to make insects, diseases, and weeds major problems in Louisiana gardens. Our mild winters, abundant rainfall, and long, hot summers allow high populations of pests to survive. Talk to gardeners from anywhere, however, and they will gladly discuss their terrible pest problems which they believe to be worse than anywhere else in the country. Dealing with occasional pests is simply a part of gardening for everyone.

Minimizing the use of pesticides, whether chemical or organic, is always a good idea. It is important to remember that the use of pesticides is only one method for controlling pests. There are other techniques gardeners should use to help prevent the severe infestations that sometimes make the use of pesticides necessary.

Introduction

One of the best defenses against pests is to keep your plants in tip-top condition through good culture. A healthy plant is more resistant to disease and withstands insect attack better than an unhealthy one. Good culture includes giving your plants proper spacing, soil, water, light, and nutrients.

Another way to avoid pest problems is through selection. Simply do not plant those plants known to be prone to insect or disease problems in your area. Choose plants that are adapted to our climate, or those which have been bred and selected for insect and disease resistance. If you have plants that constantly seem to be under attack despite your best efforts, consider removing them, and replace them with plants that you have found to be more care-free.

Crop rotation is important in flower beds that are replanted every year. Planting the same type of plants in the same soil year after year can cause a buildup in the soil of insect and disease organisms that attack that particular plant. Plant different bedding plants in your garden in different places every year whenever possible.

Proper sanitation is another important factor in controlling insect and disease problems. Stands of weeds and scrub bushes or trees growing near gardens and landscapes can serve as alternate hosts, places of breeding and refuge for pests. Always keep your yard, gardens, and adjacent areas as weed-free as possible. Flowers and fallen leaves infected with disease should be raked up, bagged, and thrown away. If left on the ground, these old leaves and flowers can harbor diseases and serve as a continuing source of plant infection.

Many disease organisms live in the soil and are splashed onto plants by rain. The application of mulch to soil under plants can reduce the incidence of these types of diseases. Mulches are also the best way to save work and reduce the use of herbicides in controlling weeds, another leading garden pest.

Keep dead branches regularly pruned out of fruit trees, shade trees, and shrubs. Dead and rotting branches can serve as points of entry for carpenter ants and sources of infection or wood rot in shade trees and shrubs.

When problems do occur, proper diagnosis is important to be able to correctly deal with the situation. There is no benefit if you use the wrong pesticide or use a pesticide when it isn't needed. Diagnosing problems is not always easy for the average gardener, but the symptoms caused by a particular insect or disease are usually distinctive enough to make diagnosis fairly certain by a capable professional. Agents at your local office of the Louisiana Cooperative Extension Service, a branch of the Louisiana State University Agricultural Center, are available to help you identify problems and recommend solutions. Most local nurseries and garden centers have individuals on staff that can help as well. If pesticides are recommended, always request the least toxic material that will do the job, and ask if something you already have might work.

Louisiana Gardening Traditions

There is a long, rich tradition of gardening in Louisiana that goes beyond the subsistence farming of the early settlers and the agriculture of later plantations and farms. Gardens have a way of springing up wherever people settle once the problems of daily survival have been taken care of. The French and Spanish settled Louisiana, and their garden styles influenced the early gardens of New Orleans and the plantations. The Port of New Orleans provided an entry point for numerous new and unusual plants from around the world so that early gardeners could grow such exotics as camellias and azaleas from the Orient as well as traditional European plants. These gardeners also made good use of plants native to their areas.

The French, who began to colonize Louisiana in the early 1700s, contributed a number of features to early gardens that can still be seen in use today. The French style has a feeling of formality. Geometric shapes, clipped hedges, straight pathways, statuary, and symmetry are characteristic. The French gave us the double rows of live oaks called *alleés* that are still seen at some plantations. The formal *parterres* composed of geometric beds edged with clipped hedges and filled with flowers also came from the French. They can still be seen at old plantations and in some modern public gardens.

Louisiana was under Spanish rule from 1769 to 1803. This legacy can be seen in the architectural features in some cities around the state. Spanish gardening traditions include enclosed courtyards, still evident in many French Quarter gardens, often with a water feature such as a fountain in the center. Gardens were often divided into four areas around the water feature. Bright, colorful, blooming plants in containers and colorful glazed tiles are characteristic of the Spanish style. Although the layout of the Spanish garden is fairly formal, the plantings tend to be more relaxed, resulting in a less formal appearance.

The English contribution to our gardening styles was a more naturalistic garden layout. In the 1800s, many formal gardens and parterres were torn out at plantations and replaced with gardens that looked more natural. Straight lines, symmetry, geometric shapes, and clipped hedges were rejected for gardens with curving walkways and plants that were allowed to develop their natural forms. During the Victorian era, beds of colorful bedding plants in the landscape became popular; in the early 1900s, the colorful mixed border style and cottage style became popular in England. All of these styles are currently in use by Louisiana gardeners.

Ready, Get Set . . . Garden!

If you've read and digested this first part of the book, you should now be sufficiently inspired and adequately prepared to jump into the following chapters to discover the when, where, how, and why for planting and enjoying a great number of plants. We couldn't include every plant that can be grown in Louisiana, but we've given you a look at some of the very best. These plants will allow you to develop a garden of which you can be proud. Have a great time in your garden!

CHAPTER ONE

Annuals

ANNUALS ARE PLANTS IN A HURRY. They sprout from a seed, grow, bloom, set seed for the next generation, and then die, all in a single growing season. The term "instant gratification" is often used when speaking of annuals—a gardener can design and plant an annual garden and watch it reach full maturity in a matter of weeks or months. The price of this rushed life and instant gratification is transience: the annual garden crescendos in a breathtaking display of color and then begins its inevitable decline. At the end of their season when they are no longer attractive, annuals are removed to make room for new plants.

Annuals are primarily used to provide color to the landscape. No other group of plants can so quickly and economically create the colorful landscape that most gardeners crave. And annuals are diverse. Through careful selection, gardeners can grow annuals of any color or color combination imaginable, during virtually any time of the year and on plants that range in height from a few inches to several feet. Annuals can be planted in beds, mixed borders, pockets among shrubs or groundcovers, pots, hanging baskets, and windowboxes.

Annuals can be divided into cool-season or warm-season plants, depending on their hardiness and temperature preferences. Cool-season annuals (such as pansies, snapdragons and calendulas) do best in the cool soils and mild temperatures of October through May. They are hardy to varying degrees, most withstanding temperatures in the low twenties or even teens. With the onset of hot weather, cool-season annuals are quick to deteriorate; then it's time to replant with warm-season annuals.

Warm-season annuals (such as torenia, marigolds and zinnias) grow and flower best in the warm to hot months of April to October. Since they are not frost hardy, they are planted after danger of frost is over, and they finish their display by the first freeze, if not before. They thrive in the extreme heat of the Louisiana summer.

Chapter One

It is important to plant the right annual in the right season, and you must choose annuals suited to the growing conditions of the planting location. While it is true that most annuals need full sun (at least eight hours of direct sun a day) to part sun (at least six hours of direct sun a day), there are some annuals that thrive in part shade (about four hours of direct sun) or shade (about two hours of direct sun.) Even annuals that like part-shade to shady locations will generally not perform as well in full shade, where they receive no direct sun at all during the day. Beds should be located away from soggy, poorly drained areas that tend to promote root and stem rot.

Wherever the bed is located, make sure it is well prepared before planting. Thoroughly turn the soil to a depth of 8 inches. Spread a 2-inch layer of compost, aged manure, fine pine bark, or peat moss, sprinkle with 8-8-8 at the rate of 1 cup per 30 square feet, and thoroughly incorporate everything into the soil of the bed. If the soil is high in phosphorus, use 1/2 cup of 15-5-10 over the bed area instead of 8-8-8.

Watch spacing when planting transplants. It's tempting to plant the young, small plants too close together, not anticipating how large they will eventually grow. If anything, annuals tend to grow larger in our state than is indicated on their tags. Ideally, the plants should grow together at maturity, completely covering the soil without excessive crowding and competition.

Once the bed is planted, mulch and thoroughly water the plants. It's a good idea to water them in with a mild fertilizer solution to get them off to a good start. Use a hose-end fertilizer applicator for large areas. Applying a soluble fertilizer twice a month, or a granular fertilizer every 4 to 6 weeks, will keep most annuals growing.

Annual plantings are not necessarily low maintenance. Keep in mind the care they will need to look attractive when deciding where, how large and how many beds to plant. Mulch will reduce problems with weeds, but weeding will still be necessary. Regular watering, pest control, and grooming (removing dead flowers and unattractive leaves) will keep them looking their best. When planted in containers, hanging baskets, and windowboxes, annuals need frequent watering and fertilization. Remember, when annuals reach the end of their attractive lives, they will need to be removed and replaced.

Alyssum

Lobularia maritima

Other Name: Sweet Alyssum
Size: 4 inches high, 10-inch spread
Type: Short-lived perennial grown as a cool-season annual
Flowers: Small, in clusters of white, pink, and purple; fragrant
Bloom Period: Fall, winter, and spring

Light Requirement:

A sweet, honey-like fragrance wafts up from low carpets of this Mediterranean plant when it blooms on warm spring days. Its tiny flowers are produced in clusters so numerous they can completely cover the plant, creating a solid carpet of white, pink, rose, lavender, or purple. Alyssum is a low-spreading plant that generally grows no taller than 4 to 6 inches and has a spread of 8 to 12 inches. It is indispensable in the spring flower garden and is outstanding as an edging, planted in pockets, or as a filler in a variety of garden beds. Plants are hardy in temperatures to the low twenties.

When to Plant

Alyssum grows easily from direct-seeding from October to November and February to March. Or try growing your own transplants or purchase them for planting October through March.

Where to Plant

Plant in full sun to part shade. Alyssum adapts well to dry, well-drained locations, but it also does well in moist, fertile soils as long as drainage is good. Its low-growing, creeping growth habit makes alyssum excellent for edging beds and for use along walkways and around containers where it will cascade attractively over the sides. Plant alyssum over areas where spring-flowering bulbs were planted. It will bloom before, during, and after the bulbs, and the bulbs will come up and bloom readily through the alyssum.

How to Plant

To prepare beds, incorporate a 2-inch layer of compost, rotted manure, or peat moss. Sprinkle general-purpose fertilizer in the bed, using 1/2 cup of 15-5-10 per 30 square feet (or 1 cup of 8-8-8 per 30 square feet if your soil is low in phosphorus). If you are direct-seeding, rake the beds carefully to remove any debris or clods. Scatter the fine seeds over the area and press into the soil. Do not cover. Water frequently, and when the seedlings come up, thin to 6 to 8 inches apart. If you are planting transplants, be sure not to set the plants deeper than they were growing previously. Water-in thoroughly and mulch.

Care and Maintenance

Water during dry weather, especially if plants are getting established. Fertilize every 6 to 8 weeks using the above fertilizers and rates. If the plants start to look shaggy during the growing season, lightly shear them back to encourage more flowers. Alyssum does not tolerate heat well, and it generally begins to look unattractive in May. Most gardeners replace it at some point with heat-tolerant bedding plants. Sometimes plants left in the ground will survive the summer and bloom well again the next cool season.

Additional Information

The fragrance is especially noticeable when alyssum is planted along paths, at entranceways, or around outdoor sitting areas. Alyssum often self-seeds. Look for volunteers in fall or spring where the plants were previously grown.

Additional Cultivars or Species

There are a number of cultivars available, especially if you purchase seeds from a catalog. All varieties are generally very reliable. 'Easter Bonnet' is an excellent blend of pastel colors, deep rose, and violet. 'Snowcloth' and 'Carpet of Snow' are compact, low-growing white varieties. 'Rosie O'Day' is a dark pink. The 'Wonderland' series is known for its especially bright colors.

Calendula

Calendula officinalis

Other Name: Pot Marigold **Size:** 12 to 18 inches **Type:** Cool-season annual **Flowers:** Cream, yellow, or orange; daisy-like **Bloom Period:** Fall to early summer	**Light Requirement:**

The edible yellow-to-orange flowers of calendula were once used to flavor pots of soups and stews, and so the common name: pot marigold. Compact dwarf varieties grow to about 12 inches and are excellent for bedding. Taller varieties, 18 to 24 inches, make fine cut flowers and look good in the middle or back of borders. The flowers are usually brilliant in shades of yellow, gold, and orange, but some varieties include creamy white shades or tints of dark red. They are daisy-like and often feature a dark disk or eye in the center, or may be fully double. The branching plants have simple, oval, medium-green leaves with hairs that feel slightly sticky to the touch. These cool-season annuals are hardy to at least the low twenties and bloom over a long period.

When to Plant

Plant seeds directly in the garden where you want the plants to grow in September to November and February to March. Transplants may be planted at the same times.

Where to Plant

Locate plantings in well-drained areas with full sun to part sun. Dwarf varieties are suitable for bedding, the front of borders or containers. Taller varieties are best for the background.

How to Plant

To prepare beds, turn the soil to a depth of 8 inches and spread a 2-inch layer of compost, rotted manure, or peat moss. Sprinkle a general-purpose fertilizer in the bed and thoroughly blend it into the soil (use 1 cup of 8-8-8 or 1/2 cup of 15-5-10 per 30 square feet). Like most bedding plants, don't plant calendulas deeper than they were growing. Water-in and mulch the bed. To direct-seed, rake the prepared bed and plant seeds according to package directions. Water frequently until the seeds come up, and then thin the seedlings to 8 to 12 inches apart. When the plants are large enough, mulch the planting.

Care and Maintenance

Calendulas are quite hardy, but would benefit from a cover on those nights when temperatures will go below 20 degrees Fahrenheit. Dead-head frequently to keep plants attractive and encourage continued flowering. Caterpillars are the only major pest and can be controlled with applications of Sevin or B.t.: always apply following label directions. Keep beds mulched to control weeds and conserve soil moisture. Plants begin to fade with summer heat and should be replaced at that time.

Additional Information

Since they are edible, calendula flowers make attractive and appropriate garnishes for food dishes. The petals are a colorful addition to salads. Taller varieties make excellent cut flowers.

Additional Cultivars or Species

'Bon Bon' is a dwarf cultivar that comes in various colors. 'Prince Mix' and 'Pacific Mix' are excellent for cutting. The cultivar 'Touch of Red' is medium height, useful for bedding or cutting, and has done well here.

Celosia

Celosia cristata

Other Names: *Celosia argentea*, Cock's Comb
Size: 8 to 36 inches, depending on cultivar
Type: Warm-season annual
Flowers: Plumes, spikes, or crested shapes in many colors
Bloom Period: Summer

Light Requirement:

Celosia has two basic flower forms. One group produces a curled, crested inflorescence that is somewhat like a rooster's comb. The other type looks more like a feathery plume—much like those ornamental grasses produce—and is the more common form used in the garden. Celosia is very heat tolerant and has been used in Louisiana gardens for generations. Old varieties, both crested and plume types, can often be seen in rural gardens where they have reseeded themselves year after year. They tend to be quite tall—3 feet or more—and are almost always vivid magenta. Modern varieties are more compact and come in many bright colors including red, yellow, orange, pink, and magenta. The simple, pointed leaves are generally green, but may be tinted with burgundy or wine red. The old types found in gardens often last all summer. New varieties planted in April normally last only until July or August.

When to Plant

Transplants can be planted in the garden from April through August. Plant seed in protected flats in February, or direct-seed in the garden in April through July.

Where to Plant

Plant in sunny locations with good drainage. Use taller varieties in the background and more compact types in beds and containers.

How to Plant

Prepare beds by turning the soil to a depth of 8 inches, and spread a 2-inch layer of compost, fine pine bark, or peat moss. Sprinkle a general-purpose fertilizer and thoroughly blend into the soil of the bed; use 1 cup of 8-8-8 per 30 square feet (1/2 cup of 15-5-10 if your soil is high in phosphorus). Water-in and mulch the bed after the transplants are planted. To direct-seed, rake the prepared bed and plant seeds according to package directions. Water frequently until the seeds come up, and then thin the seedlings to 8 to 10 inches apart. When the plants are large enough, mulch the planting.

Care and Maintenance

Caterpillars can be a major problem. Control with Sevin, B.t., or other approved insecticides following label directions. Keep beds watered in hot, dry weather, and mulch to conserve soil moisture and reduce weeds. When the central inflorescence has faded, cut it off and side shoots will continue the floral display. Fertilize moderately as celosia is easy to overfertilize. Celosia planted in the spring often finishes bloom-ing before the end of summer, and the bed must be replanted.

Additional Information

The inflorescences of celosia will dry well and retain their brilliant color if cut when mature and hung upside-down in a well-ventilated area. They are also excellent fresh-cut flowers.

Additional Cultivars or Species

There are numerous cultivars. Plume types include: 'Kimono', an ultra-dwarf, growing 4 to 6 inches; 'New Look', which has purple leaves; 'Century Mix', 'Castle Pink' (there is also a 'Castle Mix'), and 'Prestige Scarlet'—which are All-America Selection winners. Crested types include 'Chief Mix', which is long-stemmed and excellent for cutting, and 'Treasure Chest', a short, bedding cultivar in various colors. The wheat celosia (spicata type) grows to 3 feet and produces thin, feathery plumes of white, silvery pink, or dark pink depending on variety. It is excellent for cutting and drying. Look for 'Flamingo', 'Purple Flamingo', and 'Pink Candle'.

Coleus

Coleus × hybridus

Size: 1 to 2 feet	**Light Requirement:**
Type: Tender perennial grown as a warm-season annual	
Flowers: Not significant	

Several species were bred together to create today's modern coleus cultivars. These plants produce some of the most highly colored leaves found in the garden. Since the foliage supplies the color, these plants are never "out of bloom" throughout their long growing season. The colors in the leaves are amazing and include yellow, orange, chartreuse, green, purple, red, white and pink in every combination and pattern you could imagine. Native to the tropics, coleus thrives in Louisiana's hot, humid summers. The loose spikes of lavender to blue flowers are a distraction from the main display of the foliage, and are usually removed. Coleus is easily damaged or killed by even light freezes.

When to Plant

Sow seeds indoors in January or February for transplanting in April and May. Plant purchased transplants April through August.

Where to Plant

Coleus does well in part shade to full sun. Some varieties do better in full sun than others. Coleus is not picky about soil type or drainage as long as the area is not constantly wet and the soil is reasonably good. Plant in beds, borders, or containers.

How to Plant

Plant transplants in well-prepared beds improved by digging in some organic matter and a light sprinkling of a general-purpose fertilizer. If the plants are pot-bound, loosen the root system before planting at the same level they were growing. Water-in and mulch the bed.

Care and Maintenance

Pinch out the growing tips often to encourage branching. This will result in a fuller, more shapely plant. Remove flower spikes as they appear. Mealybug infestations occasionally occur on outdoor plantings (they are more of a problem on indoor plants). Control with insecticidal soap or Malathion following label directions. Fertilize every 6 to 8 weeks with a general purpose granular fertilizer, every 2 to 4 weeks with a soluble fertilizer, or once at the time of planting with a slow-release fertilizer. Coleus growing in sunny, dry areas will need to be watered regularly during the summer. Keep the beds mulched. If plants get too tall, cut them back hard and they will resprout readily.

Additional Information

Coleus are easy to root from cuttings. Root cuttings in potting soil or water in a shady area, and plant in the garden when a well-developed root system forms. The Latin name of coleus has been changed to *Solenostemon scutellariodes*, but *Coleus* × *hybridus* will most likely remain in common usage.

Additional Cultivars or Species

These vegetatively propagated varieties have proven to be sun tolerant in Louisiana based on trials done at the Burden Research Station in Baton Rouge (a branch of the Louisiana State University Agricultural Center): 'New Orleans Red', 'Pineapple', 'Alabama', 'Mardi Gras', 'Red Duckfoot', 'Red Velvet', and 'Solar Eclipse'. Seed-propagated cultivars include the 'Carefree' series, the 'Wizard' series, and the 'Fairway' series.

Cosmos

Cosmos bipinnatus and *C. sulphureus*

Size: 1 to 4 feet, depending on cultivar **Type:** Warm-season annual **Flowers:** White, pink, and burgundy; or yellow, orange, and brick red (depending on species) **Bloom Period:** Spring through fall	**Light Requirement:**

Few plants are as easy to grow from seeds as cosmos. Even beginning gardeners will be successful with this plant. The two species are quite different, but equally easy to grow. *C. bipinnatus* has fine, ferny foliage and produces single to semi-double daisy-like flowers in shades of white, pink, rosy red, and burgundy. It performs best in spring and early summer, and again in fall when daytime highs stay in the 70s and low 80s. *C. sulphureus* has foliage similar to marigolds and has smaller, single or semi-double daisy-like flowers in shades of yellow, gold, orange, and brick red. The blazing heat of midsummer will not slow this plant down one bit. Both species are generally tall growing, from 2 to 3 feet, but shorter cultivars of *C. sulphureus* are available.

When to Plant

Plant seeds of *C. bipinnatus* in the garden where they are to grow in February or March; plant transplants in March and April. Plant seeds again in September and transplants September through October. Plant seeds or transplants of *C. sulphureus* in the garden April through August.

Where to Plant

Plant in sunny areas. *C. sulphureus* is particularly well adapted to sunny, hot, dry areas.

How to Plant

Sow seeds in well-prepared seedbeds. To prepare beds, turn the soil to a depth of 8 inches, and spread a 2-inch layer of compost, rotted manure, or peat moss. Sprinkle a general-purpose fertilizer and thoroughly blend into the soil of the bed (use 1 cup of 8-8-8 or

1/2 cup of 15-5-10 per 30 square feet). Thoroughly rake the prepared bed and plant seeds according to package directions. Water frequently until the seeds come up, and then thin the seedlings to 8 to 12 inches apart. When the plants are large enough, mulch the planting. Plant transplants at the same level they were growing, 8 to 12 inches apart. Water-in and mulch.

Care and Maintenance

Cosmos needs little fertilizer to do well. Water is needed by well-established plantings only if the weather is very dry. Deadhead the plants frequently to prevent seed formation and to encourage longer flowering. Should you allow seed to set, the plants self seed easily and will come up where they grew before.

Additional Information

You can allow some flowers of *C. sulphureus* to set seed, and scatter the seeds in the bed around the original plants when they start to finish. New plants will grow and the old tired plants can be removed to make room for the next generation—a necessary procedure if you want cosmos to bloom from May to October.

Additional Cultivars or Species

Excellent *C. bipinnatus* cultivars include 'Sensation Mixed', 'Psyche Mixed', 'Seashells', 'Sonata Mixed', and the 'Versailles' series. All are 2 to 3 feet tall. Cultivars of *C. sulphureus* include the dwarf 'Ladybird Mix'—a good substitute for marigolds where spider mites have been a problem—and the 'Sunny' series, also dwarf. These cultivars are 1 to 2 feet tall. 'Bright Lights' grows 3 to 4 feet.

Dianthus

Dianthus chinensis

Other Names: Pinks, China Pink
Size: 10 to 14 inches
Type: Short-lived perennial grown as a cool-season annual
Flowers: Shades of red, white and pink
Bloom Period: Fall through early summer

Light Requirement:

Gardeners often think the common name of this outstanding cool-season bedding plant—pinks— refers to its flower color. Dianthus certainly comes in pink—and red, burgundy, white, purple, and lavender—but the edges of the petals give dianthus its common name. They are jagged—reminding one of the way pinking shears cut fabric to keep it from unraveling. The neat, well-behaved plants produce attractive mounds of dark green to blue-green narrow foliage. The 1-inch flowers are produced constantly and are born in clusters or singly. The greatest production is in the spring on plants set out the previous fall, although flowering also occurs in fall and intermittently through the winter during mild spells. Although it is generally not pronounced, a spicy, clove-like scent is produced by many cultivars of dianthus. Dianthus is one of the hardiest and most reliable of the cool-season bedding plants. It will tolerate temperatures of 15 degrees Fahrenheit with little or no damage.

When to Plant

Plant transplants September through March.

Where to Plant

Choose sunny, well-drained sites. Dianthus is intolerant of poor drainage. If drainage is a concern, plant in raised beds. The neat growth habit of dianthus makes it a good choice for containers, formal landscape designs, and flower beds. It is also effective planted in drifts, in borders, and in cottage gardens.

How to Plant

Plant in well-prepared beds that have been improved by digging in a 2-inch layer of organic matter (fine pine bark or compost) and a sprinkling of general-purpose fertilizer. Set plants 8 to 10 inches apart at the same level or slightly higher than they were growing in the containers or cell-packs. If you plant dianthus too deep, it is more prone to crown rot. If the roots of the transplants have grown into a tight ball (pot-bound), loosen the roots before planting. Water thoroughly to settle in the plants and mulch the bed.

Care and Maintenance

Other than crown rot, there are few pest problems. Proper planting in a well-drained bed is your best defense against crown rot. Water during dry periods, especially if the weather is warm. Fertilize every 6 to 8 weeks with 1 cup of 8-8-8 or 1/2 cup of 15-5-10 fertilizer per 30 square feet of bed area—or use your favorite slow-release fertilizer at the time of planting. Deadheading dianthus will keep it looking more attractive and increase flowering. It will need no protection during a typical winter throughout most of the state.

Additional Information

Dianthus has difficulty dealing with the extraordinary heat of our summers. It usually begins to look worn out by late May or early June, and should be replaced with more heat-tolerant bedding plants at that time. In certain circumstances it will survive the summer, but it often dies of crown rot in the heat and rains of late summer. The flowers of dianthus are generally single, round and flat, but may also be double (like small carnations). Dianthus is a tough plant that performs well in dry, exposed areas. The flowers are edible.

Additional Cultivars or Species

Perhaps the best cultivar for Louisiana, based on field trials at the Burden Research Station in Baton Rouge (a branch of the Louisiana State University Agricultural Center), is 'Telstar'. This dianthus, which comes in a variety of colors, is heat tolerant and may live more than one season, especially in north Louisiana. Other cultivars include 'Baby Doll', with large flowers, 'Ideal', and the 'Parfait' series. Tall-growing *Dianthus superbus* cultivars have deeply fringed, very fragrant flowers and have shown good heat tolerance even in New Orleans.

Globe Amaranth

Gomphrena globosa

Other Names: Gomphrena, Bachelor's Buttons **Size:** 1 to 3 feet depending on cultivar **Type:** Warm-season annual **Flowers:** Pink, white, red, lavender, or purple clover-like balls **Bloom Period:** Summer through fall	**Light Requirement:**

White forms of globe amaranth have been mistaken for clover, so closely do the flowers of one resemble the other. But the abundantly produced flowers of gomphrena grow on a bushy plant and come in a variety of wonderful colors. This plant is noted for its long bloom season. It is one of the most reliable bedding plants for Louisiana summer flower beds, and is truly resistant to heat and humidity. The oval green leaves are slightly fuzzy and retain their attractive appearance through the summer. The taller forms of this plant have been in cultivation for a long time, but breeders are developing more compact, dwarf cultivars that are outstanding as bedding plants.

When to Plant

Transplants are available at nurseries and garden centers in spring. Plant when danger of frost has passed in April or May through August. Gomphrena is a great choice for replacing bedding plants that play out in mid- to late summer as it can be planted even when it is very hot. For experienced gardeners, gomphrena is not difficult to start from seed in flats.

Where to Plant

Choose sunny, well-drained locations to plant globe amaranth. It does well in beds, containers, and windowboxes.

How to Plant

To prepare beds, incorporate a 2-inch layer of compost, fine pine bark, or peat moss and a sprinkling of general-purpose fertilizer in the bed—use $1/2$ cup of 15-5-10 (or 1 cup of 8-8-8, if your soil is low in phosphorus) per 30 square feet. Make sure not to set the transplants deeper than they were growing previously. Space plants 8 to 12 inches apart, depending on the cultivar. Water-in thoroughly and mulch.

Care and Maintenance

Keep beds mulched to prevent weeds and conserve moisture. If plants wilt, water thoroughly twice a week during hot, dry weather. Remove faded, tan flower heads to keep the plants looking attractive. Caterpillars can be a problem. Treat with Sevin, or the biological control, B.t., as needed and according to label directions. Fertilize once or twice in the growing season with one of the granular fertilizers mentioned above at the given rates. Water-in thoroughly after application.

Additional Information

Gomphrenas provide one of the best flowers for drying. They hold their color indefinitely. Pick them with stems for dried arrangements or without stems for use in potpourris. Dry them in a well-ventilated area.

Additional Cultivars or Species

The 'Gnome' series is very dwarf, staying under a foot, and comes in a range of colors. The 'Buddy' series is also compact and good for planting in beds. 'Lavender Lady' is pale lavender and excellent for cutting, as are various mixtures. *G. haageana,* a species native to Texas and Mexico, produces orange to red flowers. 'Strawberry Fields' is a good red cultivar of that species.

Impatiens

Impatiens wallerana

Other Names: Sultana, Busy Lizzy, Patient Lucy
Size: 8 to 24 inches
Type: Tender perennial grown as a warm-season annual
Flowers: Round, flat, 1-inch flowers in many shades of red, pink, white, and purple
Bloom Period: Summer

Light Requirement:

The number of common names indicates that this plant has been grown and loved by gardeners for a long time. Impatiens has become the most popular bedding plant in the United States, and simply can't be beat for brightening up a partly shady area. It has unbelievable stamina, flowering continuously from April until the first freezes of winter. It's hard to match that kind of performance with any other bedding plant. Breeders are developing new varieties all the time with larger flowers, new colors, and compact growth. Other than yellows and true blue, the color range is amazing. That doesn't mean that you have to plant every color available in your flower bed. Plantings of one color or a few harmonious colors are more effective than many, often clashing, colors planted together.

When to Plant

Wait until the weather is warm and settled to set out transplants (April through August).

Where to Plant

Plant in partly shady areas where there is adequate drainage.

How to Plant

Plant transplants in well-prepared beds that have been improved by digging in a 2-inch layer of fine pine bark or compost and a sprinkling of general-purpose fertilizer (use 1 cup of 8-8-8 or $^1/_2$ cup of 15-5-10 per 30 square feet). Set plants 8 to 10 inches apart at the same level or slightly higher than they were growing in containers or cell-packs. If the roots of the transplants have grown into a tight ball, loosen them before planting. Water thoroughly to settle in the plants and mulch the bed to prevent weeds and keep the soil evenly moist.

Care and Maintenance

Some varieties of impatiens get leggy by late summer. Trim them back 1/3 to 1/2 their height to reduce their size and encourage a fuller, more attractive plant. This is usually done by August. Fertilize every 6 to 8 weeks with one of the above fertilizers at recommended rates, and water-in thoroughly after application. Slugs and snails eat holes in the leaves and flowers. Control them with baits or traps as needed. Impatiens needs an even supply of moisture and will wilt if allowed to get too dry. Water deeply 2 or 3 times a week during dry weather, especially where tree roots compete for the water. Although impatiens is very tolerant of heat and humidity, it often looks a little tired in the hottest part of summer, but will recover as the weather cools off in fall.

Additional Information

You will have less of a problem with root rot if you plant in well-prepared beds that have good drainage. If drainage is a problem, plant in raised beds. Impatiens combines beautifully with ferns, hostas, gingers, caladiums, and other shade-loving plants.

Additional Cultivars or Species

A very large number of cultivars and colors have been developed, but a relatively small number are available when purchasing transplants. Commonly available types in various colors include: 'Super Elfin', very compact; 'Gem', sun tolerant; 'Accent', one of the most popular; 'Swirl' two-toned picotee; and 'Deco', dark leaves. There are also double-flowered and variegated forms of impatiens. New Guinea impatiens is a different breed altogether, and does not tolerate heat well. These plants have large, brightly colored flowers and sometimes variegated leaves. The garden balsam, *I. balsamina,* is an outstanding summer annual for full sun to part shade, and thrives on heat and humidity.

Lisianthus

Eustoma grandiflorum

Other Names: Prairie Gentian
Size: 10 to 24 inches
Type: Warm-season annual
Flowers: Beautiful single cup-shaped or double rose-like flowers in white, pink, or purple
Bloom Period: Summer

Light Requirement:

Plant breeders worked their craft on a pretty wildflower native to western North America, and transformed it into a flower of rare beauty and tough constitution. Its beauty in the garden is surpassed only by its longevity as a cut flower—lasting easily ten days in a vase. The original species grew 3 feet tall with pale purple flowers, but garden varieties are more compact and produce flowers in many shades of pink, purple, white, and violet-blue. The flowers are borne in clusters at the ends of strong stems, and the double forms look like a rose as they open. The grayish-green foliage compliments the flowers nicely, although the plant itself sometimes looks a bit awkward. Lisianthus is excellent for dry, sunny areas.

When to Plant

Lisianthus will tolerate near-freezing temperatures, but transplants are not likely to be available until warm spring weather has arrived. Plant as soon as they are available to get the most flowers. This plant is a bit of a challenge to grow from seed, so transplants are recommended.

Where to Plant

Plant in full sun where drainage is excellent. Lisianthus does well in containers alone or in combination with purslane and other plants that like it dry and sunny.

How to Plant

Plant in well-prepared beds that have been improved by digging in a 2-inch layer of fine pine bark or compost and a sprinkling of general-purpose fertilizer. Plant in raised beds if drainage is questionable. Set plants 8 inches apart at the same level or slightly higher than they were growing in pots or cell-packs. If you plant lisianthus too deep, it is more prone to crown rot. If the roots of the transplants have grown pot-bound, loosen them before planting. Water thoroughly to settle in the plants and mulch the bed.

Care and Maintenance

There are few pest problems. Proper planting in a well-drained bed is your best defense against crown rot. Water only during dry periods if the weather is especially hot. Fertilize every 6 to 8 weeks with 1 cup of 8-8-8 or $^{1}/_{2}$ cup of 15-5-10 per 30 square feet of bed area, or use your favorite slow-release fertilizer at the time of planting. Deadheading lisianthus will increase flowering. If you let it go to seed, it will tend to stop blooming. Although it has a long blooming period, it may not last the entire warm season in bloom.

Additional Information

Caterpillars will sometimes chew holes in the foliage, but damage is generally not significant. Hand pick or spray as needed. Taller cultivars may need to be staked to keep the flower stems from falling over.

Additional Cultivars or Species

'Mermaid' is a dwarf cultivar suitable for planting in beds. Taller forms, such as the 'Echo' strain and 'Heidi', are excellent for cut flowers.

Marigold

Tagetes erecta and *T. patula*

Other Names: African Marigold, American Marigold, French Marigold **Size:** 10 to 30 inches **Type:** Warm-season annual **Flowers:** Creamy white, yellow, gold, orange, or mahogany-red **Bloom Period:** Summer	**Light Requirement:**

Marigolds are flowers that almost everyone can recognize. Easy, bright, and cheerful, they are one of the flowers that many gardeners grow first. Most of the marigolds we grow are cultivars of *T. erecta*, the African marigold, or *T. patula*, the French marigold. Despite their common names, both species are native to Mexico and Central America. Currently, some seed catalogs call *T. erecta* American marigolds. Most gardeners just call them marigolds, but there are real differences between the two types. African marigolds are larger, coarser plants that grow upright 18 to 30 inches tall and produce flowers 2 to 4 inches across. French marigolds are more mounding 10- to 14-inch plants that produce flowers 1 to 3 inches wide. Cultivars of both species generally produce double flowers, but there are several single-flowered French marigolds. The color range includes shades of creamy white, pale yellow, yellow, gold, orange, mahogany-red, and some bicolors.

When to Plant

Plant seeds in garden beds March through August. Transplants can be set out from March to early October.

Where to Plant

Choose well-drained locations that receive plenty of sun. Marigolds are widely adapted to a variety of soils.

How to Plant

Marigolds are easy to grow from seed or transplants, but will perform best in well-prepared beds. Turn the soil to a depth of 8 inches, then spread a 2-inch layer of compost, fine pine bark, or peat moss. Sprinkle a general-purpose fertilizer and thoroughly blend everything into the soil of the bed—use 1 cup of 8-8-8 (or $^{1}/_{2}$ cup of 15-5-10, if your soil is high in phosphorus) per 30 square feet. Water-in and mulch the bed after the transplants are planted. To direct-seed, rake the prepared bed and plant seeds according to package directions. Water frequently until the seeds come up, and then thin the seedlings to 8 to 10 inches apart. When the plants are large enough, mulch the planting.

Care and Maintenance

Deadhead frequently to encourage marigolds to bloom as long as possible. Spider mites can be devastating. Treat with insecticidal soap, kelthane, or Malathion according to label directions. Marigolds that are planted in the spring will not last the entire warm season, so be prepared to replace them when they play out.

Additional Information

Blooming transplants of marigolds planted in October are becoming a popular substitute for chrysanthemums. They do remarkably well in October, November and early December until the first hard freeze. Spider mites are less of a problem and the plants are more compact when marigolds are planted in the fall. Marigold flower petals are edible, and are a colorful addition to salads.

Additional Cultivars or Species

African marigold cultivars include 'Climax', 'Lady', 'Antigua', 'Discovery', and 'Inca', all offering a variety of colors. 'French Vanilla' and 'Snowdrift' are white. French marigold cultivars include 'Aurora', 'Hero', 'Janie', and 'Sophia', all with various colors. *T. erecta* has been crossed with *T. patula* to create sterile hybrids such as 'Nugget' and 'Zenith'. *T. tenuifolia*, the signet marigold, is a smaller, fine-leafed species that produces small flowers. Cultivars of this species include 'Gem Mix' and 'Starfire'.

Melampodium

Melampodium paludosum

Size: 14 to 30 inches
Type: Warm-season annual
Flowers: Bright yellow single 3/4-inch daisy
Bloom Period: Summer

Light Requirement:

Melampodium is a rather new addition to the summer annual line-up. Unfortunately, no one thought of a common name for this plant before it was introduced and became popular. The name is not so unwieldy after you've learned to pronounce it. Just say mel-am-PO-dee-um. This rather large, bushy annual produces a continuous display of 3/4-inch yellow, single daisy flowers all summer. The dull, medium-green leaves are 2 to 3 inches long and provide an attractive background to the flowers. Melampodium has excellent heat tolerance and is very easy to grow.

When to Plant

Transplants or seeds may be planted in the garden anytime April through August.

Where to Plant

Any location that is well-drained and receives at least 4 to 6 hours of sun is fine. Melampodium is not picky. These tall plants are generally best planted toward the back of beds.

How to Plant

Melampodium will thrive in any average garden soil without special preparation. If the soil is poor, incorporate some organic matter and a very light sprinkling of general-purpose fertilizer. Do not be generous with the fertilizer or the plants will grow to be enormous. Space transplants about 12 to 14 inches apart. To direct-seed, rake the prepared bed and plant seeds according to package directions. Water frequently until the seeds come up, and then thin the seedlings to 12 inches apart. When the plants are large enough, mulch the planting.

Care and Maintenance

Melampodium is virtually carefree, but caterpillars sometimes eat holes in the leaves. Control with Sevin or the biological control B.t. as needed following label directions. Keep the beds well mulched to prevent weeds and conserve soil moisture. Established plants are fairly drought tolerant, but water as necessary during hot, dry weather.

Additional Information

Melampodium self-seeds readily. Often, you will see seedlings coming up among the original plants before the end of the season. A good mulch will minimize this. Volunteers transplant easily when small, and can be moved to other locations where you may want them.

Additional Cultivars or Species

Cultivars include 'Derby', the most compact. It is listed as 8 to 10 inches tall, but expect it to be 18 to 20 inches here. 'Showstar' has pointed petals and grows to be about 24 inches. 'Gold Coin' was the original cultivar and will grow 24 to 30 inches tall.

Narrow-Leaf Zinnia

Zinnia angustifolia

Other Name: *Zinnia linearis*
Size: 12 to 15 inches with an equal spread
Type: Warm-season annual
Flowers: Single daisy orange, yellow, or white
Bloom Period: All summer

Light Requirement:

The narrow-leaf zinnia has become popular only in the last few years—but it has already convinced many Louisiana gardeners of its worth in the summer flower garden. Unlike the common zinnia, this plant is undaunted by heat, insects, or diseases, and will bloom prolifically and with amazing stamina from early summer until the first frost. The flowers are less than an inch across, but are so numerous they can almost hide the narrow, dark-green leaves. Colors range from brilliant orange to gold to white—all with a golden-orange center. The plant is somewhat sprawling in habit. It looks charming cascading over the edge of a raised planter or windowbox, but may be a little too casual for a formal setting.

When to Plant

Transplants should be planted April through September. Direct seeding is not as reliable as with common zinnias, so transplants are recommended. Start seeds in flats or pots and plant in the garden when they reach sufficient size.

Where to Plant

Narrow-leaf zinnia is well adapted to hot, dry, sunny locations. Plant in well-drained beds or containers filled with a light, porous soil mix.

How to Plant

To prepare the beds, incorporate a 2-inch layer of compost, fine pine bark, or peat moss and a sprinkling of fertilizer in the bed; use 1/2 cup of 15-5-10 (or 1 cup of 8-8-8 fertilizer, if your soil is low in phosphorus) per 30 square feet of bed area. Make sure not to set the plants deeper than they were growing previously. Space plants 10 to 12 inches apart. Water-in thoroughly and mulch.

Care and Maintenance

Little additional fertilizer or watering is needed once the plants are established and growing. Keep the bed mulched to control weeds. If plants become too rangy, shear them back lightly, particularly in the late summer or early fall.

Additional Information

After a summer of blooming, these plants are often at their finest in the fall. The vibrant orange color is difficult to work into many color schemes, but the yellow—and especially the white—are easy to use.

Additional Cultivars or Species

'Crystal White', an All-America Selection winner, is a white, compact cultivar. 'Star Gold', 'Star Orange', and 'Star White' are also available, as are various mixes.

Ornamental Cabbage and Ornamental Kale

Brassica oleracea forms

Other Names: Flowering Cabbage, Flowering Kale
Size: 12-inch height, 12- to 16-inch spread
Type: Cool-season annual
Flowers: Tall clusters of pale yellow; not significant

Light Requirement:

Is it a vegetable or an ornamental? Ornamental cabbage and ornamental kale are vegetables that have been bred and selected for their beautiful foliage rather than culinary excellence. They are perfectly edible, but who would want to eat something that looks so pretty in the garden? These plants are some of the most unique that we can plant in the cool season, and are quite hardy throughout the state, requiring no protection during the winter. Both plants form large rosettes of bluish-green, thick, waxy leaves. The leaves of ornamental cabbage are smooth on the edges, while the leaves of ornamental kale are frilly and ruffled. As they begin to mature, the foliage in the center part of the plant turns beautiful colors of purple-red, rose, pink, or white. It is for this colorful foliage, rather than flowers, that these plants are grown. A well-grown planting is stunning.

When to Plant

Plant transplants in October through early December so that they can become well established before the coldest part of the winter. Start seeds in flats in August or early September.

Where to Plant

Ornamental cabbage and kale need full sun to develop their colors. Choose a well-drained location that receives at least 6 hours of sun.

How to Plant

Plant transplants in well-prepared beds that have been improved by digging in a 2-inch layer of fine pine bark or compost and a sprinkling of general-purpose fertilizer (use 1 cup of 8-8-8 or $^{1}/_{2}$ cup of 15-5-10 per 30 square feet). Set plants 12 inches apart. Sometimes ornamental cabbage and kale transplants will have a "neck," a bare stem between the lower leaves and the roots. You may plant with the neck buried in the soil up to the lowest leaves to make the plant more attractive and stable. If the roots of the transplants have grown into a tight ball, loosen them before planting. Water thoroughly to settle in the plants, and mulch the bed to prevent weeds and keep the soil evenly moist.

Care and Maintenance

It is important to keep these plants evenly moist, so mulch and water regularly when needed. Fertilize every 6 to 8 weeks as recommended above. Without good, consistent growing conditions, plants can become stunted and less showy. Watch for holes in the leaves that indicate either slug and snail damage or caterpillars. Identify the pest and use baits for the slugs and snails, and Sevin or B.t. for the caterpillars.

Additional Information

Plants are generally at their peak for about 4 to 6 weeks sometime in February through April, depending on weather, care, and when they were planted. A pointed growth from the center of the plant indicates it is beginning to flower, and the most ornamental period is over. Some gardeners leave them in to flower and appreciate them at that stage; others find the flowering stage unattractive and pull them up. Spring-planted transplants generally do not perform as well as those planted in the fall. And, yes, you may eat ornamental cabbage or kale raw or cooked.

Additional Cultivars or Species

'Color Up' is an ornamental cabbage that comes in red, white, and pink. The 'Dynasty' series also includes red, white, and pink. 'Nagoya' ornamental kale has very frilly leaves producing purple-red, rose, or creamy-white central growth. 'Peacock' is an unusual cultivar that has deeply cut, feathery leaves in red or white.

Pansy

Viola × wittrockiana

Size: 6 to 9 inches tall, 8- to 10-inch spread
Type: Short-lived perennial grown as a cool-season annual
Flowers: Red, yellow, blue, purple, white, pink, orange, and others with or without faces
Bloom Period: Fall, winter, and spring

Light Requirement:

Throughout the state no other plant is as popular as the pansy for cool-season flower beds. Pansies are reliable, very hardy (down to the low teens, and even lower), bloom like crazy and come in almost any color you could desire. The pansy has one of the widest color ranges of any garden flower, including red, purple, blue, bronze, pink, black, yellow, white, lavender, orange, apricot, and mahogany. The flowers may be of a single clear color or have two or three colors with a face. The plant itself is compact, about 8 inches in both height and spread and bears many stems. The medium-green, coarsely notched leaves are oval or heart-shaped. The fact that they are actually perennials we grow as annuals gives them great stamina. Flowering-size plants planted in the fall will bloom up to 6 months—until April or May when the heat of early summer ends the display.

When to Plant

Plant transplants October through March. A fall planting yields the best results.

Where to Plant

Full sun to part shade. They must have good drainage. Pansies are beautiful in containers, beds, borders and planted over spring bulbs, where they will bloom before, during and after the bulbs bloom.

How to Plant

Plant pansies in well-prepared beds in which a 2-inch layer of compost, fine pine bark, or peat moss has been spread and mixed in. Pansies are heavy feeders and will not perform well without adequate fertilizer. If your soil is high in phosphorus, incorporate 15-5-10 at the rate of 1/2 to 3/4 cup per 30 square feet; if not high in phosphorus, use 8-8-8 at the rate of 1 cup over the same area. Do not plant pansies deeper than they were growing to avoid crown rot. Water-in and mulch.

Care and Maintenance

Keep plants well watered, especially during establishment. Remember, pansies are heavy feeders. Fertilize once or twice a month with a soluble fertilizer for best results. Pinching off the faded blossoms will encourage longer flowering. Do not plant pansies in October if the weather is still warm, as they are prone to rot. Symptoms include yellow leaves, stunted growth, and wilt. In the southern part of the state it is usually best to wait until early November to plant.

Additional Information

Among their other great features, pansy flowers are edible and can be used in a variety of dishes. After especially cold weather, the flowers may be damaged and the foliage will look dark and water-soaked. Don't be alarmed; the plants will recover. Flower production usually diminishes in the coldest part of winter, especially in north Louisiana.

Additional Cultivars or Species

There are many series available, each with numerous colors, some with faces, some without. Look for 'Accord', 'Majestic Giant', 'Imperial', 'Crystal Bowl' (clear colors without faces), and 'Universal'. Popular pansy relatives called violas are also excellent for the garden and include *V. tricolor*, the Johnny-jump-up with purple and gold flowers, and other colors. *V. cornuta* looks like miniature pansies without faces; they produce greater numbers of smaller flowers and have a more spreading growth habit. The 'Sorbet' strain is highly recommended.

Periwinkle

Catharanthus roseus

Other Names: *Vinca rosea,* Vinca
Size: 10 to 18 inches
Type: Tender perennial grown as a warm-season annual
Flowers: Round or star-shaped, 1 to $1^1/_2$ inches
Bloom Period: Early summer to frost

Light Requirement:

"Tried and true" and "tough as nails" are clichés that apply to this plant, which has been an important part of summer flower gardens as long as most of us have been gardening. Periwinkles have been one of the most reliable heat-tolerant plants for sunny, well-drained locations for generations. This plant blooms despite the hottest weather, continuing on until frost. Like many of the bedding plants that bloom all summer, it is actually a tender perennial that will survive mild winters in coastal Louisiana to bloom again the next year. Breeders have developed many new and different colors. Rosy-red, pink, lavender, apricot, and deep purple join the traditional white, white with a red eye, and light purple. Unfortunately, a devastating disease called aerial blight (caused by the Phytophthora fungus) has made periwinkles somewhat less reliable. If you have had problems with this disease, which causes brown lesions on the stems as well as dieback and wilting of the plants, do not plant periwinkles back into that area.

When to Plant

Wait until the weather is quite warm to plant. Transplants can be planted in the garden in late April or May through August.

Where to Plant

Plant in full to part sun. Periwinkles are tolerant of hot, dry locations and must have good drainage. They are excellent in containers as well as in the garden.

How to Plant

Plant in well-prepared beds that have been improved by digging in a 2-inch layer of fine pine bark or compost and a sprinkling of general-purpose fertilizer. Plant in a raised bed if drainage is questionable. Set plants 8 to 10 inches apart at the same level or slightly higher than they were growing in pots or cell-packs. If the roots of the transplants have grown pot-bound, loosen them before planting. Water thoroughly to settle in the plants and mulch the bed.

Care and Maintenance

There are few pest problems. Proper planting in well-drained beds when the weather is warm is your best defense against Phytophthora. A mulch may also help keep the fungus from splashing from the soil onto the plants. Water only during especially dry, hot periods. Fertilize every 6 to 8 weeks with 1 cup of 8-8-8 or $1/2$ cup of 15-5-10 per 30 square feet of bed area, or use your favorite slow-release fertilizer at the time of planting. Cut plants back in late July or August as they tend to become leggy by the end of summer. They will resprout and be more bushy and attractive through the fall if you do. Flowering continues until the first freezes in December.

Additional Information

Periwinkles will frequently reseed. Look for volunteers in areas where they were growing the year before. A drug for treating a form of cancer is derived from this plant.

Additional Cultivars or Species

Classic cultivars include: 'Polka Dot', white with a red center; 'Little Blanche', pure white; 'Magic Carpet', low groundcover type with various colors; and 'Bright Eyes', white with a red eye. Newer strains with outstanding colors include the 'Tropicana' series, the 'Pretty In' series, the 'Pacifica' series, and the 'Cooler' series.

Petunia

Petunia × hybrida

Size: 12 to 18 inches
Type: Half-hardy annual
Flowers: Wide, flaring funnel-shaped in many colors
Bloom Time: Spring through early summer

Light Requirement:

Nurseries sell petunia transplants by the truck-load in the spring. The flowers are showy, come in an amazing range of colors and are produced in great abundance. Growing petunias is easy enough to make even beginning gardeners look good. So why do petunias end up frustrating so many Louisiana gardeners? The problem lies in what we are told they will do—versus what they actually can do here. We are told that petunias will bloom all summer. That may be true for more northern gardens, but it is not true for us because our summers are just too hot for them. Daytime highs in the 90s and nighttime lows in the mid- to upper 70s simply do them in. Gardeners who plant petunias in April or May are in for a rude surprise when they begin to fade out 4 or 5 weeks later. The trick to growing petunias successfully in Louisiana is early planting. Petunias are low spreading plants with medium-green leaves covered with a fine fuzz. The range of flower color encompasses everything but orange, but most commonly includes shades of red, pink, purple, and white.

When to Plant

Gardeners in south Louisiana can plant petunia transplants in their gardens as early as October. They will bloom in the fall, make root and foliage growth over the winter, and then bloom gloriously on stocky, well-established plants in March, April and May. This can be done because petunias are surprisingly hardy. They will tolerate temperatures down to 25 degrees Fahrenheit and even 20 degrees if they are covered. Petunias could survive normal to mild winters in the northern part of the state, but it's more risky. At least north Louisiana gardeners should plant as early as transplants become available in the spring, preferably by late March.

Where to Plant

Plant in well-drained locations that receive full sun to part sun for stocky, heavy-blooming plants.

How to Plant

Petunia transplants are sold in cell-packs or 4-inch pots. When planting in the fall, use smaller cell-pack transplants as they are more economical, and the small plants have plenty of time to grow before the main bloom season in the spring. Larger, well-established 4-inch pot transplants will give best results for late spring planting. To prepare beds, incorporate a 2-inch layer of compost, fine pine bark, or peat moss and sprinkle $1/2$ cup of 15-5-10 (or 1 cup of 8-8-8 fertilizer if your soil is low in phosphorus) per 30 square feet of bed area. If drainage is questionable, plant in raised beds. Make sure not to set the plants deeper than they were growing previously. Space plants 8 to 12 inches apart. Water-in thoroughly and mulch.

Care and Maintenance

Cover with sheets of fabric or plastic in the winter if temperatures below 25 degrees Fahrenheit are predicted. Petunias can survive temperatures as low as 20 without protection, but will sustain considerable damage. Water and fertilize regularly during their spring flowering season. Slugs, snails, and caterpillars eat holes in the leaves and flowers. Control slugs and snails with baits and traps and caterpillars with Sevin or B.t. Pinch back or lightly shear plants that begin to get leggy. By May, however, they are about finished and should be removed.

Additional Information

Choose floribunda or multiflora types for bedding in the garden. The large flowers of the grandifloras do not hold up to the weather as well, but are excellent in containers. Some varieties of petunias are surprisingly fragrant, particularly in the early morning or evening.

Additional Cultivars or Species

The 'Celebrity' series, the 'Cascade' series, and the 'Madness' series have done well in Louisiana. A new group, the millifloras, are dwarf with lots of smaller flowers and are represented by the 'Fantasy' series. Heat-tolerant varieties that do better in Louisiana summers include 'Purple Wave and 'Pink Wave', the 'Surfinas' and 'Supertunias'.

Salvia

Salvia splendens

Other Names: Annual Salvia, Scarlet Sage **Size:** 14 to 24 inches **Type:** Tender perennial grown as a warm-season annual **Flowers:** Robust spikes of scarlet, red, burgundy, purple, lilac, white, or pink **Bloom Period:** Summer and fall	**Light Requirement:**

If flower colors had a voice, scarlet sage would definitely yell. The red varieties of this salvia are spectacular in full bloom, yet can be almost overpowering in the landscape. New varieties of this native of Brazil have expanded the color range tremendously, and now there are soft pastel peaches, pinks, and lavenders, as well as burgundy, purple, and creamy white. This salvia, often called annual salvia, is actually a perennial, but does not survive normal Louisiana winters. Calling it annual salvia distinguishes it from salvia species that are reliable perennials (see salvias in the perennials chapter). *Salvia splendens* produces dark green, slightly scalloped, heart-shaped leaves on bushy, upright plants. The flower spikes, held well above the foliage, are densely packed with colorful tubular flowers.

When to Plant

Plant transplants April through August.

Where to Plant

Salvia is widely adaptable. It will bloom best and be more compact in full sun, but will tolerate part shade and still bloom acceptably. Excellent massed in beds or borders, its somewhat stiff, upright growth habit is best combined with other lower-growing plants in containers.

How to Plant

Annual salvia should be planted in well-prepared beds that have been improved by digging in a 2-inch layer of fine pine bark or compost and a sprinkling of general-purpose fertilizer; use 1/2 cup of 15-5-10 (or 1 cup of 8-8-8, if your soil is low in phosphorus) per 30 square feet of bed area. The fertilizer is very important as this salvia is a heavy feeder, and the foliage will be pale and the plant stunted if it is not adequately fertilized. Plant in a raised bed if drainage is questionable. Set plants about 8 inches apart at the same level they were growing in pots or cell-packs. If the roots of the transplants have grown pot-bound, loosen them before planting. Water thoroughly to settle in the plants and mulch the bed.

Care and Maintenance

Although this salvia is heat tolerant, it often seems less vigorous and the flower spikes smaller in the hottest months of July and August. Continue good care and it will revive in fall as the weather cools, and bloom until the first freeze. Trim off spent flower spikes frequently to keep the plants looking attractive. Fertilize regularly every 6 to 8 weeks with the above fertilizers and rates, or every 2 weeks with a soluble fertilizer. Leggy plants may be cut back in late summer to produce shorter, fuller plants for the fall season.

Additional Information

The bright, tubular flowers of annual salvia—especially the red varieties—are very attractive to hummingbirds. The calyx at the base of each flower is colorful and hangs on after the flower has fallen off.

Additional Cultivars or Species

'Flare' and 'Red Hot Sally' are excellent red varieties. The strains 'Salsa', 'Sizzler', and 'Hotline' come in a wide variety of colors.

Snapdragon

Antirrhinum majus

Size: 10 to 36 inches depending on the variety
Type: Short-lived perennial grown as a cool-season annual
Flowers: Spikes of tubular flowers, yellow, red, pink, white, and bicolors
Bloom Period: Spring through early summer

Light Requirement:

Snapdragons, native to the Mediterranean region, are a favorite of children, who pinch the sides of the flowers and make the "dragon's mouth" snap open and close. There are three heights: small varieties range from 8 to 10 inches; intermediates, 18 to 24 inches; and tall types, about 3 feet. The smaller types are ideal for planting in beds, while the taller varieties make excellent cut flowers. The most useful are the intermediate types, as the stems are long enough for cutting and the plants are short enough to look good in flower beds. Snapdragons are one of the hardiest and most reliable of the cool-season annuals, and will easily survive winter weather throughout the state.

When to Plant

Snapdragon transplants should be planted in October or November, since snapdragons planted in the fall outperform those planted in the spring. They will not bloom over the winter, but will spend the time becoming well established. Plant transplants in the spring, no later than March.

Where to Plant

Locate snapdragons in sunny areas that drain well. They will grow well with some shade. Short and intermediate varieties are good for beds and containers. Plant taller varieties toward the back of borders or in cutting beds.

How to Plant

Snapdragons perform best in well-prepared beds. Turn the soil to a depth of 8 inches, then spread a 2-inch layer of compost, fine pine bark, or peat moss. Sprinkle a general-purpose fertilizer such as 1 cup of 8-8-8 (or 1/2 cup of 15-5-10, if your soil is high in phosphorus) per 30 square feet, and thoroughly blend everything into the soil of the bed. Water-in and mulch the bed after the transplants are planted.

Care and Maintenance

Tall varieties will usually need to be staked. An alternative is to pinch out the growing tip when the plants are young to encourage a bushier, shorter plant. Promptly prune off finished flower spikes; this will greatly encourage the plants to bloom longer. Snapdragons are relatively heat tolerant and may continue to bloom until June or early July.

Additional Information

Although they are short-lived perennials, snapdragons rarely survive our long, hot, wet summers. On occasion, some plants may live and bloom for more than one season.

Additional Cultivars or Species

Short cultivars include: 'Bells Mix', open flower form; 'Tahiti Mix'; and 'Floral Carpet'. Intermediate cultivars include: 'Little Darling Mix', rust resistant; 'Sonnet Mix'; and 'Double Sweetheart Mix', double flowers. Tall cultivars include 'Rocket', 'Liberty', and 'Double Madam Butterfly'.

Sunflower

Helianthus annuus

Size: 1 to 10 feet depending on the variety
Type: Warm-season annual
Flowers: Daisy-like, yellow, gold, creamy white, bronze, mahogany, and orange
Bloom Period: Summer

Light Requirement:

Sunflowers are delightful plants with a cheerful (one might say sunny) disposition. If you haven't paid a lot of attention to sunflowers lately, you may think only of the gigantic yellow types. But, today's gardener has many choices when selecting sunflowers for color, height, and cut-flower or seed production. Sunflowers are among the easiest flowers to grow, and they thrive in the heat of our summers. Their quick, easy growth and large size are why children are often so delighted with them. While children get a big thrill out of growing giant sunflowers, they are a bit overwhelming for the average garden. Fortunately, plant breeders have developed a wide range of sunflower heights and a variety of colors.

When to Plant

Plant sunflower seeds or transplants in the garden anytime from March through early September. Surprisingly, sunflowers are moderately hardy and can withstand a light freeze.

Where to Plant

Sunflowers need a location that receives full sun and good drainage. They are adaptable to a variety of soils. Dwarf varieties can be used in the front of beds and borders and in containers. Tall varieties are best in the background.

How to Plant

You can start sunflower seeds in small containers filled with potting soil. Make sure the containers have drainage holes. Transplant them to flower beds when they have grown 4 to 6 inches high. Locate the containers in full sun outside to produce strong, robust transplants. You can also sow the seeds directly in a prepared garden bed. To direct-seed, rake the prepared bed and plant seeds according to package directions. Water frequently until the seeds come up, and then thin the seedlings to 12 to 24 inches apart, depending on variety. When the plants are large enough, mulch the planting. Depending on the variety, sunflowers will bloom anywhere from 55 to 75 days after the seeds sprout.

Care and Maintenance

When growing very tall sunflowers, you may want to provide a tall stake for support since the heads grow very large and heavy. The stake needs to be sturdy, pounded well into the ground, and reach at least two-thirds of the way up the plant. Water sunflowers during hot, dry weather. They will grow larger if fertilized once or twice while they are growing.

Additional Information

Some cultivars of sunflowers produce edible seeds. Seed heads are ready to harvest when the back of the head is brown and dry. Remove seeds by brushing them out with your hand and store them in air-tight containers in your refrigerator. Sunflower seeds make tasty snacks—raw or roasted—and can be used in salads and other dishes.

Additional Cultivars or Species

The selection from seed catalogs these days is incredible: 'Music Box', dwarf with 4-inch flowers of various colors; 'Sunspot', 2-foot plants with 10-inch flowers; 'Teddy Bear', 1-foot plants with double flowers; 'Valentine', lemon-yellow 4-inch flowers on a 4-foot plant; 'Autumn Giant', 6- to 10-inch flowers of various colors on a 6- to 8-foot plant; 'Russian Giant', 8- to 10-foot plants that produce huge flowers and are good for seed.

Wax Begonia

Begonia × semperflorens-cultorum

Size: 18 inches high, 12 inches wide
Type: Tender perennial used as a warm-season annual
Flowers: Red, pink, or white in clusters
Bloom Period: Spring to fall

Light Requirement:

A bed of well-grown wax begonias in full bloom is an incredible sight. Each plant can clothe itself in flowers, creating a solid carpet of blooms that dazzles the eye. The individual flowers are not particularly attractive (although there are some lovely doubles). It is the ability of these plants to produce flowers so prolifically and over such a long period of time that makes begonias so popular. The oval foliage may be bright green, green-tinged red, or bronzy-red, and has a waxy sheen that gives this begonia its name. Begonias sometimes survive mild winters in New Orleans in protected locations, especially if well mulched, but for most Louisiana gardeners they last only one season. That season, however, is from April to early December, with flowers virtually the whole time.

When to Plant

Transplants should be set out in garden beds from April through the summer.

Where to Plant

Begonias need a well-drained but moist location. They flower best if they receive 4 to 6 hours of morning sun, and shade from the hot afternoon sun. There is a trend to use begonias in full sun, and they will do reasonably well until July and August. Then, the combination of intense light and high temperatures will begin to take its toll. Begonias also do well in shady areas, but the plants are not as compact and do not flower as heavily. They are excellent for containers.

How to Plant

To prepare beds, incorporate a 2-inch layer of compost, fine pine bark, or peat moss and 1/2 cup of 15-5-10 (or 1 cup of 8-8-8, if your soil is low in phosphorus) per 30 square feet of bed area. If drainage is questionable, plant in raised beds. Make sure not to set the plants deeper than they were growing previously. Space plants 8 to 10 inches apart. Water-in thoroughly and mulch.

Care and Maintenance

Wax begonias are susceptible to root and crown rot if not cared for properly. Make sure beds drain well, and do not plant too deep. Proper watering is also important. Begonias must receive an even supply of water, but a common mistake is to water lightly and often—sometimes every day. This greatly encourages the possibility for rot. Water deeply no more often than once or twice a week. Begonias in sun need more water than those in shade. Fertilize occasionally with a soluble fertilizer. Avoid granular formulations as the granules can lodge in the foliage when scattered over the bed and cause damage to the leaves.

Additional Information

Because they grow over such a long period, you may need to trim back the plants occasionally to keep them shapely, especially in late summer. Feel free to do so as needed; they will resprout vigorously with a little extra fertilization. The trimmings root easily in loose potting soil; when rooted, they can be planted in the garden or containers.

Additional Cultivars or Species

The 'Cocktail' series is a popular and reliable bronze-leaved cultivar with flowers in white 'Whisky', pink 'Brandy', white-edged rose 'Rum', or rose 'Gin'. 'Wings Hybrid' has unusually large flowers. There are numerous others, including cultivars with double flowers and variegated foliage. The tuberous begonias, *B.* × *tuberhybrida,* are difficult and unreliable, particularly in the southern part of the state.

Wishbone Flower

Torenia fournieri

Other Name: Torenia
Size: About 12 to 14 inches
Type: Warm-season annual
Flowers: Numerous blue, violet, purple, pink, and rose, usually with a yellow throat
Bloom Period: Summer

Light Requirement:

Versatile and very reliable, the wishbone flower is named for the way its stamens join together to form a wishbone shape. This native of Vietnam does well in full sun to part shade, and provides a tremendous display of blue, purple, lavender, rose, pink, or white flowers over a very long period. The blue-flowered types are welcome in shady areas where the colors of most shade-loving, warm-season plants tend to be red, pink, or white.

When to Plant

Start seed indoors in February to plant out beginning in April. Plant transplants from April through the summer.

Where to Plant

It's hard to find plants that will perform equally well in the full, hot sun or in shady areas, but torenia makes it look easy. It is not particular about soil type or drainage, as long as the soil does not stay bone dry or constantly soggy.

How to Plant

Wishbone flower will thrive in any average garden soil without special preparation. If the soil is poor, incorporate some organic matter and a very light sprinkling of general-purpose fertilizer. Space transplants about 8 to 10 inches apart. To direct-seed, rake the prepared bed, scatter the fine seeds on the surface, and press in. Water frequently until the seeds come up, and then thin the seedlings to 8 inches apart. When the plants are large enough, mulch the planting. They are also easy to start in flats and transplant into beds.

Care and Maintenance

You should never claim a plant is fool-proof, but torenia nearly is. There are no major insect or disease problems to worry about. Water during hot, dry weather and keep the beds mulched to prevent weeds and conserve soil moisture.

Additional Information

Torenia self-seeds with abandon, but rarely becomes a nuisance. Look for volunteers where plants grew previously. They are easy to transplant into desired locations—even when they have started blooming—if you keep them well watered.

Additional Cultivars or Species

The standard species is medium blue with dark-blue markings. 'Clown Mix' is a seed-grown cultivar that introduced many new colors. 'Panda' is a compact cultivar that comes in blue and pink. Also worth planting is *T. baillonii*, 'Suzie Wong', a low-growing plant that produces numerous deep yellow flowers with a black throat in partly shaded areas.

Zinnia

Zinnia elegans

Other Names: Common Zinnia, Old Maids, Youth-and-Old-Age
Size: 12 to 36 inches
Type: Warm-season annual
Flowers: Single and fully double, daisy-like, red, yellow, orange, white, and purple
Bloom Period: Summer

Light Requirement:

Ask gardeners if they know what zinnias are, and most of them will say yes. Ask if they are growing them in their gardens, and most of them will say no. What a pity! Zinnias have been grown in American gardens for generations, and deserve their reputation for being one of the most attractive and easiest-to-grow annuals. Zinnias come in many heights, flower sizes and forms. Some are less that 1 foot tall with round flower heads less than 1 inch across, while others tower 3 feet tall and bear 7-inch blossoms on strong, wiry stems. Breeders have developed the color range to include apricot, rose, cream, violet, pale yellow, and even green—as well as the familiar bright red, purple, yellow, and orange. Multicolored and striped cultivars are also available.

When to Plant

Plant seeds in garden beds March through August. Transplants can be set out during the same period.

Where to Plant

Choose well-drained locations that receive plenty of sun. Zinnias are widely adapted to a variety of soils.

How to Plant

Zinnias are easy to grow from seed or transplants, but will perform best in well-prepared beds. Turn the soil to a depth of 8 inches, then spread a 2-inch layer of compost, fine pine bark, or peat moss. Sprinkle a general-purpose fertilizer such as 1 cup of 8-8-8 (or 1/2 cup of 15-5-10, if your soil is high in phosphorus) per 30 square feet, and thoroughly blend everything into the soil of the bed. Water-in and mulch the bed after the transplants are planted. To direct-seed, rake the prepared bed and plant seeds according to package directions. Water frequently until the seeds come up, and then thin the seedlings to 8 to 10 inches apart. When the plants are large enough, mulch the planting.

Care and Maintenance

Deadheading zinnias will promote more flowering. Caterpillars and powdery mildew are the worst problems you are likely to encounter. Treat caterpillars with Sevin, B.t., or other approved pesticides. Treat powdery mildew with daconil. Use products according to label directions.

Additional Information

Zinnias make outstanding, long-lasting cut flowers.

Additional Cultivars or Species

The following cultivars have performed well in Louisiana: 'Cut and Come Again', 2-foot, well-branched, various colors; 'Dreamland' series, 4-inch flowers in bright colors on compact 16-inch plants; 'Peter Pan' series, similar to 'Dreamland' with informal flowers; 'Ruffles' series, $2\frac{1}{2}$-foot plants with informal 4-inch flowers in various colors; 'Thumbelina', 10-inch plants with $1\frac{1}{2}$-inch flowers of various colors. In addition to common zinnias, *Z. haageana*, the Mexican zinnia, is available in two cultivars: 'Persian Carpet' and 'Old Mexico'. These produce 18- to 24-inch spreading plants with 2-inch red and yellow bicolor flowers. There are many more available, especially from seed catalogs.

CHAPTER TWO

Bulbs

FLOWERING BULBS HAVE A LONG TRADITION of use in Louisiana gardens and are one of our most enduring herbaceous plant materials. It is not unusual to see bulbs blooming around an old homestead long after the house is gone. Sometimes a double row of daffodils marks the old pathway that led up to a front door, or a clump of summer-blooming crinums planted long ago produces rosy pink trumpets in an otherwise wild meadow.

This group of plants provides an excellent way to introduce color and interest into the landscape. The term bulb is used for any fleshy below-ground structure produced by a plant, including true bulbs, tubers, corms, rhizomes, and tuberous roots. It is important to know that these structures differ significantly from one another, for these differences can influence how a plant is planted and propagated.

Bulbs can be broadly divided into two categories: those that bloom in the spring and those that bloom in the summer. Spring-flowering bulbs bloom between January and April. They are planted from September through November, except for tulips and hyacinths, which are planted in December through early January after a 6- to 8-week chilling in the vegetable bin of a refrigerator. Many spring-flowering bulbs do not rebloom reliably in Louisiana. The farther north in the state you garden, the more likely a larger variety of spring bulbs will rebloom. Tulips and hyacinths rebloom sporadically if at all in coastal Louisiana, but they may rebloom for several years in the northern part of the state. Summer-flowering bulbs bloom roughly from May through September and are generally planted in March through May.

No matter what kind of growing conditions you have, from shady to sunny and from dry to wet situations, at least a few kinds of bulbs will thrive there. Most bulbs prefer good drainage, although calla, canna, crinum, spider lily, Louisiana iris, and gingers are a few exceptions. Full to part sun is important to most of these plants for healthy growth and flowering, but there are several, such as caladiums and gingers, that do fine in shadier spots.

Chapter Two

Buy bulbs of the best quality. Bargain-priced bulbs are not a good deal when the flowers they produce are small or nonexistent. When choosing loose bulbs at a local nursery or garden center, pick out the largest, plumpest bulbs in the bin. They should be firm with no obvious cuts, soft spots, or damage from insects or disease.

Many bulbs have a dormancy period after the foliage dies off. This period generally occurs in the winter for summer-flowering bulbs and during the summer for spring-flowering bulbs. As bulbs enter dormancy, growth stops and the foliage becomes yellow, then brown. At that time, the foliage may be trimmed back to the ground. Be sure to place markers where the dormant bulbs are located; sometimes it's hard to remember exactly where they are when nothing shows above ground, and you can accidentally dig into them with a shovel if you're not careful. Most bulbs may be left in the ground all year long with proper mulching for winter protection. A few summer bulbs should be lifted and stored during their dormant period.

Avoid removing any foliage from a bulb when it is healthy and green, for it is the leaves that manufacture the food which is stored in the bulb. Removing healthy foliage reduces the plant's ability to create food, weakens the bulb, and decreases flowering. However, seed pods that sometimes form after a bulb has bloomed should be removed to avoid draining the plant of energy.

Bulbs perform best if they are planted into well-prepared beds. Remove any weeds from the area and turn the soil over to a depth of 8 inches. Spread a 2-inch layer of organic matter such as compost, fine pine bark, peat moss, or aged manure over the bed, sprinkle a general-purpose fertilizer appropriate for your area at label recommendations (such as 8-8-8 at one cup per 30 square feet of bed area), and thoroughly incorporate it all into the bed. If drainage is poor, plant bulbs in raised beds, or choose bulbs tolerant of moist soils.

When growing spring-flowering bulbs, you will find there is a long delay between planting in fall and bloom the following spring, but there is a way to provide color in the bed before the bulbs come into flower. After the bulbs are in the ground, plant over them with low-growing cool-season annuals such as alyssum, violas, or pansies. These annuals cover the bare soil and provide color before, during, and after the bulbs flower.

Amaryllis

Hippeastrum spp. and hybrids

Other Name: St. Joseph's Lily
Zones: 8 and 9
Size: 18 to 24 inches
Type: Semi-evergreen
Flowers: Large, showy trumpets in red, pink, and white
Bloom Period: April

Light Requirement:

Amaryllis is the undisputed queen of the spring bulb garden. There is not another spring-flowering bulb that can compare with the spectacular beauty of a clump of amaryllis in bloom. While Northern gardeners must grow amaryllis in pots protected over the winter, these bulbs are hardy when planted into garden beds in Louisiana, particularly in the southern part of the state. Each large bulb produces several medium-green strap-shaped leaves about 2 inches wide and 1 1/2 feet long (they grow longer in the shade). The flowers are produced in clusters of four at the top of thick stems held well above the foliage, and they range in size from 5 to 10 inches across, depending on the variety.

When to Plant

Bulbs are usually available in the fall. Here's the tricky part—they should not be planted into the garden until late March or April.

Where to Plant

Plant in well-drained beds that receive 4 to 6 hours of sun a day. Amaryllis will tolerate more sun, but the foliage may take on a yellowish tint and the plants will need more watering.

How to Plant

When you buy bulbs in the fall, they must be planted into pots. Choose a container that will comfortably hold the bulb with about an inch clearance between the bulb and the rim of the pot. Partly fill the pot with a good, well-drained potting soil, place the bulb in the pot, and finish filling the pot with soil. When the task is done, the neck and a little of the top of the bulb should be showing. Water often enough to keep the soil moist, and place the pot in a sunny window. Amaryllis potted in the fall will bloom indoors during the winter. Once planted into the garden, amaryllis will bloom in April every year. Keep your amaryllis indoors until April, and then plant them into a well-prepared bed outside. Plant at the same level they were growing in their containers, with the necks above ground level. Mulch after planting.

Care and Maintenance

Amaryllis usually go semi-dormant to dormant in the winter, depending on how cold it gets. Keep bulbs well mulched with pine straw to protect them from severe freezes. Trim off the foliage when it yellows. Fertilize in March or April, and again in June. Unless you are breeding amaryllis or intend to grow some from seeds, prune off the flower stalk where it emerges from the bulb when flowering is complete. This will prevent the bulb from wasting energy on seedpod production. Dig and divide bulbs in early March or after flowering every 3 or 4 years.

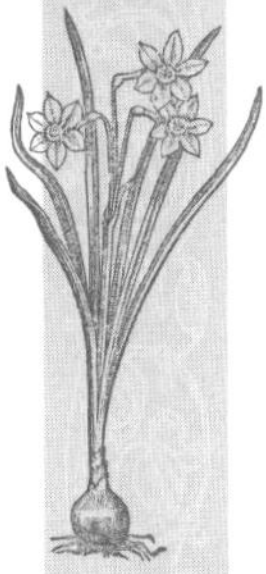

Additional Information

Purple blotch disease causes dark-red splotches on the foliage. Prune off badly infected leaves and treat with an appropriate fungicide. Some garden-grown amaryllis plants are infected with viruses and show pale-green streaks or blotches in their foliage. A virus may decrease the vigor of the plants. There is no cure—a virus is contagious, and infected plants should be discarded.

Additional Cultivars and Species

H. × *Johnsonii,* the vigorous and reliable St. Joseph's lily, is red with a white stripe on each petal. *H. vittatum,* white with red veins, is common in New Orleans gardens. Modern Dutch hybrids are large and showy but may not be as vigorous in the garden as the old types.

Bearded Iris

Iris × germanica

Zones: 8 and 9
Size: 2 feet
Flowers: Large, showy; purple, yellow, blue, white, pink, and many other colors
Bloom Period: Spring to early summer
Light Requirement:

The gorgeous orchid-like flowers of bearded irises make these plants tremendously popular. The flowers come in an amazing range of colors and color combinations, and the flower stalks vary in height from 18 to 36 inches. The foliage, 18 to 24 inches tall, is an attractive bluish green, sword-shaped and arranged in a fan at the ends of creeping, fleshy rhizomes. Relatively easy to grow in the northern part of the state, bearded irises are less reliable the farther south you garden.

When to Plant

Plant iris rhizomes or plants in fall. Container-grown plants can be planted in spring or early summer.

Where to Plant

Locate iris plantings where they will get at least 6 hours of sun a day. The beds must be well drained. Raised beds give best results in south Louisiana.

How to Plant

Till the soil to a depth of 6 to 8 inches. Spread a 2-inch layer of organic matter (fine pine bark is best if your soil is heavy), and sprinkle with 15-5-10 at the rate of 1/4 cup per 10 square feet of bed area. Use 1/3 cup of 8-8-8 per 10 square feet if your soil is low in phosphorus. If your soil is a heavy clay, spread 2 inches of builders sand over the area. Thoroughly blend all amendments into the existing soil and rake smooth. Plant irises so that the rhizome is just below the soil surface, water-in, and mulch the beds to prevent weeds.

Care and Maintenance

Do not overwater. Bearded irises like to be grown somewhat dry, especially in summer. To keep the plants looking neat, trim off faded flower stalks and foliage when it yellows. Fertilize each year as indicated above after plants finish flowering. Divide in September or October. Dig up clumps, discard the old unsprouted rhizomes, and trim the foliage of the young, growing rhizomes back to 6 to 8 inches. Replant at the same depth they were growing. Do not divide bearded irises more often than every 3 or 4 years.

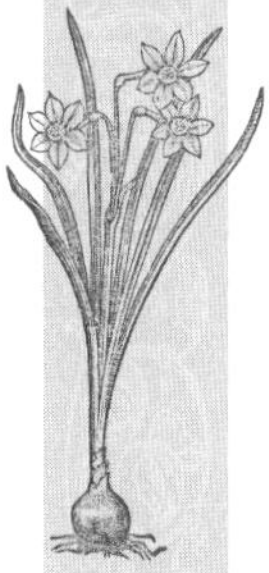

Additional Information

Many bearded iris varieties will grow in south Louisiana but fail to bloom. Bacterial soft rot destroys many iris plantings in coastal areas. In north Louisiana, the best bearded iris varieties are relatively care-free.

Additional Cultivars or Species

The old cultivar white flag, *Iris* × *albicans,* is a reliable spring bloomer throughout the state. It is often confused with the Florentine iris, *I.* × *germanica* var. *florentina,* which is taller and less common. As its name implies, white flag is usually white, but there is also a blue form called 'Madonna'.

Butterfly Ginger

Hedychium coronarium

Other Name: Butterfly Lily
Zones: 8 and 9
Size: 4 to 6 feet
Type: Dormant in winter
Flowers: Fragrant, white
Bloom Period: Summer

Light Requirement:

Gingers are a wonderful group of plants for shady Louisiana gardens, especially those in the southern part of the state. Gardeners in northern Louisiana will be able to grow several of the hardiest types, and these gingers are certainly worth including in the garden. Ideal for moist, shady areas, gingers lend a lush, tropical look to the summer landscape. Although no ginger is difficult to grow, butterfly ginger is one of the easiest. Strong stems bear two rows of 12- to 18-inch-long medium-green leaves along opposite sides. The flowers are produced at the tips of the stems, emerging from a green cone-like structure. Each flower is perfectly shaped like a white butterfly and produces a rich, sweet fragrance that is especially noticeable in the evening. Butterfly ginger is outstanding planted close to an outdoor sitting area.

When to Plant

Plant rhizomes or growing plants in late March through August. Butterfly gingers can be transplanted any time during the summer as long as they are kept well watered afterward.

Where to Plant

Locations that receive no more than 4 to 6 hours of daily sun are best. Butterfly gingers will bloom well with as little as 2 hours of sun or dappled light. Moist, fertile soils encourage vigorous growth. Avoid dry areas.

How to Plant

Set plants into the ground so that the rhizomes are just below the soil surface. Any good garden soil is fine, but gingers will respond well to generous amounts of compost, rotted manure, or peat moss dug into the bed before planting. To stimulate lush growth, add 15-5-10 at the rate of 1 cup per 30 square feet when turning in the organic matter. Water-in and mulch to conserve moisture and control weeds. Tall plants may need to be temporarily staked until they get established.

Care and Maintenance

Each butterfly ginger shoot produces only one bloom spike. When the flowers have faded, you can trim off the spent spike or cut the entire shoot down to the ground. The latter is recommended if the foliage has been damaged by insects or if the clump is becoming crowded. The rhizomes will send up more shoots to replace whatever you remove. Water as needed during hot, dry weather; fertilizer applications are optional. Dig up clumps of butterfly ginger, divide them, and replant in late spring at least every other year to keep the plants under control and growing where you want them. When the foliage turns brown after the first hard freeze, cut it back to the ground and mulch with a thick layer of leaves or pine straw to protect the rhizomes.

Additional Information

Although it is not poisonous, this is not a ginger suitable for flavoring food. In coastal southeast Louisiana, gardeners can plant edible ginger (*Zingiber officinale*) rhizomes purchased at the supermarket into beds during the warm summer months. Many gingers will survive north Louisiana winters if provided a thick mulch of pine straw over their rhizomes in early December.

Additional Cultivars or Species

Hedychium flavum has yellow-orange flowers. *H. gardneranum*, Kahili ginger, produces large, showy spikes of pale yellow flowers with red stamens. Other excellent gingers: *Curcuma petiolata*, hidden lily ginger; *Alpinia zerumbet*, shell ginger; and *Amomum compactum*, round cardamon. There are many other wonderful gingers too numerous to list here. We recommend you explore this group of plants.

Caladium

Caladium × hortulanum

Zone: 9
Size: 12 to 18 inches
Type: Dormant in winter
Flowers: Not significant

Light Requirement:

It's hard to beat caladiums for summer-long color in shady areas. The color is provided by the remarkable foliage, which can be splashed, spotted, banded, and patterned in every imaginable combination of red, rose, pink, white, and green. The leaves are usually heart-shaped like their larger relatives the elephant ears, but there are also cultivars with narrower leaves called strap-leaf or lance-leaf types. Caladiums have many uses in the landscape. Mass plantings are dramatic, especially when just one variety is used. Caladiums are beautiful planted along walkways, in front of large shrubs, and in beds with ferns, gingers, impatiens, and other shade-loving plants.

When to Plant

Caladiums tubers can be planted indoors in pots or flats in February or March to get a head start on the season. Unsprouted tubers or growing plants should not be planted in the garden until April in south Louisiana or May in the northern part of the state.

Where to Plant

Choose areas that are well drained but tend to stay moist. All caladiums prefer some shade during the day and grow most luxuriously in partial-shade conditions. Many gardeners are currently trying to grow caladiums in full sun. If you try this, keep the plants well watered. The strap-leaf types are better adapted to sunny areas, as are those varieties with heavily textured leaves—but the fact remains that they just aren't as happy in full sun. Caladiums are excellent in containers and windowboxes.

How to Plant

Beds should be generously amended with compost, rotted manure, or peat moss. Till the soil to a depth of 6 to 8 inches. Spread a 2-inch layer of organic matter, and sprinkle with 15-5-10 at the rate of 1/4 cup per 10 square feet of bed area. Use 1/3 cup of 8-8-8 per 10 square feet if your soil is low in phosphorus. If your soil is a heavy clay, spread 2 inches of builders sand over the area. Thoroughly blend all amendments into the existing soil and rake smooth. Plant unsprouted tubers one inch below the soil surface and sprouted tubers at the same level they were growing in their containers. Water-in and mulch the bed after planting to conserve soil moisture and control weeds.

Care and Maintenance

Keep caladiums well watered during hot, dry weather. Fertilize as indicated above in July to stimulate continued leaf production. Caladiums begin to go dormant in late September or October. When foliage is no longer attractive, lift the tubers with the foliage attached and lay them out in a sheltered location. When the foliage has turned tan and papery, pull it from the tubers. Store tubers in net bags, burlap sacks, cardboard boxes, or paper bags in a location that will not freeze over the winter. Caladiums left in the ground over the winter in New Orleans frequently come back up in the spring if the location is well drained.

Additional Information

Caladiums produce an interesting flower, but since the foliage is the main feature of this plant, remove flower buds or flowers as they appear. Pest problems are minor. Caterpillars, snails, and slugs occasionally chew a few holes in the leaves.

Additional Cultivars or Species

Cultivars commonly available include 'Rosebud', 'Carolyn Wharton', 'Candidum', 'White Christmas', and 'Pink Symphony'. There are many others. 'Candidum Junior' and 'Miss Muffet' are dwarf cultivars.

Canna

Canna × generalis

Zones: 8 and 9
Size: 2 to 6 feet, depending on cultivar
Type: Dormant in winter
Flowers: Large, showy; orange, scarlet, yellow, rose, and other colors
Bloom Period: Summer

Light Requirement:

Canna is a plant that yells "tropical" at the top of its lungs yet is remarkably hardy. If you don't like flamboyant plants, pass canna by. Its brilliant flowers and green, burgundy, or variegated foliage make a strong statement in the garden. Though some gardeners describe cannas as garish, others see these colorful, easy-to-grow plants as indispensable in the landscape. Cannas tolerate a tremendous range of growing conditions, from dry, sunny beds to shaded aquatic gardens.

When to Plant

Plant rhizomes or growing plants any time from April to August.

Where to Plant

Cannas will grow just about anywhere. Flowering is best in full to part sun, but they will bloom with as little as 3 hours of direct sun. Growth is fastest in moist, fertile soil, but these plants are not picky. Cannas are good additions to aquatic gardens. When planted in containers, dwarf cultivars are great for brightening up decks and patios with flowers all summer long.

How to Plant

The expression "Just stick it in the ground" certainly applies to cannas. Plant rhizomes just below the soil surface in average garden soil. Face the growing point in the direction you want the plants to grow. Water-in and mulch. For aquatic planting, plant in a generous-sized pot with heavy garden soil, and place so that the water's surface is a couple of inches above the rim of the pot. When planting in containers, use a good-quality, well-drained potting soil.

Care and Maintenance

Each canna shoot produces only one bloom spike, and when the flowers have faded, you can trim off the spent spike or cut the entire shoot down to the ground. This severe cutting is recommended if the foliage has been damaged by insects or if the clump is becoming crowded. The rhizomes will send up more shoots to replace whatever you remove. Water as needed during hot, dry weather; fertilizer applications are optional. Dig up clumps of cannas, divide them, and replant in late spring at least every other year. This practice will keep the plants under control, growing where you want them. When the foliage turns brown after the first hard freeze, cut it back to the ground and mulch with a thick layer of leaves or pine straw to protect the rhizomes.

Additional Information

Cannas would be perfect except for a pest called the canna leaf-roller. This caterpillar can cause terrible damage by chewing holes in the leaves, turning the leaves brown, and binding the leaves and flower buds together with silk. This pest is active all summer, creating the need for repeated applications of acephate, Sevin, or B.t. according to label directions. In south Louisiana where the canna leaf-roller is especially bad, some gardeners just give up and either accept the damage or stop planting cannas.

Additional Cultivars or Species

'Tropical Rose' is an excellent seed-grown dwarf cultivar with rose-pink flowers. The Pfitzers are a group of dwarf varieties with flowers in many colors. 'The President' is a popular tall-growing red cultivar. There are many others with a wide variety of flower colors. *Canna indica* grows wild and shows up in many gardens. It has small red flowers with narrow petals and sets copious amounts of seed. It can become weedy.

Crinum

Crinum species and hybrids

Other Names: Milk-and-Wine Lilies, St. John's Lily
Zones: 8 and 9
Size: Varies with species, from 2 to 4 feet
Type: Evergreen, killed back by hard freezes
Flowers: White, pink, rose, and burgundy clusters of trumpets on stalks
Bloom Period: Spring to late summer (depending on type)

Light Requirement:

Crinums have long been part of gardening in the South, but they have recently fallen out of favor with landscape architects and nurseries. They are rarely seen in new subdivisions and landscapes, and many new gardeners have never even heard of them; these tough, long-lived bulbs are far more common in old neighborhoods and in rural areas, where gardeners still count on sharing with friends to acquire many of their plants. Crinums have been passed on from gardener to gardener for generations. Clumps of crinums can live on long after the gardener who planted them is gone. The strap-shaped leaves are broad and often wavy. They emerge from the tops of the bulbs to form a mound, or arch up and over like amaryllis, or radiate out from a central point. This is a large group of species and hybrids, and there is a lot of variation within the group. The often-fragrant flowers are produced in clusters at the end of thick stalks. Many look like trumpet lilies or amaryllis and come in colors of white, pink, rose, and burgundy, sometimes with stripes. The milk-and-wine lilies get their name from their milky white flowers which have a broad wine-red stripe down each petal. Flowering occurs from spring to late summer, depending on type.

When to Plant

Plant crinum bulbs in spring through late summer. Plants should have a chance to get established before winter.

Where to Plant

Crinums are amazingly adaptable to a wide variety of growing conditions. Full sun to part shade suits the majority of them. Most crinums tolerate poorly drained heavy soils, and some will even grow in wet conditions. They also thrive in well-drained soils.

How to Plant

Despite their tough nature, crinums benefit from good soil preparation. Enrich the spot where the bulbs will be planted with generous amounts of organic matter. Plant the bulbs deep, about 12 to 18 inches down. This will discourage the production of offsets and produce a large (crinum bulbs can be huge) single bulb and improve flowering. Spacing will depend on the size of the species or cultivar planted. Water-in and keep the bulbs well mulched.

Care and Maintenance

Feed in late spring and midsummer. A general-purpose fertilizer applied around the plant in moderation is fine. A topdressing of rotted manure or compost is also recommended. The foliage will freeze back during especially cold winters. When it does, trim it back and make sure the bulbs are covered with a thick layer of pine straw for protection. They will return vigorously in the spring. Prune off faded flower stalks as they occur.

Additional Information

Most crinums grow very well when planted alongside garden ponds, and they look lovely in those locations. They are striking as specimen plants in beds with other plants or by structures in the garden.

Additional Cultivars or Species

A few of the species and cultivars: *Crinum moorei*, *C. americanum*, *C. asiaticum*, *C. scabrum*, *C. bulbispermum*, *C.* × *powellii* 'Alba', *C.* 'Ellen Bosanquet', *C.* 'Emma Jones', and *C.* 'Mrs. James Hendry'.

Dutch Iris

Iris × hollandica

Zones: 8 and 9
Size: 18 to 24 inches
Type: Dormant in summer
Flowers: Blue, purple, white, yellow, and other colors
Bloom Period: Spring

Light Requirement:

Surprisingly few traditional spring-flowering bulbs return reliably year after year for us, particularly in the southern part of the state. Most are good for only one or maybe two seasons. Dutch irises are quite reliable; they will come back to brighten your spring garden for many years. The "×" that you see in the Latin name of some plants indicates that they are not a true species but a hybrid plant resulting from a cross between two species. *I. × hollandica* was created by crossing *I. xiphium* and *I. tingitana*. Like most irises, the beautiful flowers are complex in shape. Several flowers are produced one at a time at the top of 1 1/2- to 2-foot-tall stems. The foliage is narrow and grassy in appearance.

When to Plant

Plant bulbs October through November.

Where to Plant

Bulbs will rebloom best if they receive at least 4 to 6 hours of sun a day. The site should be well drained; these plants are good to use in raised bed plantings.

How to Plant

Loosen the soil in the area where the bulbs are to be planted to a depth of 6 to 8 inches, and dig in a 2-inch layer of organic matter. If your soils are acidic, incorporate some lime along with the organic matter. Plant the bulbs 3 to 4 inches deep, spaced 2 to 3 inches apart. Water-in and mulch the area or plant over with white alyssum.

Care and Maintenance

Fertilize with a general-purpose fertilizer in February. Dutch iris usually bloom in March or April. You must wait for the foliage to begin to turn yellow before you cut it back. This will allow the bulb to store the maximum amount of food and ensures there will be flowers next spring.

Additional Information

Dutch irises make outstanding cut flowers; plant enough for indoor arrangements. Since the foliage is not particularly attractive, plant clumps of Dutch irises among other plants.

Additional Cultivars or Species

Many cultivars are available. 'Wedgwood' is a classic light blue. Try 'Golden Harvest', 'Blue Ribbon', or 'White Wedgwood'. The Spanish iris, *I. xiphium,* is one of the parents of the Dutch iris.

Gladiolus

Gladiolus × hortulanus

Other Names: Sword Lily, Glads
Zones: 8 and 9
Size: 30 to 40 inches
Type: Dormant late summer to spring
Flowers: Many-flowered spikes of red, yellow, pink, purple, orange, and other colors
Bloom Period: Summer

Light Requirement:

Gladiolus means "little sword" in Latin. This name and the common name "sword lily" refer to the pointed, blade-shaped leaves produced by this plant. Despite its popularity as a cut flower, gladiolus with its strong, upright growth and one-sided spikes of flowers often looks somewhat awkward in the garden. A single row of glads, each leaning in a different direction, does not contribute a positive effect. Try planting glads in groups among other plants, and make sure they do not fall over.

When to Plant

Corms should be planted from early February through early March. Since the bloom time of each plant is rather short, gardeners often plant a succession of corms at 2-week intervals to provide a longer bloom period. Early planting ensures that the corms will bloom before the intense heat of summer, and they will be less likely to suffer severe damage from gladiolus thrips.

Where to Plant

Plant in well-prepared beds with excellent drainage. Glads need 6 to 8 hours of sun to grow strong stems and stay upright. These plants usually look best when planted in groups among lower-growing shrubs or herbaceous perennials.

How to Plant

Loosen the soil in the area where the bulbs are to be planted to a depth of 6 to 8 inches, and dig in a 2-inch layer of organic matter and a sprinkling of general-purpose fertilizer. Plant the corms 4 to 5 inches deep; planting at this depth will help the plants remain upright. Water-in and mulch over the area.

Care and Maintenance

If plants begin to fall over, they must be staked. Watch for stippling in the foliage or flowers. This is damage caused by gladiolus thrips, the major pest of glads in our area. Spray with acephate, carefully following label directions. Glads left in the ground will sometimes rebloom, especially if the bed is well drained, although they most often play out in a couple of years. Corms can be dug up when the foliage yellows in late summer, stored in a frost-free location, and planted out the next year.

Additional Information

If you cut your gladiolus for indoor arrangements and want the corms to rebloom the following year, leave at least 4 or 5 leaves to produce a large blooming-size corm.

Additional Cultivars or Species

Gladiolus byzantinus, the Byzantine gladiolus, is a reliable, long-lived perennial that is treasured as a garden flower in the South. Its spikes of magenta flowers appear in early summer. Plant corms in the fall. They may be left in the ground all year. *G. natalensis* is called the parrot gladiolus and was one of the principle species used to create the modern hybrids. It produces spikes of hooded yellow and orange flowers, and it is a reliable perennial whose corms do not need to be lifted and stored.

Louisiana Iris

Iris spp. and hybrids

Zones: 8 and 9
Size: 16 to 36 inches
Type: Semi-Evergreen
Flowers: Shades of burgundy, pink, blue, purple, lavender, white, and yellow
Bloom Period: March through May

Light Requirement:

The Louisiana iris species are *Iris fulva, I. brevecaulis, I. nelsonii,* and *I. giganticaerulea*. Only in Louisiana can we find all four of these closely related species. They will cross with one another, but with no other species of *Iris* except *I. hexagona*. Although there are other iris species native to Louisiana, only these four and their hybrids are called the Louisiana irises. Their hybrids are noted for their exceptional color range, which is greater than any other group of irises, and they have become popular garden plants in many countries. Wherever they are grown they are called Louisiana irises. They have become our state's floral ambassador to the world. It's a pity that more Louisiana gardeners haven't discovered this wonderful group of plants. There should be at least one or two in every garden.

When to Plant

The best time to plant Louisiana irises is August through October when they are most dormant. This is also an excellent time to dig and divide your irises, though most gardeners purchase container-grown irises in the spring when they are in bloom in order to select the flower shapes and colors they prefer.

Where to Plant

Plant Louisiana irises where they will get at least 6 hours of sun a day. Planting in areas that are too shady will reduce flowering. The original species grow in open moist to boggy areas in full sun. The hybrids do well under average garden conditions. You may also plant Louisiana irises in aquatic gardens and along the edges of ponds in shallow water.

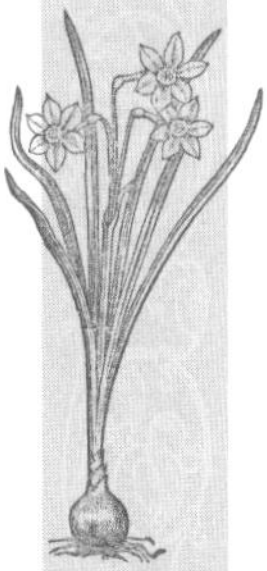

How to Plant

Remove weeds from the area to be planted, till the soil to a depth of 6 to 8 inches, and spread a 2-inch layer of organic matter such as compost, rotted manure, or peat moss. Sprinkle 1 cup of 8-8-8 or 1/2 cup of 15-5-10 (if your soil is high in phosphorus) per 30 square feet. Plant so that the top of the rhizomes are just showing, and make sure the roots are well covered. Water-in and mulch the beds, being sure to cover the rhizomes to prevent sunscald. Potted Louisiana irises may be placed into aquatic gardens with the water's surface a couple of inches above the pot rim. These irises may also be planted in shallow water or in the banks around ponds with the rhizomes just below the soil surface.

Care and Maintenance

The main growing season for Louisiana irises is October through May. Fertilize in October and February at the rates recommended above, and keep the plants well watered during this period. The foliage may become unattractive in late summer, particularly if the plants are planted in a dry location. Trim the foliage back and vigorous new growth will begin in the fall. Plants growing in aquatic or boggy conditions are less likely to enter a pronounced dormancy.

Additional Information

Louisiana irises are not susceptible to many serious insect and disease problems. Leaf miners can cause white streaks in the foliage as they eat out the green tissue; a systemic insecticide applied when they are first noticed and then as needed will usually do a good job. Rust is a fungus disease that causes numerous small spots, first yellow, then brown, on the foliage. There is no treatment. Remove and dispose of infected leaves promptly.

Additional Cultivars or Species

There are numerous outstanding hybrid cultivars. A few are 'Easter Tide', a lavender and pale yellow bicolor; 'Acadiana Sunset', burgundy with yellow signals; 'Creole Fantasy', purple; 'Cajun Country', deep red; 'Clara Goula', ruffled white; and 'Deneb', pink.

Narcissus

Narcissus spp.

Other Names: Jonquils, Paperwhites, Daffodils
Zones: 8 and 9
Size: 8 to 16 inches
Type: Dormant in summer
Flowers: Yellow and white, occasionally orange and pink
Bloom Period: Spring

Light Requirement:

Lumping all of the narcissus together is not really fair to this group of diverse spring-flowering bulbs, but to get into the classification of all the major narcissus divisions would take a chapter in itself. Most gardeners are familiar with daffodils, and many know paperwhites and jonquils. These bulbs are among the most-loved and best of the spring-flowering bulbs we grow in our gardens. Closer to the coast, fewer types will readily rebloom year after year, but in the northern part of the state, daffodils and other narcissus are some of the most enduring of the spring bulbs. There are many narcissus cultivars that can become a lasting part of your garden and brighten your heart each spring, no matter which part of the state you live in.

When to Plant

Bulbs should be planted October through early December. Choose large, firm, and preferably double-nosed bulbs (double-nosed bulbs are not always available for some of the smaller-flowered varieties).

Where to Plant

Plant in a well-prepared bed that drains well. Avoid low areas that retain water. If you want your bulbs to rebloom, they must receive at least 4 to 6 hours of direct sun.

How to Plant

Large bulb types should be planted 4 to 6 inches deep, and smaller bulbs 3 to 4 inches deep. Space bulbs about 4 inches apart. They are most effective planted in groups, but they can also be scattered in informal drifts or planted in formal rows.

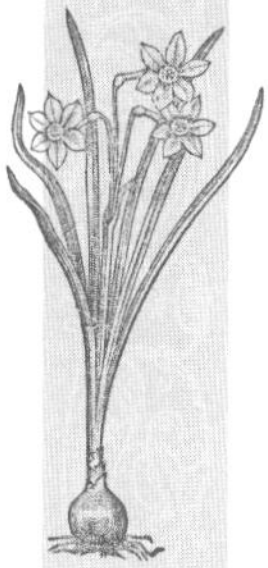

Care and Maintenance

Do not cut the foliage of narcissus plants until it begins to turn yellow in late spring or early summer on bulbs you expect to rebloom. Some varieties do not rebloom well in certain parts of the state. In particular, large trumpet daffodils tend to do better in north Louisiana. You may fertilize the bulbs immediately after flowering with a general-purpose fertilizer appropriate for your area.

Additional Information

These bulbs needn't be dug and stored after blooming. Indeed, clumps can stay in the ground without dividing for several years. After 5 to 7 years, clumps of bulbs may become crowded and will bloom better if divided and the largest bulbs replanted.

Additional Cultivars or Species

The following narcissus cultivars should repeat bloom throughout the state. There are certainly others that would do well, particularly in north Louisiana, but these make a good beginning. *N. tazetta* (Paperwhite) cultivars 'Ziva', 'Galilee', 'Chinese Sacred Lily', 'Soleil d'Or', and 'Erlicheer'; *N. jonquilla* (Jonquil) cultivars 'Campernelle', 'Trevithian', 'Sweetness', and 'Golden Scepter'; *N. cyclamineus* cultivars 'February Gold', 'Peeping Tom', and 'Tete a Tete'; *N. triandrus* (Angel's Tears) cultivars 'Thalia', 'Ice Wings', 'Silver Chimes', and 'Hawera'; and *N. pseudonarcissus* (Daffodil) cultivars 'Carlton', 'Ice Follies', 'Mount Hood', and 'Fortune'.

Philippine Lily

Lilium philippinense var. *formosanum*

Other Names: *Lilium formosanum,* Asian Trumpet Lily
Zones: 8 and 9
Size: 5 feet
Type: Dormant in winter
Flowers: Clusters of 3 to 10 white trumpet flowers
Boom Period: Late summer through fall

Light Requirement:

Looking for all the world like an Easter lily on steroids, the Philippine lily can be a dramatic sight in July and August when it comes into bloom. Lilies as a group have their ups and downs when grown this far south. Many of the Asiatic lilies and Oriental lilies tend to be relatively short-lived, playing out after a few years. This is not true of the Philippine lily, which thrives in our climate. The leaves are about 6 inches long, narrow, lance-shaped, and arranged all around the tall, erect stems. The blooms are spectacular. The large white trumpets are 5 inches across and 7 inches long. Young plants may produce only 3 flowers at the top of the plant, but older plants produce a cluster of up to 10, and established bulbs form a clump with several stems.

When to Plant

Spring or early summer is best so the plants will have a chance to become well established before they come into flower.

Where to Plant

Good drainage is important. If the area where you want to plant the lilies is not well drained, plant them into a raised bed. Philippine lilies thrive in full sun but bloom well as long as they get at least 5 or 6 hours of direct sun. In less sun, plants will be taller and will probably need to be staked.

How to Plant

Plant into a bed that has been improved by digging a 2-inch layer of organic matter and a sprinkling of general-purpose fertilizer (15-5-10 or 8-8-8 if your soil is low in phosphorus). Plant bulbs 3 to 4 inches deep; set plants at the same level they were growing in the ground or in their containers.

Care and Maintenance

These tall lilies will occasionally need to be staked, particularly when in bloom or if you want to let the seedpods ripen for the seed. If you do not intend to save the seeds, trim off the faded flowers when a cluster is finished.

Additional Information

Seed produced in the late summer and fall germinate readily. Harvest the seeds when the pods turn yellow and start to split slightly. They can be planted in pots for later transplanting into the garden or right into the garden, and they usually bloom the second year. They make wonderful gifts for your gardening friends, who will all want one when they see yours blooming.

Additional Cultivars or Species

Lilium longiflorum, the Easter lily, is a reliable rebloomer across the state. Save plants after the holiday and plant them in a well-drained bed that receives morning sun. They will increase and bloom for years to come. The brown-spotted orange tiger lily, *L. lancifolium*, grows to about 4 feet and blooms in June or July. Try the Madonna lily, *L. candidum*.

Snowflake

Leucojum aestivum

Zones: 8 and 9
Size: 1 foot
Type: Dormant in summer
Flowers: White, nodding bells
Bloom Period: April

Light Requirement:

Snowflakes are among the most robust and reliable spring-flowering bulbs. In Louisiana, where snow in winter is fairly rare, a plant with the name "snowflake" has a certain allure. Snowflakes bloom in April with white, bell-like flowers that dangle from strong stems in clusters of two to six. They are produced in the midst of clumps of rich green foliage that is similar to that of narcissus. Children find the flowers irresistible. Each of the 6 white petals that make up a flower has a green dot on its tip. This detail seems to imbue the flowers with a certain enchantment, and children will go from flower to flower counting the spots. The strong foliage persists well into summer (often until June), when it finally yellows and should be cut back. Even novice gardeners will find this excellent repeat bloomer almost foolproof.

When to Plant

Snowflake bulbs are planted along with other spring-flowering bulbs. You'll find them for sale in fall; they can be planted in October through November.

Where to Plant

Any garden bed that has good soil and receives at least 4 to 6 hours of sun will work well. Snowflakes are not as picky about drainage as are many spring bulbs, particularly when they are in active growth; but it is best to avoid areas that tend to stay soggy during the summer.

How to Plant

Plant bulbs into beds with good garden soil. New beds should be improved by digging in organic matter and a light sprinkling of general-purpose fertilizer. You can plant the bulbs in established beds with little or no special preparation, as they are adaptable and undemanding. The bulbs should be planted 3 to 4 inches deep and 2 to 3 inches apart. Plant in clusters of 6 or more bulbs for the best effect.

Care and Maintenance

Trim off faded flowers when they are finished blooming, but delay cutting back the foliage until it has turned yellow. You will not need to dig and divide the bulbs more often than every 3 to 5 years.

Additional Information

When the foliage is cut back in midsummer, plant heat-tolerant bedding plants around the clump to fill in the gap. Be careful not to dig into the bulbs while doing this, or you will injure them.

Additional Cultivars or Species

Leucojum vernum is another species sometimes offered in catalogs. It is not as reliable as *L. aestivum*.

Spider Lily

Lycoris radiata

Other Names: Naked Ladies, Hurricane Lily
Zones: 8 and 9
Size: 12 to 15 inches
Type: Dormant in summer
Flowers: Clusters of light-red flowers
Bloom Period: September

Light Requirement:

When a gardener tells you he is having trouble with his naked ladies, there is no need to be scandalized. He's (we hope) just using one of the more colorful names for this traditional Southern bulb. These bulbs bloom on stalks before they send up any foliage, so they look rather naked when blooming. They bloom in September, the month when most hurricane activity occurs; hurricane-conscious gardeners in the Deep South have dubbed them hurricane lilies. Most gardeners, though, call them spider lilies, a name given to several plants whose flowers have thin petals and a "spidery" appearance. The foliage sprouts in October and persists until spring when it yellows and disappears. The foliage is an attractive bluish green with a silver stripe running down the middle, and it lies close to the ground.

When to Plant

Plant bulbs in spring or summer before September. Spring-planted bulbs will not sprout until fall.

Where to Plant

Avoid densely shaded, poorly drained areas, or the bulbs will not thrive or bloom well. Planting under deciduous trees works very well. The trees lose their leaves in winter when the spider lily foliage is growing, so the foliage will receive plenty of sun; when the trees leaf out in spring, the bulbs will be dormant. They also do well planted in lawn areas—when the foliage is growing, lawns are dormant and not being mowed.

How to Plant

Plant bulbs 3 to 4 inches deep. Bed preparation is not crucial, especially when planting in a lawn area.

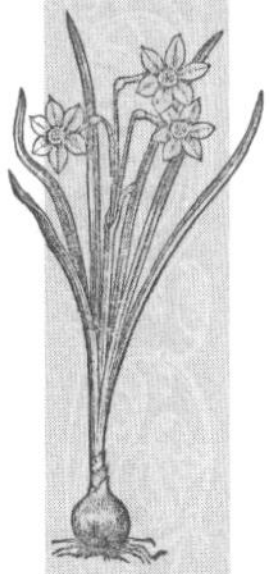

Care and Maintenance

Little care is needed when spider lilies are planted in a good location. Do not cut off the foliage while it is green. About every 5 to 7 years, the bulbs may begin to become crowded and flowering will be reduced. When the foliage begins to yellow in spring, dig up the bulbs, separate them, and replant. Share the extras with your friends. Do not divide too often.

Additional Information

Occasionally an exceptionally cold winter will damage the foliage. When this happens, the bulbs will bloom sparsely or not at all the following September. Naturally no one remembers to blame the freeze that happened months before.

Additional Cultivars or Species

Lycoris africana is a larger-growing chrome yellow species. The foliage is larger, more upright and noticeable in the garden. It may not be quite as reliable as *L. radiata,* but it usually blooms every year and is quite attractive. *L. radiata* Alba is a white form.

C H A P T E R   T H R E E

Groundcovers and Ferns

WHEN IT COMES TO HOME LANDSCAPING, most of us generally plant our trees, shrubs, and flower beds, then cover all remaining soil surface areas with turfgrasses. Sometimes I think we rely too much on grass lawns. They require constant maintenance, and sometimes they can be . . . well . . . boring. A group of plants called groundcovers is a lower-maintenance alternative that can tremendously enhance home landscapes. Groundcovers can reduce maintenance, beautify problem areas, and create a whole new landscape dimension.

The term groundcover is applied to low-growing plants, other than turfgrass, used to cover areas of the landscape. Perennial evergreen plants that have a sprawling or spreading habit are commonly used. Groundcovers create an effect in the landscape that is impossible to achieve with turfgrass, providing variation in height, texture, and color that enriches the surroundings.

In addition to the beauty they offer, groundcovers have practical uses. They provide barriers to foot traffic (most people won't walk through them) and can guide traffic movement through a site. Some groundcovers are effective in erosion control. Others, because they don't have to be mowed, reduce maintenance in problem areas such as steep slopes, under low-branched trees and shrubs, where the roots of large trees protrude, confined areas where lawn mowing is difficult, or shade where grass will not grow.

Whatever type of groundcover you choose, proper preparation of the planting area will ensure good establishment and faster growth. First remove all existing unwanted vegetation such as lawn grass or weeds. This can be done physically or you can use a herbicide such as glyphosate (following label directions), but in either case, do a thorough job. Then till the soil to loosen it. If you are working under a tree, use a turning fork to minimize damage to the tree's roots, and avoid severing roots larger than an inch in diameter. Two or three inches of additional soil may be added near the bases of older trees if necessary. Do not exceed $1^{1}/_{2}$ inches over the most active tree roots. After the soil is broken up, spread 2 inches of organic matter (compost, fine pine bark, peat moss, or rotted manure) over the area. Sprinkle 15-5-10 fertilizer at the rate of $^{1}/_{2}$ cup per 30 square feet, or 8-8-8 at the rate of 1 cup per 30 square feet if your soil is low in phosphorus, and work everything in. Rake the area smooth and you will be ready to plant.

Plant most groundcovers October through April to take advantage of the cool, moist weather that encourages successful establishment.

There are many hardy ferns that can be planted in the shady areas of your landscape as groundcovers or for other uses. The different species range in size from under a foot to as much as three feet. The leaves of ferns are called fronds, and they provide the primary ornamental feature of the plants.

Ferns do not produce colorful flowers; their attributes are more subtle and refined. It would be inaccurate to say that ferns are just green—they come in many shades from chartreuse to deep olive, and some produce fronds that are tinted with red or silvery variegations.

Some of the ferns used in the landscape are evergreen, and some are deciduous. Some of the evergreen ferns may suffer damage or loss of their fronds during severe winters, but they more often retain their foliage throughout the winter season. If they are frozen back, they will reliably return from their roots.

One of the best things about ferns is that they are easy to grow. Not susceptible to any major insect or disease problems, they are one of the plants you can just about plant and ignore. They will grow best in areas that receive one to four hours of direct sun or dappled light during the day; morning sun is greatly preferred.

The majority of ferns do best in a soil that is consistently moist. They do well in Louisiana because of our high rainfall and humidity. Prepare beds for ferns as recommended for groundcovers. During dry periods you may need to water your landscape ferns. Mulching a fern planting with your favorite mulch is highly recommended to conserve soil moisture and reduce weeds.

As time goes by, many ferns will grow into fairly large clumps. Should you need to divide your ferns, the best time is in late winter or early spring.

Autumn Fern

Dryopteris erythrosora

Other Name: Japanese Shield Fern
Zones: 8 and 9
Size: 12 to 18 inches
Type: Evergreen

Light Requirement:

When gardeners think of ferns, they usually think "green." There are certainly no ferns that rival caladiums for brilliantly colored foliage, but autumn fern, in its own subtle way, is different from most other ferns: its new fronds emerge and unfold a rich coppery red. This beautiful color contrasts wonderfully with the plant's dark-green, shiny, mature fronds. Autumn fern is evergreen, especially in the southern part of the state, retaining its beautiful appearance in the winter shade garden.

When to Plant

The fronds of autumn fern can be injured by temperatures in the low twenties. To allow the plant to become well established before going through its first winter in the ground, plant it in March through May for best results (especially in north Louisiana where temperatures in the teens are typical in winter). Planting in the summer from containers is fine if the plants are kept well watered during establishment.

Where to Plant

Locations that receive 2 to 4 hours of morning sun or less are preferred. A moist soil rich in organic matter will produce best growth.

How to Plant

Plant in a well-prepared bed generously enriched with organic matter. Plant at the same level the fern was growing in the container, being careful not to bury the crown. Water-in and mulch after planting.

Care and Maintenance

Water thoroughly during hot, dry weather. Occasionally trim off brown fronds. If the autumn fern is frozen back in winter, cut off the damaged fronds and mulch over the crown. Autumn ferns will come back reliably from the ground.

Additional Information

Autumn fern is extremely well behaved in the garden. It stays put and doesn't run all over the place. It is attractive as a single specimen or in mass plantings. Coppery-red new fronds are produced all summer long.

Additional Cultivars or Species

Other species are *Dryopteris Cycadina* , *D. seiboldii,* and *D. Filix-mas.*

Holly Fern

Cyrtomium falcatum

Zones: 8 and 9
Size: 24 inches high, 30 inches wide
Type: Evergreen

Light Requirement:

In gardening lingo, the term *ferny* has come to mean "delicate and fine-textured." Well, this description does not apply to the holly fern. "Bold and coarse-textured" would be more accurate. The fronds are pinnately compound, and each leaflet resembles a toothed, dark-green, shiny holly leaf rather than something belonging to a fern. A large, well-established planting looks more like a planting of shrubs than ferns. Holly fern's texture and tough constitution make it a wonderful plant to use in the landscape.

When to Plant

Plant from containers in spring through early summer before the weather gets into the 80s. Plant divisions in March or April.

Where to Plant

Choose an area that receives 2 to 4 hours of sun a day. Holly ferns will grow in more sun if kept well watered, but their foliage will tend to look yellowish-green. Moist but well-drained soils are best (although holly ferns will tolerate dry conditions better than many ferns).

How to Plant

Holly ferns grow from a crown. Be careful not to plant too deep and bury the crown, or the plant may rot. Enrich the soil of the planting area with organic matter before planting. Water-in and mulch the bed when you finish. Holly ferns are able to grow quite a bit larger than the plants you buy at the nursery; leave about 2 feet between plants, even though this may seem like too much space at first.

Care and Maintenance

Water during dry, hot weather, especially new plantings. Thrips can be a problem, and they may cause the foliage to become faded and grayish in appearance. Spray with Orthene 75S according to label directions at the first sign of damage. Prune off damaged fronds. Especially severe winters will occasionally damage the foliage. Prune in spring to remove freeze damage, and the plants will vigorously replace the lost growth.

Additional Information

Although the leaves look like holly leaves, they have no spines and are not prickly. Holly fern is wonderful for providing rich texture in the shade garden. The fronds often produce sporangia on the backs of their leaflets. These dark-brown, slightly raised spots sometimes alarm gardeners, who think they are some sort of pest—but they are natural and only indicate a healthy plant.

Additional Cultivars or Species

C. falcatum 'Butterfield' and 'Rochfordianum' have deeply serrated and fringed leaflets. 'Compactum' is a dwarf form and 'Fortunei' has dull rather than shiny leaves.

Maidenhair Fern

Adiantum capillus-veneris

Other Names: Southern Maidenhair Fern, Venus's Hair Fern	**Light Requirement:**
Zones: 8 and 9	
Size: 12 to 18 inches	
Type: Deciduous	

The common name of this fern is difficult to understand, until you look at the stems of the fronds. They are very thin—almost as thin as human hair. This is among the most delicate-looking ferns. The fronds of maidenhair differ from those of many ferns in that they are not feather shaped, and they do not grow from a central crown. On a maidenhair you will see many small, triangular, light-green leaves dancing from ground level to about 18 inches above the ground, in no particular arrangement. The thin black stems are not readily visible, and the leaflets seem to hover with no apparent support. The overall effect is delightful.

When to Plant

Maidenhair ferns are dormant in the winter. Most gardeners will find the plants available at local nurseries in the spring, and that's a good time to plant them. They can be planted from containers during the summer, but extra care must be taken to keep them well watered in hot, dry weather. Plant divisions March through April.

Where to Plant

Avoid areas subject to hot, dry wind. A sheltered, shady location that stays evenly moist is best. A few hours of morning sun is fine as long as the plants receive adequate water. The soil should be rich in organic matter.

How to Plant

Plant into a well-prepared spot that has been generously enriched with organic matter. Dig at least 2 to 3 inches of compost or well-rotted manure into the area before planting. If you garden in a part of the state that has acidic soils, add lime during soil preparation; maidenhair ferns prefer alkaline soil. Mulch plants with rotted leaves, pine straw, cypress mulch, or finely ground pine bark.

Care and Maintenance

Prune back dead fronds when winter frosts have killed them. Keep the planting well mulched through the winter to protect the rhizomes in the ground. Maidenhairs do not tolerate dry conditions. Water generously and prune off any brown fronds that may occur during the summer.

Additional Information

Maidenhair ferns are excellent for small areas and combine easily with other shade-loving plants. They are great in containers alone or in combination with other plants that like similar growing conditions. They look nice in hanging baskets and wall baskets where the fronds tend to cascade over the sides. The fronds are nice additions to fresh flower arrangements.

Additional Cultivars or Species

Adiantum pedatum, the northern maidenhair fern, is more difficult to grow here, particularly in south Louisiana.

Sword Fern

Nephrolepsis exaltata

Zones: 8 and 9
Size: 24 to 30 inches
Type: Evergreen

Light Requirement:

Upright, feathery fronds shaped like the blade of a sword give the fern its warrior name. The most you could do with this "sword," however, is tickle someone's nose with it. The light- to medium-green fronds add an interesting texture to shady gardens. You wouldn't call this fern graceful—the slightly arching, erect fronds seem a bit too rigid for that. Still, it looks great against a wall or dark hedge and lends itself well to formal plantings. Sword fern is also striking as a specimen plant, or planted over a larger area as a groundcover.

When to Plant

Since sword fern is subject to freeze injury during cold winters, plant in spring so plants will have an entire growing season to establish before their first winter in the ground. Divisions should be dug and planted in March or April.

Where to Plant

Choose shady areas or those that only get a few hours of morning sun. Sword fern will tolerate a fair amount of sun if kept well watered, but push it too far and you'll see fronds bleached yellow with brown edges.

How to Plant

Set plants into well-prepared beds generously enriched with organic matter, at the same level they were growing in their containers. Make sure you eliminate all weeds in the bed before planting. Water-in and mulch the area when plants are in the ground. If growing them in containers, use a well-drained potting soil rich in organic matter.

Care and Maintenance

Fronds will often turn brown in winter, especially in the northern part of the state; sword fern is more reliably hardy south of Alexandria. After fronds have turned brown, trim them back and mulch over the crowns. If the winter is mild and the fronds stay green, you may still cut them back in March to encourage growth of fresh, new fronds.

Additional Information

Sword fern is outstanding in containers on patios, decks, or porches, and can even be grown indoors in a bright window. Sword ferns in containers outside should be brought indoors when temperatures below freezing are predicted.

Additional Cultivars or Species

Nephrolepsis exaltata 'Bostoniensis', the famous Boston fern, is a mutation of the sword fern that has long, arching fronds that hang down. Outstanding in hanging baskets, it should be protected from freezing temperatures in winter when grown in containers or baskets. The Boston fern has mutated into many other cultivars, most of which are best grown in containers and protected from cold—but it would be interesting to try a few in the ground in warm coastal sections of the state. You never know.

Wood Fern

Thelypteris kunthii

Other Names: Marsh Fern, Shield Fern, Maiden Fern **Zones:** 8 and 9 **Size:** 24 to 36 inches **Type:** Deciduous	**Light Requirement:**

This fern can just appear in your garden. Such an event is not at all uncommon in New Orleans, particularly in older neighborhoods. Wood fern is native to Louisiana and seems to find its own way to spots that suit it. The wide, graceful, yellow-green fronds contrast well with many plants and combine nicely with just about everything. It spreads fast enough to warrant close watching, and it may spread beyond its allotted area, but extras can be easily transplanted in spring.

When to Plant

Wood fern is deciduous, dormant in the winter, so nurseries are not likely to have them for sale before March. March is a excellent time to plant them, though they can be planted at any time from containers if extra care is taken to water summer plantings. Divisions may be dug and planted February through April. The creeping rhizomes can be cut with a shovel into clumps that contain several fronds.

Where to Plant

Wood fern will grow in a variety of soils. Loose soils amended with organic matter are best, as are shady areas or those that get a few hours of morning sun. But a fern that grows between the bricks in my patio can't be that particular!

How to Plant

Plant in any good garden soil. Adding some organic matter to the soil before planting will make the wood fern more vigorous and faster growing. Water-in thoroughly and mulch after planting.

Care and Maintenance

The fronds can become ragged by late summer, especially in hot, dry weather. If they do, feel free to cut them back to the ground. The plants will rapidly replace them with fresh, new growth. Fertilize lightly with a general purpose granular fertilizer after cutting back to stimulate new growth. In winter, wood fern fronds brown with the first hard freeze and the plants go dormant. Cut them back to the ground and mulch.

Additional Information

The yellow-green fronds are unique, an outstanding characteristic of this fern. The color brightens shady areas and perks up the plants growing around it.

Additional Cultivars or Species

Thylepteris torresiana, Mariana maiden fern, can be grown in southern Louisiana.

Asian Jasmine

Trachelospermum asiaticum

Zones: 8 and 9
Size: 10-inch-deep mat
Type: Evergreen
Flowers: Yellowish white
Bloom Period: Rarely blooms

Light Requirement:

Most groundcovers are suitable for either shade or sun; Asian jasmine is remarkable in that it will do equally well in shade and sun and everything in between. If you want to plant a groundcover in an area that extends from shady into sunny conditions, this is the one to choose. Good for planting in large areas, its reliability and fast rate of growth have made it one of the most popular and widely used groundcovers in Louisiana. The 1- to 1½-inch-long, shiny, pointed, dark-green leaves give a planting an elegant look. Asian jasmine is a running vine, but it does not climb vertical surfaces as does English ivy and is not so driven to climb as its relative Confederate jasmine (*Trachelospermum jasminoides*). It will occasionally meander up a tree trunk if the bark is rough enough, or weave through fences, and it can overwhelm small shrubs planted in it.

When to Plant

Plant in October through March to give it a chance to become established during the cool, moist weather during that period. It will use that time to produce a strong root system which can support rapid growth during its first summer.

Where to Plant

Plant in sun or shade in well-prepared areas. Asian jasmine is very tolerant of a wide range of soils.

How to Plant

Loosen the soil and incorporate 2 to 3 inches of finely ground pine bark, compost, or peat moss into the area. Fertilizer may be added at this time, using 15-5-10 at the rate of 1 cup per 30 square feet. Plant gallon containers 18 to 24 inches apart. Small 4-inch-pot-sized plants should be planted 8 to 12 inches apart. Water-in and mulch newly planted areas to suppress weeds and encourage faster spreading. Complete coverage usually takes 2 growing seasons. Until then, weed as necessary by hand or with an appropriate herbicide, following label directions.

Care and Maintenance

When used as a groundcover, Asian jasmine looks its best when kept sheared to a height of 4 or 5 inches. This should be done in late winter each year. This running vine will not stop growing at the edge of a bed, so the edges will have to be trimmed as well. Watering during hot, dry weather is beneficial to new plantings. Fertilize with 15-5-10 in April and July each year at the above rate to stimulate rapid growth. Maintain weed control, although Asian jasmine's vigorous growth will suppress most weeds.

Additional Information

Avoid planting small shrubs or perennials in a bed with Asian jasmine, as it will simply swallow them up in the absence of constant pruning. Even large shrubs will occasionally need to have the vine removed from them. There are better, less-aggressive groundcovers for mixed plantings and small, tight areas. Extended periods of temperatures in the low teens can damage Asian jasmine, but it will reliably and rapidly grow back. Cut back damaged growth in early spring. A purple tint in the leaves is normal in winter and does not indicate damage.

Additional Cultivars or Species

T. asiaticum 'Variegatum' is an attractive variegated form. 'Asia Minor' is a bushy dwarf with small leaves. The cultivar 'Nortex' has narrower leaves with silver-gray veins.

Aspidistra

Aspidistra elatior

Other Name: Cast Iron Plant
Zones: 8 and 9
Size: 2 to 3 feet
Type: Evergreen
Flowers: Not significant

Light Requirement:

Aspidistra was a popular parlor plant during Victorian times and earned its common name, cast iron plant, by being tolerant of poor growing conditions. You would have to look hard to find a tougher, more reliable plant for difficult shady areas of the landscape. This herbaceous perennial is rather tall for a groundcover, but in a large-scale setting (such as under a live oak), it is very effective when planted over a large area. The bold foliage is rich, dark-green, and slightly shiny. It emerges from the ground rolled up like a tube, and then opens up into a broad spear shape tapered at the tip and at the base where it is connected to the petiole. Aspidistra forms slowly spreading clumps. The 1-inch brownish purple flowers are produced at the base of the leaves; most gardeners never notice when they appear.

When to Plant

Since it is planted in shady areas, aspidistra may be planted from containers anytime, even in the heat of summer if kept well watered. Planting divisions is best performed in spring, but this plant is so tolerant that it is often successfully divided and transplanted in summer.

Where to Plant

Aspidistra must be planted in the shade. When planted in areas that are too sunny, the foliage turns yellow and becomes ragged in appearance. Moist soils rich in organic matter encourage vigorous growth. Aspidistra competes well with the roots of trees and grows well when planted beneath the trees. It also makes an outstanding container plant; it is used this way effectively at Longue Vue House and Gardens in New Orleans. Although hardy in the ground in north Louisiana, aspidistra may not be reliable in outside containers during cold winters.

How to Plant

Plant in well-prepared beds that have been improved by incorporating a 2-inch layer of organic matter into the soil. Make sure plants are planted no deeper than they were growing in their containers. Divisions may need a little support to hold up the leaves until the roots establish. Water-in and mulch the bed after planting. Clumps spread slowly, so space them no more that 2 feet apart for coverage in a reasonable amount of time.

Care and Maintenance

Keep the planted area well mulched to suppress weeds and conserve soil moisture. Supplemental summer irrigation may be necessary during hot, dry weather, especially for new plantings. Fertilize in April or May with a complete fertilizer appropriate for your area. To keep the planting looking its best, prune out the occasional yellow or brown leaves that appear. White scale will sometimes show up on aspidistra. It doesn't seem to bother the plant much and can be controlled with an oil spray used according to label directions.

Additional Information

Aspidistra will grow in the deep shade that few other plants will tolerate. Its bold, tropical-looking foliage makes an outstanding contribution to the shady landscape. It combines wonderfully with fine-textured ferns.

Additional Cultivars or Species

Aspidistra elatior 'Variegata' has creamy white streaks in its foliage. A dwarf variety, *A.* 'Milky Way', has small, low-growing leaves spotted with white.

Creeping Lily Turf

Liriope spicata

Zones: 8 and 9
Size: 8 to 10 inches
Type: Evergreen
Flowers: Spikes of pale lavender
Bloom Period: Summer

Light Requirement:

There are only a few groundcovers reliable enough to plant in large areas. Creeping lily turf is easy enough, tough enough, and spreads fast enough to make it excellent even for relatively large plantings in the shade. This plant is similar in appearance to monkey grass (*Ophiopogon japonicus*), but its leaves are slightly wider and it grows taller. The foliage is very dark green and attractive all year. It spreads by means of underground runners, and if properly planted and maintained, can spread rapidly to cover an area in 2 years. Growth is thick and it does a good job out-competing weeds. The pale-lavender flower spikes are produced in summer—although nice, they are not particularly showy.

When to Plant

Plant creeping lily turf any time, but fall planting is best: it allows the plants to become established during the cool, moist winter so they will be ready to grow vigorously the following spring and summer.

Where to Plant

This groundcover needs a shady location that receives no more than a few hours of sun a day. Planting in full sun will lead to yellow, poor-quality foliage. It is excellent in shady areas where turfgrass will not grow and competes well with a tree's root system. Do not use it to edge beds as you would its relative, liriope (*Liriope muscari*), or it will run back into the bed and become a problem.

How to Plant

Plant into well-prepared beds for fastest coverage. Remove all weeds from the area and till the soil to a depth of 6 to 8 inches. Spread a 2-inch layer of organic matter (compost, finely ground pine bark, or peat moss) and a sprinkling of 15-5-10 at the rate of 1/2 cup per 30 square feet (or 1 cup of 8-8-8 where soil phosphorous levels are low). Add a 2- to 3-inch layer of coarse sand to heavy clay soils. Thoroughly incorporate all into the bed and rake it smooth. Divide gallon-size clumps into 2 to 3 pieces and plant them 6 to 10 inches apart. Plant 4-inch-size clumps without dividing. The closer together you plant them, the faster the coverage will be. Water-in and mulch the area to suppress weeds and encourage spreading.

Care and Maintenance

Keep new plantings of creeping lily turf well watered during the summer. Established plantings rarely need to be watered. Keep weeds under control with occasional hand weeding. To encourage maximum growth, fertilize at the rate above in April and July. Water thoroughly immediately after application.

Additional Information

Creeping lily turf works well in beds planted with shade-loving shrubs and large perennials, but it may be too aggressive to interplant with low-growing perennials.

Additional Cultivars or Species

Liriope muscari is a clumping relative that grows taller and has wider leaves. It is sometimes used as a groundcover, but the plant does not produce runners, making it more difficult to establish even coverage over a large area.

English Ivy

Hedera helix

Zones: 8 and 9
Size: 4 to 6 inches
Type: Evergreen
Flowers: None produced in groundcover plantings

Light Requirement:

English ivy is a classic plant with which almost everyone is familiar. As a groundcover it is good for shady areas, but it will grow in sunny situations if kept well watered. In full sun the foliage tends to yellow slightly. It is a vine that spreads by running along the soil surface, but if it encounters a vertical surface such as a tree trunk or wall, it can, and generally will, grab hold and climb. English ivy is quite hardy and will retain its dark-green 3- to 5-pointed leaves all winter no matter how cold it gets. There are a tremendous number of varieties. The small-leaved dwarfs are good for small areas and detail work.

When to Plant

Plant November through March to take advantage of cool, moist winter conditions for establishment. Container-grown plants can be planted any time, but summer plantings will require more care during establishment.

Where to Plant

Shady to partial-sun areas are best. Avoid planting near walls or other vertical structures if you don't want the ivy to climb on them. It's generally not too difficult to keep the vine off vertical surfaces by occasionally trimming it away. To avoid rot diseases, do not plant in wet or poorly drained areas.

How to Plant

Gallon-size plants spaced 1 to 2 feet apart will produce fastest coverage, but smaller-size plants spaced closer together will also work. Plant into a well-prepared bed enriched with organic matter, and mulch the area to control weeds, conserve soil moisture, and encourage spreading.

Care and Maintenance

To stimulate rapid growth, fertilize with a 15-5-10 fertilizer at the rate of 1 cup per 30 square feet in April and July. Established plantings do well with just the April feeding. Water in dry summer weather, especially if growing plants in a sunny area. Scale, an occasional problem, can be controlled with oil sprays. Fungus stem and root rot can cause significant damage, especially in the southern part of the state. The application of an appropriate fungicide can help.

Additional Information

You may be concerned about the health of a tree if English ivy has been allowed to grow up into it. Rest assured that no harm will be done to the tree if you like the way the ivy looks and want to let it grow. English ivy is also attractive when used as a vine on walls and other structures.

Additional Cultivars or Species

There are many, many cultivars of English ivy. The larger, unvariegated types are best for use as groundcovers. *Hedera canariensis,* Algerian ivy, is a related species that can be used like English ivy. It has larger leaves and is not as hardy, though it is hardy throughout Louisiana.

Japanese Ardisia

Ardisia japonica

Zones: 8 and 9
Size: 10 inches
Type: Evergreen
Flowers: Tiny, light pink, followed by red berries
Bloom Period: Summer to fall

Light Requirement:

This evergreen groundcover has unfortunately been widely used in commercial plantings, often where it gets so much sun that the foliage yellows and becomes unattractive. In the right location, Japanese ardisia produces a carpet of medium-green leaves in a whorled arrangement along upright stems about 8 to 10 inches tall. It spreads by underground stolons. The 1/4-inch pinkish-white flowers are produced in small clusters. They are barely noticeable when they appear, but the scarlet-red berries that follow in November, though not numerous, are eye-catching.

When to Plant

Container-grown plants can be planted any time, but will require more watering and care when planted during the heat of the summer. Plant fall through spring to take advantage of the cool, moist winter weather during establishment.

Where to Plant

Avoid hot, sunny, dry areas where this plant is bound to fail. Japanese ardisia is beautiful when planted under trees or in front of large shrubs like Indica azaleas. It likes soils that are evenly moist; wet or poorly drained soils may encourage root rot.

How to Plant

A well-prepared bed is important for this plant to spread properly. Turn the soil 6 to 8 inches deep and spread over it a 2- to 4-inch layer of finely ground pine bark or compost. Sprinkle with 15-5-10 at the rate of 1/2 cup (or 1 cup of 8-8-8 if soil phosphorus is low) per 30 square feet, and thoroughly incorporate everything into the soil. Rake smooth and plant. Japanese ardisia is often purchased in 4-inch pots for groundcover planting. Space plants 8 to 12 inches apart. When plants are removed from the pots, unwrap the stolons which are usually coiled up, and spread them out into the soil. Water-in and mulch the bed to discourage weeds and speed growth of the groundcover.

Care and Maintenance

If foliage is burned by severe freezes, cut it back in spring to encourage new growth. Feed in spring and again in summer as prescribed above. Keep the area well mulched until complete coverage is achieved.

Additional Information

Japanese ardisia is not terribly aggressive and combines well with ferns, hostas, toad lily (*Tricyrtis*), and other shade-loving perennials.

Additional Cultivars or Species

Ardisia japonica 'Gulf Green', 'Ito-Fukurin', 'Red Tide', and 'White Caps' are variegated forms that do not grow as vigorously as the species and should be used only for small plantings.

Monkey Grass

Ophiopogon japonicus

Other Name: Mondo Grass
Zones: 8 and 9
Size: 8 to 10 inches
Type: Evergreen
Flowers: No ornamental value

Light Requirement:

One of the most widely planted and reliable groundcovers, monkey grass has very thin, fine-textured foliage that is dark green with a faint luster. It is grassy in appearance, but actually belongs to the Liliaceae (lily) family. An excellent replacement for turfgrass in shady areas, it spreads moderately fast by means of underground stolons. The small flowers and dark-purple fruit are hidden by the foliage and contribute nothing to its ornamental value: the beauty of monkey grass is in its foliage. This outstanding groundcover is suitable for large areas.

When to Plant

October through March planting is preferred in order to take advantage of the cool, moist growing conditions of winter for establishment. Planting from containers can be done any time, but plants will require more care if planted in the heat of summer. Plant divisions in spring.

Where to Plant

Plant in shade to part sun. The foliage will become yellowish if planted in too much sun.

How to Plant

Plant into well-prepared beds enriched with organic matter and a general-purpose fertilizer. Make sure all weeds have been thoroughly eradicated before planting. Space small clumps (divide up larger ones if necessary) 6 to 8 inches apart. Water-in and mulch the area with 2 inches of bark, cypress mulch, or ground pine straw.

Care and Maintenance

Water new plantings regularly during hot, dry weather. Established plantings are care-free. Every few years, cut back monkey grass in February or early March. This will remove any accumulation of brown leaves and stimulate vigorous new growth, improving the appearance of the planting.

Additional Information

Monkey grass is sometimes used to edge beds, but this is not usually a good idea. Since the plant spreads by underground stolons, it eventually will creep backwards into the bed and may have to be removed.

Additional Cultivars or Species

O. japonicus 'Nana' or 'Kyoto Dwarf' is a small-growing cultivar only 2 inches high. Spread is very slow and it is best used for detail work (like between steppingstones). The foliage of *O. japonicus* 'Varigatus' is striped white. *O. planiscapus* 'Arabicus' has narrow, dark-green leaves that look almost black.

Strawberry Geranium

Saxifraga stolonifera

Other Name: Strawberry Begonia	**Light Requirement:**
Zones: 8 and 9	
Size: 4 inches	
Type: Evergreen	
Flowers: Small, white	
Bloom Period: April	

Why in the world would strawberry and geranium be found together in the name of a single plant? Well, this low-growing groundcover forms a rosette of leaves and sends out long runners that produce small new plants on their ends, just like strawberries; and the foliage, if you use your imagination, looks sort of like a geranium. In truth, comparing the foliage to a geranium doesn't really do it justice. It is round with scalloped edges, dark green, and exquisitely veined and netted with silver. The underside of the leaf and the leaf stem are tinted red. It must have reminded someone of rex begonias, thus its other common name. In the spring, loose clusters of small, white flowers on 8- to 10-inch-tall stems dance above the foliage for about four weeks.

When to Plant

Strawberry geranium is hardy and best planted October through March to take advantage of the cool, moist weather of winter for establishment. The plant grows easily from divisions planted in spring.

Where to Plant

In the deep South, we must give this plant plenty of shade; several hours of direct sun on a summer afternoon will burn the foliage. Strawberry geranium will not thrive in dry soil, so make sure the area stays moist.

How to Plant

Do not bury the crown when planting, as this may lead to crown rot. Space plants about 8 inches apart into a well-prepared bed. Water-in and mulch to conserve soil moisture and prevent weeds. In a favorable location, spread is fairly rapid.

Care and Maintenance

Fertilize with a general-purpose fertilizer such as 15-5-10 or 8-8-8 in April. Cut back faded flower stalks when they finish flowering, and keep the plants well watered in the heat of summer.

Additional Information

It is easy to propagate strawberry geranium from the small plants at the ends of its runners. Dig them up and replant them in spring. This plant is best suited for small areas and detail work; it is beautiful around shady pools, along walkways, or for edging beds.

Additional Cultivars or Species

S. stolonifera 'Tricolor' is a variegated form with green, white, and pink leaves. It lacks the vigor of the species and is best used in containers.

CHAPTER FOUR

Ornamental Grasses

MANY GARDENERS THINK IT ODD TO TALK about ornamental grasses because some of our worst garden weeds are grasses. Crabgrass, torpedo grass, wild Bermudagrass, and Johnson grass are persistent, difficult-to-control pests with which many of us are all too familiar. Unfortunate experiences with these plants are bound to make many Louisiana gardeners reluctant to purposefully plant grasses into flower beds or borders.

But this reluctance is unnecessary, because ornamental grasses are truly attractive and not rampantly aggressive, and like their weedy cousins, they are tough and susceptible to virtually no insect or disease problems. Ornamental grasses are an excellent choice for gardeners trying to create a landscape that is more self-reliant, requiring less spraying, fertilization, and maintenance.

The term "ornamental grass" is applied to grasses and grass-like plants that are used chiefly for their beauty. This is a large and complex group of plants with wide ranges of growth habit and culture. In a strict sense, true grasses are members of the Poaceae or grass family. Many other plants that we think of as grasses are actually sedges and rushes, which belong to different families altogether. These other plants, along with the true grasses, comprise the bulk of the plants we call ornamental grasses. Gardeners across the country are discovering that the great variety of sizes, shapes, and colors of ornamental grasses add texture, motion, and grace to the landscape.

Ornamental grasses grow well in a wide variety of soils; many will even do well in poorly drained areas. Extensive bed preparation is not usually necessary. Do remove all weeds from the area and turn the soil before planting. The incorporation of a 2-inch layer of compost, aged manure, or peat moss into the bed will help the grass establish and grow more vigorously.

Most ornamental grasses go dormant in the winter and turn brown, and this dead growth needs to be cut back before the new, fresh growth sprouts in the spring.

Chapter Four

When to cut back ornamental grasses in Louisiana depends to a large degree on your preferences and even to some extent on where you garden. If you like the appearance of the dormant grass, wait until February to cut it back. Otherwise, cut it back in late fall or early winter as soon as it begins to appear less attractive to you. The further south you garden in Louisiana, the less dormant landscapes are in winter. A fountain of brown, dead grass looks decidedly out of place in an otherwise green winter garden in south Louisiana, no matter how beautiful the form.

You'll enjoy combining ornamental grasses with other plants in your landscape. They take their place in beds and borders easily, enriching neighboring plants with their presence. Combine maiden grass (*Miscanthus sinensis*) varieties with bold-leafed tropicals like gingers, cannas, or crinums. Pink pentas and blue daze make just one possible combination with purple fountain grass (*Pennisetum setaceum* 'Rubrum').

These rugged plants can also function as important structural features of the landscape. Tall grasses such as pampas grass (*Cortaderia selloana*), vetiver (*Vetiver zizonioides*), and giant reed (*Arundo donax*) can be used to divide the landscape into distinct spaces and are effective as hedges or screens.

Don't overlook the use of ornamental grasses in containers, particularly those that tend to be evergreen. Species and varieties of *Carex* and *Acorus* are striking when planted alone or as accents in a mixed container.

We are all familiar with the use of low-growing running grasses such as St. Augustine and centipede. In the minds of most gardeners, all other grasses are simply weeds. But it's time to take a look at this other category of grassy plants and appreciate what it can add to our landscapes.

Giant Reed Grass

Arundo donax

Zones: 8 and 9
Size: 10 to 15 feet
Type: Semi-evergreen in south Louisiana, freezes back in north Louisiana
Flowers: Large (2-foot) tan spikes
Bloom Period: Fall

Light Requirement:

The wind blowing through giant reed grass makes a delightful rustling sound. This is appropriate; the semi-woody stems are used to make reeds for wind instruments. Other than bamboo, this is the most massive of the ornamental grasses, and can effectively be used as a screen or large accent. The foliage has a slight bluish cast and is arranged in rows along opposite sides of the main stem. Each leaf is about 1 1/2 feet long, and the overall impression is of a giant corn plant. Unlike many other plants native to the Mediterranean region, giant reed grass thrives in the humid, rainy summer climate of Louisiana. Its texture is bold and coarse, yet it has grace in its movements and growth habit. It is an excellent choice for creating a tropical look, and is hardy in the northern part of the state. The dramatic flower heads that appear at the ends of the tall canes in fall are silvery tan with a faint burgundy tint; they add interest to the plant and persist into winter.

When to Plant

You can plant container-grown giant reed grass from spring through late summer, though spring is best (after danger of frost has passed). Gardeners often obtain this plant as divisions from friends; they should plant these gifts in the spring.

Where to Plant

Giant reed grass grows best in full sun. It is effective as an accent in the background of a garden or as a screen.

How to plant

Plant at the same level as the plant was growing in the container into well-prepared beds with good drainage. Like most ornamental grasses, it is not picky about soil type. Water plants during hot, dry weather while they establish during their first year. Remember that this will be a very large plant, so leave plenty of space around it. For a screen, space plants at least 5 to 8 feet apart.

Care and Maintenance

Fertilize in the spring as new growth emerges using a granular fertilizer with a 3:1:2 ratio such as 15-5-10. Irrigation during the summer is generally not necessary, but keep plants well mulched to conserve soil moisture and control weeds. The upper canes usually survive most winters, especially in the southern part of the state, but the foliage is often browned and unattractive by the end of winter. For that reason it's usually best to cut the canes down to the ground in early spring before new growth emerges. The fresh new canes and foliage grow very rapidly, and by early to midsummer the plants will have attained most of their former size. This plant forms large clumps that spread moderately fast, so don't let it grow into areas where you don't want it.

Additional Information

The canes often lean over or sprawl by late summer or fall, particularly after high winds. They can be tied up or staked if more upright growth is desired. Canes that have fallen over can be selectively pruned out. Clumps may be reduced in size by dividing them in the spring as new growth emerges. The flowers dry well when cut and hung upside down in a well ventilated area, and they make dramatic additions to large-scale arrangements.

Additional Cultivars or Species

Variegated giant reed grass (*Arundo donax* 'Variegata') is a striking and commonly grown cultivar. Its new growth is stunningly white as it emerges in the spring, but the variegation with green streaks becomes softer and more subtle as the canes mature. Its growth and care are the same as the species.

Pampas Grass

Cortaderia selloana

Zones: 8 and 9
Size: About 8 to 10 feet tall with an equal spread
Type: Evergreen, though subject to winter injury
Flowers: Large silvery-white fluffy panicles
Bloom Period: Late summer

Light Requirement:

Although ornamental grasses as a group are just now beginning to catch on with Louisiana gardeners, pampas grass has long been a popular plant in the area. Like its relative the giant reed grass, pampas grass is one of the largest ornamental grasses—but its texture is entirely different. Instead of a coarse look, the foliage is very fine and grows up into a fountain-like mound. The individual leaves are very narrow and arch out gracefully, often curling on the ends. This stately grass is native to the Argentine pampas where it has evolved the ability to survive the wildfires that occasionally occur. Indeed, some gardeners who live in areas where burning is permitted will burn back their plants in late winter to get rid of dead, brown foliage—and the plants grow back just fine. The flower spikes produced in late summer are among the most attractive produced by ornamental grasses. The silvery plumes on tall stalks held above the foliage look like enormous feather dusters and persist over a long period.

When to Plant

Spring planting is preferred, but you may plant container-grown pampas grass any time after danger of frost has passed through late summer. Plant divisions in spring.

Where to Plant

Pampas grass needs a sunny location with plenty of room. Soil type is not important, but the area should not stay constantly wet. The plants make dramatic accents. Make sure you allow room for this large clumping grass to spread about 8 feet. It looks great in the back of beds and borders; since it doesn't send out runners, it is well behaved. Pampas grass can also be used to create privacy screens or to divide the landscape into areas.

How to Plant

Plant pampas grass at the same level it was growing in its container into well-prepared beds that are free of weeds. Be careful not to plant it too deep or the crown may rot, particularly if drainage is not good. Water-in and mulch after planting. To create a privacy screen or hedge planting, space the plants at least 8 feet apart.

Care and Maintenance

Pampas grass is tough and not susceptible to any insect or disease problems. Particularly in south Louisiana, it is fairly typical for the plants to sustain no winter injury. Simply prune away last year's old flowers in spring. If the winter is cold enough to cause significant damage to the foliage, prune back the plants in late winter or early spring. This is best accomplished while wearing long sleeves and gloves to protect your arms and hands and using manual or power hedge shearers. A machete may also be used (carefully!). Clumps can be lifted and divided if they grow too large, but this is quite an undertaking. The roots are very tough. Pampas grass is quite drought tolerant; other than watering during hot, dry weather their first year after planting, no irrigation is necessary.

Additional Information

Pampas grass leaf edges are very finely serrated and very sharp. They can and will inflict shallow, painful cuts similar to paper cuts if you handle them incorrectly. Always be careful when reaching into the plant. This quality makes pampas grass particularly effective as a barrier. It would be virtually impossible to force your way through an established planting. The fluffy, white flower heads make beautiful additions to dried flower arrangements. Spray them lightly with hairspray to keep them intact.

Additional Cultivars or Species

C. selloana 'Rubra' produces flower plumes with a pink tint. *C. selloana* 'Sun Stripe', 'Silver Comet', and 'Variegata' have green-and-white-striped foliage. For smaller areas, try the dwarf pampas grass, *C. selloana* 'Pumila', which grows to about 4 feet with a spread of 3 feet.

Variegated Acorus

Acorus gramineus 'Variegatus'

Other Name: Grassy-Leaved Sweet Flag
Zones: 8 and 9
Size: 6 to 12 inches
Type: Evergreen
Flowers: No ornamental value

Light Requirement:

This useful plant from the Far East looks like a tiny variegated iris when viewed up close, but it is actually a member of the Araceae family (which includes philodendrons). The very narrow leaves grow from the ends of creeping rhizomes in a fan arrangement and are upright, arching only slightly toward their ends. The overall look is of a clump of grass. The foliage is striped with creamy white and stays attractive all year long. The flowers are produced at the base of the plant and are not noticeable. Acorus produces a slowly spreading clump that is well behaved in the garden.

When to Plant

Plant from containers any time, but spring or early summer is preferable. Plant divisions in spring.

Where to Plant

Although acorus will grow in full sun if the location is sufficiently moist, the plants seem to do better when they receive some shade during the day. Acorus is not particular to soil type. It will grow in everything from well-drained beds to boggy areas and may even be used in aquatic gardens.

How to Plant

A well-prepared bed where organic matter has been incorporated into the soil will encourage the clumps to spread faster. Plant acorus so that the rhizome is showing slightly above the soil surface, then water-in and mulch over the area. Because of their relatively small size and evergreen foliage, acorus are excellent for use in container plantings. This plant is also great for detail work along pathways, in the front of mixed perennial beds, as individual clumps, or planted in drifts. Acorus may be planted in a container using heavy garden soil and placed in an aquatic garden with the water level no more than a couple of inches above the rim of the pot.

Care and Maintenance

Every few years, cut the plants back in late winter or early spring if there is an accumulation of old, brown foliage. This will encourage fresh new growth and improve the appearance of the clump. Fertilize using a general-purpose fertilizer with a 3:1:2 ratio (such as 15-5-10) in March or April. Use aquatic fertilizer tablets for plants growing in aquatic gardens. White scale can be a common problem, and acorus is susceptible to spider mites. Both pests may be effectively controlled with oil sprays used according to label directions. Clumps can be divided in spring if desired.

Additional Information

The common name "grassy-leaved sweet flag" comes from three characteristics of this plant: it has a grassy texture, its rhizome has a sweet smell when broken open, and it resembles irises (often called flags). For a dynamic effect, combine acorus with red-flowering impatiens, cardinal flower, or red wax begonias. It also makes an attractive addition to the aquatic garden, contrasting texturally with the other aquatic plants.

Additional Cultivars or Species

Acorus gramineus 'Ogon' has yellow variegated leaves with a very fine texture. *A. gramineus,* the standard species, has shiny, dark-green leaves. Another larger species, *A. calamus,* grows to 3 feet and has leaves an inch wide, giving it a coarser, more iris-like appearance.

Variegated Japanese Sedge

Carex morrowii 'Variegata'

Zones: 8 and 9
Size: 10 inches
Type: Evergreen

Light Requirement:

Sedges are very similar in appearance to grasses. They are distinguished from them by stems that are triangular rather than round in cross-section. Botany students use the phrase "sedges have edges" to help them remember the difference. Members of the family Cyperaceae—this is a large group of plants—often grow in moist or boggy situations. All Louisiana gardeners are familiar with nut grass (or coco grass or nut sedge). This sedge is one of our worst weeds—but such is not true of all sedges. There are a number of species in the genus *Carex* that are very attractive and well-behaved garden plants. Variegated Japanese sedge is a low, mounding plant with thin leaves that swirl out from a central growing point. The leaves are striped lengthwise with creamy white and are attractive year-round. The flowers appear in the spring and are of no ornamental value. The little brown spikes can be cut off if you so desire, or left on to fade away.

When to Plant

Container-grown variegated Japanese sedge is usually available at local nurseries and can be planted anytime. Divisions are best planted in March or April.

Where to Plant

Avoid hot, dry, sunny areas when planting. This plant is an excellent choice for moist (even wet), partly shady spots. It is effective as an edging or individual accent, or planted in drifts. It combines beautifully with coarser-textured plants such as hosta or toad lily (*Tricyrtis*).

How to Plant

Prepare the area by removing any weeds and incorporating a generous amount of organic matter such as compost, rotted manure, or peat moss into the bed. Plant at the same level it was growing at the nursery, being careful not to bury the crown. Water-in and mulch after planting

Care and Maintenance

Fertilize in March using a general-purpose granular fertilizer with a 3:1:2 ratio such as 15-5-10 (or a 1:1:1 ratio such as 8-8-8 if your soil is low in phosphorus). Every 2 or 3 years, cut the clump back to remove the accumulation of brown foliage that occurs over time. It is very important to do this in early spring before new growth appears; if done after new growth has emerged, the plants will sulk the rest of the summer. If desired, divide clumps in late February or March. Mulching the planting is, as usual, a good idea to control weeds and conserve soil moisture. New shoots will occasionally revert to the solid green of the original species, and if not removed, may tend to take over. Keep an eye out for them.

Additional Information

This plant is graceful in its growth. The fine leaves tend to arch up, then trail on the ground around the central crown. Push through the foliage in a circular motion with your hand, as if you were stirring a pot. The result will be a spiral pattern of foliage around the central crown, creating a lovely effect.

Additional Cultivars or Species

Carex buchananii, the leatherleaf sedge from New Zealand, produces very fine, upward-growing, reddish-brown leaves that arch over and spiral slightly at their tips. A plant with brown leaves may sound odd, but it is really quite effective when combined with other plants as an accent in beds or in containers. You may wish to try *C. plantaginea*, *C. elata* 'Bowles' Golden', and *C. texensis*.

Variegated Japanese Silver Grass

Miscanthus sinensis 'Variegata'

Other Name: Eulalia Grass
Zones: 8 and 9
Size: 5 to 6 feet high, 4 to 6 feet wide
Type: Goes dormant in winter
Flowers: Pinkish-tan flower spikes
Bloom Period: Summer to fall

Light Requirement:

Miscanthus sinensis has mutated into a bewildering array of cultivars, many of which are among the most beautiful and useful of the ornamental grasses. Variegated Japanese silver grass is one of the most lovely. This medium to large grass possesses a graceful fountain-like form that is poetry in motion when brushed by a breeze. Each of the thin leaves is striped with creamy white down its middle. The overall effect from a distance is that of a pale, almost-white plant. The pinkish-tan plumes are held on tall stems well above the foliage and are quite attractive, combining well with other plant materials. They are produced in July, adding interest all the way into winter.

When to Plant

Container-grown plants are best planted in spring through early summer.

Where to Plant

Variegated Japanese silver grass grows best in full sun and well-drained to wet locations. Use it in the background of flower beds or perennial borders, or as a specimen plant to accent an area of your landscape. It grows large, so make sure the location you choose for it provides enough room. As is true of many of the larger ornamental grasses, plants purchased at the nursery are not nearly as large as the grass will eventually become.

How to Plant

Plant at the same level it was growing in its container. As for most ornamental grasses, extensive bed preparation is not necessary, but planting into soil that has been enriched by the addition of organic matter such as compost, rotted manure, or peat moss will encourage establishment and vigorous growth. Water-in and mulch after planting.

Care and Maintenance

Variegated Japanese silver grass is ideal for the low-maintenance landscape. No special care is required, and the plant is not susceptible to any major insect or disease problems. Fertilize in March or April with 15-5-10 to encourage vigorous growth, though this is usually not crucial for good performance. When the grass goes dormant for the winter, it turns tan; you may cut it back to the ground any time after that. At least cut the clump back by early March before new growth begins to appear.

Additional Information

The flowers, fresh or dried, make interesting additions to decorative arrangements. Like most *Miscanthus* cultivars, variegated Japanese silver grass is very nice planted near aquatic features in the landscape. It works well with any color scheme.

Additional Cultivars or Species

There are more *Miscanthus* cultivars than can be practically listed here. Three nice variegated cultivars are *Miscanthus sinensis* 'Silverfeder', 'Cabaret', and 'Cosmopolitan'.

Zebra Grass

Miscanthus sinensis 'Zebrinus'

Zones: 8 and 9
Size: 6 feet
Type: Dormant in winter
Flowers: White plumes
Bloom Period: Late summer

Light Requirement:

This plant is a real attention-getter. Most variegated ornamental grasses are striped lengthwise, but zebra grass has yellow bands that run horizontally across the leaf, giving the foliage a very different and striking look in the landscape. The foliage arches gracefully but is held fairly upright, creating an attractive form. The flowers are off-white with a faint burgundy tint, a welcome addition to the late-summer garden. They are held well above the foliage on long stalks and wave gracefully in the slightest breeze.

When to Plant

Spring planting is preferred, but you may plant container-grown zebra grass any time after danger of frost has passed through late summer. Plant divisions in spring.

Where to Plant

The growth is more sturdy and less likely to lean over when planted in full sun, but the plant will do well in some shade. Plant in any good garden soil, well drained or wet. Because of its size, use this plant toward the back of beds. Its striking variegation makes it an outstanding accent plant. It is effective when shown off in a large container.

How to Plant

Plant at the same level it was growing in its container. Extensive bed preparation is not necessary, but planting into soil that has been enriched with the addition of organic matter such as compost, rotted manure, or peat moss will encourage establishment and vigorous growth. Water-in and mulch after planting.

Care and Maintenance

No special care is required for this excellent low-maintenance plant which is not susceptible to any major insect or disease problems. Fertilize in March or April with 15-5-10 to encourage vigorous growth, though this is not crucial for good performance. When the grass goes dormant for the winter, it turns tan; you may cut it back to the ground any time after that. At least cut the clump back by early March before the new growth begins.

Additional Information

Don't be alarmed if the new growth on your zebra grass emerges without horizontal yellow bands. New growth is bright green, and the variegation will show up as the foliage matures. Stalks of zebra grass foliage make outstanding additions to fresh flower arrangements.

Additional Cultivars or Species

Miscanthus sinensis 'Stricta', porcupine grass, is similar but more upright.

C H A P T E R   F I V E

Palms

VISITORS TO NEW ORLEANS ARE IMMEDIATELY STRUCK by the presence of numerous palms planted along streets and in home landscapes. The palms, more than any other plants, make these visitors realize they are in a milder climate. Only in the southernmost areas of the United States can palms be grown successfully in the ground outdoors, and they create a look that cannot be duplicated by any other plant material. Palms are a visual signal that says "tropical."

Although you will find palms used more extensively in New Orleans than anywhere else in Louisiana, gardeners throughout the state can make use of these wonderful and diverse plants. The palms included in this chapter are among the hardiest and most reliable for north Louisiana and some of the nicest ones best used in the southern part of the state.

A palm is a woody plant, but the trunk is not made of the kind of wood like the wood of trees that have annual growth rings and bark; the internal structure is very different and looks more fibrous. This structure is quite strong and helps palms stand up to high winds. It is also the reason the trunks of palms, unlike those of most trees, do not increase in diameter with age. The trunk does not taper toward the younger, upper part—it is the same diameter all the way down, giving the trunk a unique columnar appearance. If anything, the lower trunk can be thinner due to erosion or loss of outer coverings. This structure means the trunk cannot heal itself like most trees, and it is important to avoid injury. Some palm species have a smooth, uniform trunk like the cabbage palm (*Sabal palmetto*); others may have adhering leaf bases like the jelly palm (*Butia capitata*) or matted, hairy trunks like the windmill palm (*Trachycarpus fortunei*).

Another unique characteristic of palms is that they do not branch. A single growing point produces the trunk and the foliage. If this place of growth should be killed, the palm cannot regenerate a new one, and it dies. Never cut a palm back to try to control its height.

Chapter Five

The leaves of palms are called fronds, and these are usually large and dramatic. Palms have two basic forms of leaves—pinnate or feather-shaped fronds, and palmate or fan-shaped fronds. With most palm species, the leaves form a compact crown at the top of the trunk. Compact means concentrated at the top; the fronds themselves may spread out considerable distances. Those of the Canary Island date palm, for instance, can reach out 10 to 15 feet in all directions.

When planting palms (or any other trees, for that matter), it is not recommended that the soil in the planting hole be changed or amended with organic matter such as compost, manure, peat moss, or fine pine bark. Use of these additives will make it harder for the roots to become properly established because the roots will not live in the planting hole but will grow far out into the surrounding native soil. It is best for the roots to adjust to the soil they will actually live in, rather than to start off in one type of soil and then have to make a transition into another.

Dig the hole two to three times as wide as the rootball and just deep enough to accommodate it. Thoroughly pulverize the soil you remove from the hole. The rootball should sit on firm, undisturbed soil. Place the palm into the hole, making sure you are planting it at the same level it was growing previously. Next, fill the hole halfway with the thoroughly pulverized soil that was removed to make the hole. Firm the soil by pressing firmly with your foot (do not pack it tight!), or add enough water to settle the soil, which will remove undesirable air pockets. Finish filling the hole and firm again or add water. (Either firm with your foot or use water—don't do both.) A low berm may be built around the edge of the planting hole to facilitate watering later on. Apply a mulch to help conserve soil moisture and prevent weeds, and give the plant one final soaking to settle everything in. Bracing may be necessary for taller specimens to help stabilize them until the roots get established. Be careful to use a method that will not damage the trunk, as palms cannot heal the wounds.

The selection of palms that can be grown successfully in our state is limited compared to that of south Florida or the southern coast of California, but there are enough species, and diversity among them, to satisfy most gardeners who want to add that tropical touch to their landscapes.

Cabbage Palm

Sabal palmetto

Other Name: Sabal Palm
Zones: 8 and 9
Size: 25 to 30 feet
Type: Evergreen, fronds may brown in severe winters
Flowers: Not significant

Light Requirement:

The cabbage palm is native from North Carolina down to Florida, and it is hardy enough to grow in the northern part of Louisiana. Its single trunk may be smooth or covered with the criss-cross pattern of old leaf bases. Its 3- to 6-foot fan-shaped fronds curve under gracefully. The leaf-stalk or petiole does not bear spines. Flower stalks reach 2 to 3 feet in length. They produce numerous whitish flowers followed by round, shiny, black fruit which is 1/3 inch in diameter. Cabbage palms are well adapted to poorly drained areas and have a moderate growth rate. They are generally hardy down to 15 degrees Fahrenheit.

When to Plant

Wait until the soil has warmed up in late spring to early summer to plant or transplant cabbage palms. May through August is the best time. A warm soil is important for root growth and proper establishment.

Where to Plant

Choose a location that receives partial to full sun. Locate cabbage palms away from existing trees whose canopy might eventually overshadow the palms. They are adapted to a wide variety of soil types.

How to Plant

Since the roots of cabbage palms die back to the base of the trunk when severed, the palms are transplanted with a relatively small rootball. Generally, palms should be planted at the same depth they were growing before, but cabbage palms may be planted 1 to 2 feet deeper with good results. Dig a hole as deep as and 2 to 3 times the diameter of the rootball, and position the tree in the hole. If the tree is balled in burlap, cut any cords and pull back the burlap one-third to halfway down the rootball. Thoroughly break up the soil removed from the hole, and backfill with this soil (do not add any amendments such as compost or peat moss) until the hole is half filled. Firm the soil in the hole to remove air pockets, finish filling the hole, and firm again. Apply a generous amount of water to finish settling the soil, and mulch. Smaller containerized palms will not need any support; taller specimens may need to be braced for 1 to 2 years until established, and they may require professional installation.

Care and Maintenance

Other than having to water newly planted palms regularly during hot, dry weather, the gardener will find cabbage palms to be remarkably care-free. No pruning is required other than removing brown fronds and flower stalks. In poor or sandy soils, the application of 15-5-10 fertilizer in late spring will encourage growth, but this is usually optional. Should winter freezes brown back the fronds, remove them in the spring. New growth may not occur until mid- to late summer, so do not be too hasty to decide that the palm is dead.

Additional Information

The tender growing point is edible and gives this palm its common name. Harvesting it will kill the plant, however; this is not something the average gardener should undertake.

Additional Cultivars or Species

The Texas palmetto, *Sabal mexicana*, is similar in appearance to the cabbage palm, but is larger and has larger, coarser fronds. It is widely planted in New Orleans and appears to be at least as hardy as the cabbage palm.

Canary Island Date Palm

Phoenix canariensis

Zones: 8 and 9
Size: 30 to 50 feet
Type: Evergreen, but fronds may be damaged in winter
Flowers: Not significant

Light Requirement:

The Canary Island date palm is one of the largest and most prominent palms in New Orleans and can be seen planted along neutral grounds and in area landscapes. Its graceful, feathery fronds grow very large, 15 to 20 feet long. The trunks on these palms are stout when young, up to four feet thick. Older, taller palms usually have trunks that are thinner and smoother, especially toward the base. The round orange fruit is about one inch across and is produced in large, heavy clusters. The palms are reliably hardy down to 15 degrees Fahrenheit, and most returned after the severe 11-degree freeze in New Orleans in 1989.

When to Plant

Canary Island date palms should be planted or transplanted in summer, May through August, when the ground is warm. This will encourage root growth and establishment.

Where to Plant

This palm is excellent for street planting in any area where it can be allowed to spread to 30 feet and grow 40 feet tall. Needless to say, it is best used in large-scale situations. Plant in full sun in well-drained soil.

How to Plant

Canary Island date palms are commonly sold as young trees in containers with little trunk development. They are easy to plant and establish at this size. Larger specimens with well-developed trunks are best planted professionally. Plant at the same depth they were growing in their containers. Dig a hole as deep as the rootball and 2 to 3 times its diameter, and position the tree in the hole. Thoroughly break up the soil removed from the hole, and backfill with this soil (do not add amendments such as compost or peat moss) until the hole is half filled. Firm the soil in the hole to remove any air pockets, finish filling the hole, and firm again. Water-in to settle the soil, and mulch. Smaller containerized palms will not need any support; taller specimens may need to be braced for 1 to 2 years until established.

Care and Maintenance

These palms look best if the old brown fronds are removed annually. Water newly planted Canary Island date palms regularly during hot, dry weather. The application of a general-purpose fertilizer in late spring will encourage growth if the palm has been planted in poor or sandy soil, but this is usually optional. Should winter freezes brown back the fronds, remove the fronds in the spring. New growth may not occur until mid- to late summer, so do not be hasty to decide the palm is dead.

Additional Information

The fruit of the Canary Island date palm is not an edible date. Once these palms begin to reach heights of 20 feet or more, the old fronds must be removed by professionals. (The cost of that should be considered when selecting this species.)

Additional Cultivars or Species

P. dactylifera is the true date palm. It is generally not reliably hardy in the state, though the cultivar 'Deglet Noor' is reported to be hardy down to 10 degrees Fahrenheit for short periods. *P. reclinata*, the Senegal date palm, is a smaller, clumping species that is occasionally planted in New Orleans but is not reliably hardy in the long run.

Chinese Fan Palm

Livistona chinensis

Zone: 9
Size: 10 to 15 feet
Type: Evergreen, but subject to winter injury
Flowers: Not significant

Light Requirement:

The large fan-shaped fronds of the Chinese fan palm are among the most graceful of the fan palms. The fronds reach up to six feet across, and the ends of all the leaflets droop down, giving the fronds a weeping effect that is very attractive. This single-trunk palm is relatively slow growing, but the spreading fronds require an area at least six feet wide. The leaf bases cling to the trunk after old fronds have been pruned away, giving the trunk a rough appearance. Most gardeners purchase young container-grown plants. With these plants, it will be several years before a trunk becomes apparent. Chinese fan palms are hardy down to 20 degrees Fahrenheit, and many will come back in protected locations after 11- to 15-degree episodes.

When to Plant

Wait until the soil has warmed up to plant or transplant Chinese fan palms. A warm soil is important to root growth and proper establishment. May through August is the best planting time.

Where to Plant

These palms do best when they receive some shade, and can even tolerate a fairly shaded location. They will be less susceptible to winter injury if they are planted under the protection of a large tree or near a structure such as a wall or house.

How to Plant

Most gardeners buy Chinese fan palms as young trees in containers with little trunk development. They are easy to plant and establish at this size. Plant these palms at the same depth they were growing in their containers. Dig a hole as deep as the rootball and 2 to 3 times its diameter, remove the palm from its container, and position it in the hole. Thoroughly break up the soil removed from the hole, and backfill with this soil (do not add any amendments such as compost or peat moss) until the hole is half filled. Firm the soil in the hole to remove any air pockets, finish filling the hole, and firm again. Thoroughly water-in the palm, and mulch the planting area.

Care and Maintenance

Should the fronds be damaged by winter freezes, prune them off in spring. Young plants may be covered for protection until they get too big. Fertilize in late spring with 15-5-10 to encourage growth. Keep newly planted trees well watered during their first summer.

Additional Information

When it is young, this palm is useful for providing lush, tropical foliage that looks similar to that of split-leaf philodendron. As the tree ages and develops a trunk, lower-growing plants can be planted under it to fill in the area.

Additional Cultivars or Species

The Australian fan palm, *L. australis*; the ribbon fan palm, *L. decipiens*; and the Taran palm, *L. saribus* are all listed as hardy in Zone 9. As far as we know, these palms have not been grown in New Orleans, and there is no information on how hardy they would be in south Louisiana.

Dwarf Palmetto

Sabal minor

Other Name: Palmetto
Zones: 8 and 9
Size: 6 to 8 feet
Type: Evergreen
Flowers: Not significant

Light Requirement:

This outstanding small-growing palm is native to Louisiana and may be found from Texas to Florida and South Carolina. It is hardy throughout our state. It may grow very slowly to 6 to 8 feet tall, or remain trunkless and smaller, 3 to 5 feet. The fan-shaped leaves are 1 to 3 feet wide. The leaf stems do not have teeth and are up to 3 feet long. The dwarf palmetto produces clusters of numerous white flowers from May to June, followed by black fruit $^3/_8$ inch in diameter later in the year. It thrives in wet, swampy areas in the wild. It is an outstanding choice for landscaping shady, poorly drained areas or for planting near ponds or water features.

When to Plant

Dwarf palmetto palms should be planted in summer, May through August, when the soil is warm. This will encourage root growth and establishment. These palms are very difficult to transplant from the wild because of their large subterranean root systems.

Where to Plant

Plant in well-drained to wet areas. In the wild, palmettos often grow under the shade of trees, so shaded to partly shaded areas in the landscape are fine. This relatively small-growing species is more appropriate to smaller-scale landscapes than are the larger-growing palms.

How to Plant

Since they are difficult to transplant, gardeners should purchase young, seed-grown trees in containers. Plant dwarf palmettos at the same depth they were growing in their containers. Dig a hole as deep as the rootball and 2 to 3 times its diameter, remove the palm from its container, and position it in the hole. Thoroughly break up the soil removed from the hole, and backfill with this soil (do not add any amendments such as compost or peat moss) until the hole is half filled. Firm the soil in the hole to remove any air pockets, finish filling the hole, and firm again. Thoroughly water-in the palm and mulch the planting area.

Care and Maintenance

Other than occasional grooming, little care is needed. Prune off old fronds as they become unattractive. Only unusually severe winters will brown the foliage in north Louisiana. Should that happen, trim off the brown foliage in the spring.

Additional Information

This palm is an excellent choice for native landscapes, and can be used as a shrub rather than as a tree. It is sometimes difficult to find at nurseries.

Additional Cultivars or Species

The saw palmetto, *Serenoa repens*, is also native to Louisiana and should be hardy throughout the state. It is a small palm very similar to dwarf palmetto but distinguished by the teeth along its leaf stems. The foliage varies from yellow-green to blue-green. It can grow in shady, poorly drained areas.

Mediterranean Fan Palm

Chamaerops humilis

Other Name: European Fan Palm
Zones: 8 and 9
Size: 3 to 8 feet tall, 6 feet across
Type: Evergreen, but subject to winter injury
Flowers: Not significant

Light Requirement:

The Mediterranean fan palm has the distinction of being the only palm native to Europe. Under unusual circumstances, it may reach a height of 20 feet, but it typically grows no taller than 8 feet. It is a multitrunked, clumping palm. As it suckers from the base, the Mediterranean fan palm creates a mounding mass of foliage instead of the classic growth pattern most people associate with palms. The fronds are stiff and fan-shaped and grow about 2 feet across. The petiole is slender with rows of teeth. The trunks are often hidden by the foliage, but as the plant ages, they will become more noticeable. This relatively slow-growing palm is a good choice for small areas.

When to Plant

As is true of all palms, the Mediterranean fan palm should be planted during the warm months of May through August. The warmth of the soil during summer encourages root growth and establishment.

Where to Plant

Choose a well-drained location that gets plenty of sun. Because of its smaller size and slow rate of growth, Mediterranean fan palm may be planted into relatively small landscapes. Allow about 6 feet for it to spread.

How to Plant

Mediterranean fan palms are usually sold in containers. Plant these palms at the same depth they were growing in their containers. Dig a hole as deep as the rootball and 2 to 3 times its diameter, remove the palm from its container, and position it in the hole. Thoroughly break up the soil removed from the hole, and backfill with this soil (do not add any amendments such as compost or peat moss) until the hole is half filled. Firm the soil in the hole to remove any air pockets, finish filling the hole, and firm again. Thoroughly water-in the palm and mulch the planting area.

Care and Maintenance

Should the fronds become damaged by winter freezes, prune them off in spring. Young plants may be covered for protection until they get too big. Fertilize in late spring with 15-5-10 to encourage growth, and keep newly planted trees well watered their first summer.

Additional Information

Purchased plants may have only a single trunk or growing point, but more will develop with age. If you wish to keep the plant to a single trunk, remove the suckers as they appear. Its relatively small size makes Mediterranean fan palm an excellent choice for courtyards and sheltered patios, and it appreciates the protection afforded by those locations.

Additional Cultivars or Species

This is the only species in its genus. The cultivars 'Canariensis' and 'Robusta' are listed.

Needle Palm

Rhapidophyllum hystrix

Other Names: Porcupine Palm, Blue Palmetto **Zones:** 8 and 9 **Size:** 6 feet **Type:** Evergreen **Flowers:** Not significant	**Light Requirement:**

This slow-growing, clumping palm is native from South Carolina to Florida and west to Mississippi. It is considered the hardiest palm and will withstand temperatures to minus six degrees Fahrenheit. Gardeners in northern Louisiana can plant it with absolute confidence. Forming a rounded mound of foliage, the leaves are fan-shaped and usually no more than 2 1/2 feet across. The trunks are generally hidden by the foliage. The leaf stems are short, and their bases are covered with dark fibers in which are embedded very sharp spines six to eight inches long. Except that they do not have a tuft of feathers at one end, they look for all the world like the darts used with blow guns. (Unless someone is reaching into the plant, it is not hazardous.)

When to Plant

Wait until the soil has warmed up in late spring to early summer to plant or transplant needle palms. May through August is the best time. A warm soil is important for root growth and proper establishment.

Where to Plant

Plant in a well-drained area that receives full sun to partial sun. Allow for a spread of 6 feet, even though it will take a small plant quite a while to grow that large.

How to Plant

Dig a hole as deep as the rootball and 2 to 3 times its diameter, remove the palm from the container, and position it in the hole. If the tree is balled in burlap, cut any cords and pull back the burlap one-third to halfway down the rootball. Thoroughly break up the soil removed from the hole, and backfill with this soil (do not add any amendments such as compost or peat moss) until the hole is half filled. Firm the soil in the hole to remove air pockets, finish filling the hole, and firm again. Apply a generous amount of water to finish settling the soil, and mulch.

Care and Maintenance

Keep the palm well watered during its first summer after planting. Occasionally prune off old, unattractive fronds as they occur (watch out for the needles!). It is unlikely that you will ever have to prune off freeze-damaged growth. If soils are poor, fertilize with 15-5-10 in April or May to stimulate growth.

Additional Information

The needle palm grows into a shape more like a shrub than a palm, and it can be used as such in the landscape—in a foundation planting, for instance. This palm is hard to find. It would be used much more in Louisiana if more people were aware of it and if nurseries would carry it.

Additional Cultivars or Species

There are no cultivars or additional species of *Rhapidophyllum* listed.

Windmill Palm

Trachycarpus fortunei

Zones: 8 and 9
Size: 15 to 20 feet
Type: Evergreen
Flowers: Not significant

Light Requirement:

The windmill palm is another very hardy palm that is quite reliable in northern Louisiana. Numerous specimens thrive in Shreveport. Wonderfully proportioned, it has the look of the classic cabbage palm without the massive size. A mat of dark-brown fibers woven together (they actually look like burlap) coats the trunk of a younger palm. As the tree ages, the lower part of the trunk loses its covering and appears much thinner. The leaves are fan-shaped, dark green, and two to three feet in diameter. The head of the windmill palm is compact, reaching only about five feet across. Windmill palms are moderately slow growing. Where there is room, they are particularly attractive planted in groups of three.

When to Plant

Since a warm soil is important for root growth and proper establishment, May through August is the best time to plant windmill palms.

Where to Plant

Plant in full to part sun in a well-drained area. The compact growth of these plants makes them useful in a variety of landscape situations. They are excellent around swimming pools, as accents in formal landscapes, and around patios.

How to Plant

Windmill palms are sold both in containers and balled in burlap. They should be planted at the same depth they were growing at the nursery. Dig a hole as deep as the rootball and 2 to 3 times its diameter, remove the tree from the container, and position it in the hole. If the tree is balled in burlap, cut any cords and pull back the burlap one-third to halfway down the rootball. Thoroughly break up the soil removed to create the hole, and backfill with this soil (do not add any amendments such as compost or peat moss) until the hole is half filled. Firm the soil in the hole to remove any air pockets, finish filling the hole, and firm again. Apply a generous amount of water to finish settling the soil, and mulch. Smaller palms under 5 feet will not need any support; taller specimens may need to be braced for 1 to 2 years until they are established.

Care and Maintenance

Other than occasional grooming, little care is needed. Prune off old fronds as they become unattractive. In northern Louisiana, only unusually severe winters will brown the foliage. Should that happen, trim off the brown foliage in the spring. Keep the palm well watered during the first summer after planting. Once established, windmill palms are quite drought tolerant. Fertilize in May with 15-5-10 to encourage growth.

Additional Information

One generally doesn't associate palms with China, but the windmill palm is native to the central and eastern parts of that country. This helps explain its relatively hardy nature.

Additional Cultivars or Species

There are no cultivars of *T. fortunei* listed, and other species of *Trachycarpus* are not in common use.

CHAPTER SIX

Perennials

GARDENERS ARE GIVING INCREASING ATTENTION to the ways hardy, herbaceous perennials can be used in the landscape. Home gardeners and commercial landscapers alike are becoming more aware of the rich potential this wonderful group of plants holds. Perennials offer a certain permanency to the flower garden, and provide abundant color and and beauty in return for the care they require.

Perennials are sometimes defined as plants which live for more than two years, but this definition includes trees, turfgrasses, and shrubs. When used by horticulturists, the term perennial generally refers to a group of herbaceous (non-woody) plants most frequently grown for their colorful flowers or attractive foliage.

Perennials have been underutilized in Louisiana in the past because of a general assumption that they don't do well here, and it is true that some of the classic perennials of Northern gardens won't grow in our state. Many perennials, however, thrive under our growing conditions; we just need to choose varieties adapted to our climate. The perennials used in our gardens should have a tolerance to diseases favored by heat and humidity. Try to select those that have a reputation for heat tolerance.

In addition to being adapted to our climate, perennials should be selected according to the conditions of the planting site. Some perennials such as purple loosestrife, cardinal flower, and Louisiana irises are tolerant of poor drainage, but most require excellent drainage. Light preference varies from shade-loving plants to those that need full sun.

Height, spread, color, plant habit, and time and length of bloom should also be given careful consideration when selecting perennial plants for the landscape.

One of the most important factors in perennial-growing success is careful bed preparation. Remember, unlike beds of annuals, which are replanted two or three times a year, perennials live for years. There will be fewer chances to rework the beds. Extra effort at the beginning will pay off in the long run.

First do a thorough job of removing unwanted vegetation from the planting area. If it is a new bed, this may include lifting any grass sod that currently covers the area. If it is an existing bed that has become overrun with weeds, you will have to physically dig out the weeds, roots and all, or kill off the weeds with a herbicide, such as glyphosate, prior to reworking the bed. Beds should be dug to a depth of at least 8 to 10 inches as many perennials are deep rooted. Most perennials prefer soils that are rich in organic matter. Heavy clay soils should be amended with sand and compost or fine pine bark to improve drainage. Sandy soils can be improved with the addition of compost, peat moss, or aged manure. Lime or fertilizer should be added according to soil-test results. Contact your local office of the Louisiana Cooperative Extension Service, a branch of the Louisiana State University Agricultural Center, for information on soil testing. Good drainage is essential to successfully growing most perennials; in some cases, raised beds may be necessary.

Planting perennials is like putting money in a savings account: it pays you interest. Most perennials that do well will eventually become overcrowded and need to be divided. Mature clumps can be dug in fall or late winter, then cut or pulled apart. Divisions should usually contain three to five shoots or growing points. Discard any weak or diseased divisions. Now you have more plants than you started with—that's your "interest".

Perennials are tough. Unlike annuals, which are gone after one season, perennials have the ability to live for years. A perennial bed planted with carefully chosen well-adapted plants has the ability to provide color and interest season after season, year after year, without constant replanting.

Artemisia

Artemisia ludoviciana

Other Name: Western Mugwort
Zones: 8 and 9
Size: 3 feet
Type: Dormant in winter
Flowers: Not significant

Light Requirement:

There are not a lot of reliable silver-leaved perennials in the Deep South—most of these plants developed their protective silver coverings to protect them from dry environments. Silver-leaved perennials often rot in the hot, wet weather of mid- to late summer in Louisiana, but there is an exception: *Artemisia ludoviciana* can tolerate the hottest, wettest weather. Its rather fine foliage consists of silver-gray, narrow, lance-shaped leaves. The small flowers, produced in clusters at the top of the stems, are barely noticeable. This enthusiastic plant is best used in the back of the border, where it will form a beautiful background of silver filigree to pinks, lavenders, and purples or more vivid reds and yellows.

When to Plant

Plant October through early December and late February through April.

Where to Plant

Artemisias are well adapted to hot, dry, and sunny locations with poor soil. They require good drainage.

How to Plant

Plant in beds that have been improved with the addition of organic matter and a sprinkling of all-purpose granular fertilizer. If planted in an existing, well-maintained garden bed, little or no improvement of the soil is necessary. Set plants into the ground at the same level they were growing in the pot.

Care and Maintenance

When there is sufficient growing space, the artemisia is relatively care-free. There are no major insect or disease problems. Additional fertilizer or abundant, late-summer growth may cause floppy, sprawling plants. If this is a problem, provide support or trim back the plant. Artemisia can spread. Watch for sprouts in unwanted locations and remove them promptly. Dig and divide every 2 or 3 years, in late winter or early spring, to maintain control.

Additional Information

The aromatic foliage can be cut, dried, and used for dry arrangements or crafts. Wait until the plant comes into bloom before harvesting.

Additional Cultivars or Species

A. ludoviciana 'Silver King' grows 2 to 3 feet and is the most commonly grown cultivar; 'Silver Queen' has foliage that is more deeply cut; 'Valerie Finnis' has foliage that is wider and grows 18 to 28 inches. *Artemisia* × 'Powis Castle' is a fine-textured silvery-green plant, growing 24 to 30 inches, that has performed very well in Louisiana. A much lower-growing perennial plant with silvery-white leaves is dusty miller, *Senecio cineraria*. It is often grown as an annual, but is surprisingly hardy. It survives mild winters in the northern and most winters in the southern part of the state.

Blue Phlox

Phlox divaricata

Other Name: Louisiana Phlox
Zones: 8 and 9
Size: 12 to 15 inches
Flowers: Clusters of lavender-blue to purple
Bloom Period: Spring

Light Requirement:

This native wildflower offers a lovely blue to purple contrast for April azaleas. Spring bloom and the winter presence of medium green, shiny foliage increase the popularity of blue phlox for the landscape. The pale lavender-blue to purple flowers are 3/4 to one inch across and produced in clusters at the ends of the stems. Blue phlox is offered in local nurseries as Louisiana phlox since it is native to the state.

When to Plant

Plants in containers are usually purchased in the spring when in bloom and may be planted then. Fall or late-winter planting is preferred.

Where to Plant

Blue phlox will grow in full sun if the bed stays moist, but it seems to be happiest with part sun to part shade. Drainage is not critical as long as the bed does not stay constantly wet. Use blue phlox in front of shrub plantings (especially azaleas) or in front of borders and beds.

How to Plant

Set plants into a spot that has been improved with 2 inches of compost, rotted manure, or peat moss worked into the soil. A light sprinkling of fertilizer may be added. Plant the plants at the same level they were growing in their containers, water them thoroughly, and mulch.

Care and Maintenance

After flowering, cut the plants back halfway and remove faded flower heads to encourage new growth from the base. Foliage quality through the summer is good in moist, partially sunny locations, but plants may go semi-dormant in dry, sunny spots. Divide in late winter as needed, generally no more often than every 3 years. Fertilize in early May with 8-8-8, 1 or 2 teaspoons per plant. Use 15-5-10 if your soil is high in phosphorus.

Additional Information

Blue phlox is not very competitive and more aggressive plants can crowd it out. Choose mixed plantings carefully.

Additional Cultivars or Species

Cultivar 'Laphamii' is dark violet-blue. 'Fullers White' is white. 'Chattahoochee', a hybrid cultivar, has lavender-blue flowers with reddish-purple centers.

Chrysanthemum

Dendranthema × morifolium

Other Names: *Chrysanthemum × morifolium*, Mums
Zones: 8 and 9
Size: 10 to 18 inches
Flowers: Double or single, daisy-like, in clusters, pink, red, yellow, purple and other colors
Bloom Period: Fall

Light Requirement:

The undisputed queen of the fall flower garden, chrysanthemums are beautiful, reliable, and easy to grow. From October through early December, they put on a show of flowers in a tremendous variety of colors, shapes, and sizes. Garden varieties are compact and suited for the landscape. The greenhouse varieties developed for pots and sold by florists are usually too leggy in the garden, as are the cut-flower varieties.

When to Plant

Plant blooming plants in the fall, when they become available. Plant divisions from existing clumps in late winter or early spring when plants are dug and divided.

Where to Plant

Chrysanthemums are relatively adaptable and undemanding. They need a location that gets at least 6 hours of sun and has reasonable drainage.

How to Plant

Prepare the area for planting by incorporating a 2-inch layer of organic matter and a light sprinkling of general-purpose fertilizer (8-8-8 or 15-5-10) into the soil. Plant the mums at the same level they were growing in their containers, water thoroughly, and mulch.

Care and Maintenance

When plants have finished flowering, lightly shear them back. They will often bloom again. In winter, when the tops have been browned by frost, cut them to the ground and mulch. Divide clumps every few years when new sprouts appear in late winter or early spring. Pinch or trim plants back once or twice during the summer to encourage them to be full, bushy, and more compact. Do not cut them back after the middle of July. Fertilize in March and again in July. Pest problems are not typical, but aphids occasionally show up. Treat with insecticidal soap. Caterpillars that eat the foliage and flower buds can be controlled with Sevin or the biological pesticide B.t.

Additional Information

Chrysanthemums are stimulated to bloom by the longer nights of fall. On occasion, after a mild winter in south Louisiana, mums will grow early enough in the spring to benefit from nights long enough to initiate flowering. This spring to early summer display of flowers will not prevent fall bloom. Cut plants back when flowers fade.

Additional Cultivars or Species

Garden mums that have performed well in Louisiana include 'Lipstick', red; 'Tinkerbell', purple; 'Grandchild', pink; 'Stardom', lavender-pink; 'Ruby Mound', red; 'Jackpot', yellow; 'Ryan's Pink', large, soft pink. Another reliable cultivar is *Dendranthema* × *rubellum* 'Clara Curtis', a single rose-pink with yellow centers on 24-inch plants.

Comfrey

Symphytum officinale

Other Name: Boneset
Zones: 8 and 9
Size: 18 inches high, 24 inches wide
Type: Evergreen
Flowers: Small, bell-shaped, white or rose
Bloom Period: Summer

Light Requirement:

This medicinal herb sneaked into the chapter on perennials because it is attractive and absolutely effortless to grow. Bold, quilted, dark-green leaves add a coarse texture to the border that contrasts beautifully with other perennials. The curled spikes of bell-shaped white or rose flowers are not spectacular, but they provide a charming touch. Comfrey grows to 14 to 18 inches tall with a spread of about 24 inches and fits well into the middle border, providing textural contrast.

When to Plant

Plant from containers anytime. Fall or early spring is best. Plant divisions in late winter or early spring.

Where to Plant

Choose a location that receives 4 hours or more of direct sun. Good drainage is preferred, but comfrey is adaptable.

How to Plant

Plant into an area prepared by incorporating a 2-inch layer of compost, rotted manure, or peat moss. Comfrey grows from a crown and must be planted at the same level it was growing in the container. Water thoroughly to settle the soil around the roots. Add mulch.

Care and Maintenance

Cut foliage back to the ground if damaged by freezing. Comfrey often stays green through the winter. Remove individual yellowed leaves during the summer. Fertilize in April or May with a light application of a general-purpose fertilizer to stimulate good growth. (In a fertile soil this is optional.)

Additional Information

The name "boneset" refers to the plant's ancient medicinal use for healing broken bones. Comfrey can heal a monotonous border with its bold leaves!

Additional Cultivars or Species

S. officinale 'Variegatum' has leaves attractively edged in creamy white. There is a similar comfrey, *S.* × *uplandicum*, that also has a variegated form.

Daylily

Hemerocallis spp. and hybrids

Zones: 8 and 9
Size: 12 to 36 inches
Type: Evergreen
Flowers: Flat or trumpet-shaped, a variety of colors
Bloom Period: Summer

Light Requirement:

Few gardeners need an introduction to the daylily. It is tough, reliable, and popular. Its flowers rise 12 to 36 inches (sometimes more) above its thick, grass-like foliage. The color range is tremendous, especially when you consider that the first breeders began with only yellow, orange, and burgundy. You can find lilies with flowers in many shades of peach, creamy white, lavender, red, purple, rose, and pink, in double and single forms, and ranging in size from two to six inches. In Louisiana, the evergreen and semi-evergreen varieties are most successful.

When to Plant

Fall and early spring are the best times to set out plants. Container-grown daylilies can be planted while in bloom. Daylilies are best divided and replanted in the fall.

Where to Plant

Daylilies need at least 6 hours of sun. Older types of daylilies can be seen growing in ditches along side roads, but modern varieties prefer sunny beds with good drainage.

How to Plant

Prepare the bed by turning the soil to a depth of 8 to 10 inches. Mix a 2-inch layer of fine pine bark or compost and 8-8-8 fertilizer (1/3 cup per square yard) into the soil. Plant daylilies at the same level they were growing in their containers. Do not bury the crowns. Water and mulch the plants. Raised beds are recommended when inadequate drainage is a problem.

Care and Maintenance

Groom daylilies by removing faded flowers when all have finished blooming. Fertilize in spring (see rate in How to Plant section). Keep the beds well mulched to prevent weeds and conserve soil moisture. Established daylilies are fairly drought tolerant, but an occasional deep watering during hot, dry weather is beneficial. Every 3 to 5 years, divide in late fall when clumps become crowded. The daylily aphid is a common pest. Look for it primarily in the spring when it feeds in the heart of the plant causing deformed leaves. Treat with acephate. Spider mites occur infrequently and can be controlled with kelthane or insecticidal soap.

Additional Information

Daylily flowers and flower buds are edible. Pickled daylily buds are delicious. The name "daylily" arose because each flower lasts only one day before it fades. Even though each flower lasts but a day, many flowers are produced over a long period.

Additional Cultivars or Species

Many gardeners have favorite varieties of daylilies. Select those with the size and flower color to enhance your garden, using evergreen and semi-evergreen types. Be warned: if you begin to collect varieties of daylilies, it may be difficult to stop.

Hosta

Hosta spp. and hybrids

Other Name: Plantain Lily
Zones: 8 and 9
Size: 12 to 15 inches
Type: Dormant in winter
Flowers: Lavender or white, bell-shaped, on tall stalks
Bloom Period: Summer

Light Requirement:

Until recently, it was believed that hostas would not thrive in Louisiana. Today, hostas grow in and enhance shady gardens throughout the state, though they often don't achieve the size or vigor of plants grown farther north. The foliage of hostas is distinctly ornamental. It is bold, strap-shaped to paddle-shaped, deeply veined, often slightly shiny, and may be various shades of green, blue-green, chartreuse, or variegated in white or yellow. The lavender or white flowers are produced on rather awkwardly tall stems, but are a pleasant surprise.

When to Plant

Plants are available at nurseries in spring. Plant as early as possible so plants can become established before the weather gets too hot. It is often worthwhile to buy larger plants.

Where to Plant

Hostas are excellent for shady areas that receive only a few hours of morning sun. Although they like moist soil conditions, good drainage is important. They combine beautifully with ferns and other shade-loving plants.

How to Plant

Soils high in organic matter are preferred. Plant in beds that have been generously amended with compost, rotted manure, or peat moss. Add a sprinkling of general-purpose fertilizer such as 8-8-8 or 15-5-10 when turning in the organic matter. Plant hostas so that the crown is at or slightly above soil level. Water thoroughly and mulch.

Care and Maintenance

Keep the plant well watered and mulched. Fertilize in April. Hostas are rather slow to establish and may take several years to reach their full size. Snails and slugs enjoy the foliage, so beware—treat regularly with baits or traps. When the flowers have faded, trim off the tall stems. In the fall, the foliage yellows and may be removed. We recommend you mark the growing sites, as these plants may be otherwise forgotten when they are dormant. Hostas are slow to begin growth in the spring, after other perennials have pushed through the soil.

Additional Information

Clumps may be divided in spring just as new growth begins to appear. They spread so slowly that division is needed infrequently.

Additional Cultivars or Species

There are numerous species and hybrids available, but there is little information on how well some of them perform in Louisiana. *H. sieboldii* has green leaves edged with white. *H. fortunei* has large, blue-green leaves; *H. sieboldiana* bears puckered blue leaves. 'Aureomarginata' has leaves edged in yellow; *H. plantaginea* has light-green leaves and fragrant white flowers on tall stems. *H. undulata* 'Albomarginata' is a small plant with wavy, white-variegated leaves.

Lantana

Lantana camara

Other Name: Ham and Eggs
Zones: 8 and 9
Size: 12 to 30 inches
Type: Evergreen
Flowers: 1-inch clusters of small flowers in yellow, orange, red, and white
Bloom Period: Summer

Light Requirement:

Some gardeners remember lantanas as a hobo—the common pink- and yellow-flowered ham and eggs plant that grows like a weed in vacant lots and along the railroad tracks. New cultivars of this shrubby perennial expand the color range of the flowers and include plants that are more attractively compact and produce more flowers over a longer season. Dwarf cultivars form low, mounding plants about 12 inches high and spreading about two feet. Taller, upright types grow two to three feet high with a similar spread. The color range includes clear yellow, orange, magenta, creamy white, red and pink, often with several different colored flowers appearing on the same plant.

When to Plant

Lantanas should be planted after the weather is warm and settled, from April through August.

Where to Plant

Sunny areas are best, although a few hours of shade per day present no problem. Lantanas are well adapted to hot, dry conditions but will thrive in the average garden bed. Good drainage is important.

How to Plant

Careful bed preparation is not critical, as these plants have retained much of the vigor that allows wild lantanas to thrive in difficult locations. If the soil is poor, the addition of some organic matter and a light sprinkling of general-purpose fertilizer is recommended. Plant lantanas at the same level or slightly higher than they were growing in the container. If the plants are pot-bound, loosen the roots before planting. Water thoroughly and mulch.

Care and Maintenance

If the plants become too large, trim back to control size and to encourage a bushier plant. This is especially important with taller varieties. Some varieties tend to produce flowers in cycles, blooming, stopping, then blooming again. Trimming off any seeds that set will minimize the cycle syndrome. Lantanas usually freeze to the ground in north Louisiana; thick mulch applied at the plant base often ensures another blooming season. They also freeze to the ground in southern Louisiana, but are more reliably perennial.

Additional Information

The hot dog days of summer are made for lantanas. While other plants languish in the heat, lantanas produce a continuous display of flowers until fall. Hummingbirds and butterflies are attracted to the blooms, providing even more color for the garden. Insects and diseases pose little problem for lantanas.

Additional Cultivars or Species

Some excellent low, mounding cultivars include 'New Gold', gold; 'Gold Mound', gold; 'Silver Mound', creamy white; 'Lemon Drop', light yellow; 'Patriot Rainbow', pink and yellow; and 'Lemon Swirl', green and yellow variegated leaves, yellow flowers. Among the taller cultivars that nurseries offer are 'Irene', burgundy red; 'Dallas Red', orange-red; and 'Christine', dark pink. There is an excellent trailing lantana, *L. montevidensis,* which is low-growing with light-purple flowers; a white form of the trailing variety is also available.

Liriope

Liriope muscari

Other Name: Lily Turf
Zones: 8 and 9
Size: 12 to 18 inches
Type: Evergreen
Flowers: Spikes of small, light-purple flowers
Bloom Period: Summer

Light Requirement:

Liriope is so widely used that some gardeners consider it a cliché. This virtually indestructible perennial is a classic for the Louisiana landscape. Liriope, a standard edging plant for beds, is far more versatile than our imaginations often allow. It can be used in individual clumps for accent (particularly variegated types), planted into drifts in borders, or added for detail in small areas, containers, and planters. Liriope forms a dense clump of long, narrow, dark-green leaves emerging from the ground in a graceful arch. They may grow from 12 to 20 inches tall in the largest cultivars. The attractive spikes of lavender-blue flowers in early to midsummer are showy, though not spectacular.

When to Plant

October through March is the best time to plant, taking advantage of cool, moist weather for plants to become established. Liriope can be planted from containers during the summer if they are regularly watered. Plant divisions in late winter or spring.

Where to Plant

Liriope prefers part sun to shade, but will grow in full sun if planted in soil rich in organic matter and watered consistently. Excellent drainage is not crucial, but avoid soggy areas.

How to Plant

Prepare the bed by turning the soil to a depth of 8 to 10 inches. Blend 2 inches of fine pine bark or compost with a sprinkle of 8-8-8 (at a rate of 1/3 cup per square yard) and add to the soil. Plant liriope at the same level it was growing in its container. Water deeply and mulch. Large containers of liriope may be divided into several pieces before planting, especially when used as a border or added to a planted area. Plants to be used for specimens or accents should be left intact.

Care and Maintenance

Fertilize liriope plantings in March with a general-purpose fertilizer appropriate for your area. Established plantings rarely need to be watered. Cut back the plants to within a few inches of the ground every few years to remove the accumulation of brown foliage. This should be done in late February or early March.

Additional Information

Liriope is often used as a groundcover, but that job is better done by its spreading relative creeping lily turf, *L. spicata*.

Additional Cultivars or Species

There is a liriope to suit the personality of almost every garden and gardener. *L. muscari* 'Variegata' has creamy-white variegated leaves; 'Aztec' has white variegated leaves which appear silvery. It is an excellent accent plant. 'Monroe #1' is the only white-flowered variety, while 'Samantha' has rosy-pink flowers. 'Majestic' has dark-green foliage and can reach 2 feet. 'Big Blue' is another large cultivar, growing to 20 inches with attractive flower spikes. Check your nursery for other varieties.

Mist Flower

Eupatorium coelestinum

Other Name: Wild Ageratum
Zones: 8 and 9
Size: 24 to 36 inches
Type: Dormant in winter
Flowers: Fluffy clusters of blue
Bloom Period: Fall

Light Requirement:

A drive along the highways in October may offer the sight of a remarkably beautiful, blue-lilac wildflower with dark-green, hairy, heart-shaped leaves. It is often found blooming beside the brilliant-yellow narrow-leaved sunflower (*Helianthus angustifolius*). The combination of blooms and contrasting leaves makes a striking fall wildflower display. The mist flower, a native wildflower, is gaining in popularity among Louisiana gardeners. The fall bloom is a welcome addition to gardens that frequently rely on the chrysanthemum for the only autumn color. The blue-lilac mist flower combines wonderfully with the yellows, oranges, rusts, and burgundies provided by mums. This perennial is so similar to the common garden ageratum (*Ageratum houstonianum*) that it is also called wild ageratum.

When to Plant

Plants are often available in the perennial section of nurseries in spring. Young plants can be transplanted March through May. Older clumps divided in March supply many new plants.

Where to Plant

In the wild, mist flower may grow in hard, dry clay or in damp soils along ditches; it may grow in full sun or part shade. It is not picky! It will thrive in any garden bed that receives 4 to 6 hours of sun. It is a tall robust plant that looks best in the middle or back of beds and borders.

How to Plant

Plant in any reasonably good soil. Little or no preparation is required; this attractive flower doesn't want or need to be pampered. If mist flower is planted in rich, loose soil, and watered and fertilized regularly, it will grow and spread aggressively.

Care and Maintenance

Sporadic flowering may occur during the early summer, but the main display is in fall. You may cut mist flower back once or twice during the summer to encourage a shorter, bushier plant if you like. Discontinue pruning in August. No watering or fertilization is needed, and there are no pest problems. Mist flower spreads by underground runners, self-seeds, and may appear in unexpected locations. Remove unwanted growth promptly.

Additional Information

Mist flower combines beautifully with ornamental grasses, and the soft blue-lilac puffs of flowers fit any color scheme. It is best suited to a natural landscape or wild garden. With the restraining hand of an attentive gardener, it can be tamed to flourish in a more controlled situation.

Additional Cultivars or Species

E. maculatum, Joe-pye weed, is a large, attractive plant, but is not for the small garden. It grows 5 to 7 feet tall and 3 to 4 feet wide—it is an imposing presence and excellent in a large border. It produces large rosy-pink flower heads up to 18 inches in diameter. 'Gateway' is a named cultivar that is somewhat shorter. *E. fistulosum* is similar and grows well in moist sites.

Obedient Plant

Physostegia virginiana

Zones: 8 and 9
Size: 2½ to 3 feet
Type: Dormant in winter
Flowers: Tall showy spikes of lavender pink or white
Bloom Period: Summer

Light Requirement:

The obedient plant is a great perennial for beginners. Say "grow" and it will grow. Occasionally its vigorous spreading habit leads gardeners to say, "Stop growing!" The colorful spikes of lavender-pink, snapdragon-like flowers ensure the continued popularity of this tall plant. It adjusts beautifully to the back of the bed or border and combines with cool colors like blue, pink, lavender, and purple. (Please keep it away from tomato red, orange, and gold.)

When to Plant

Plant from containers anytime. Fall or early spring is best, when plants become available at nurseries. Plant divisions obtained from old, established clumps in late winter or early spring.

Where to Plant

Full sun will produce luxurious plants, but obedient plant adapts to a variety of growing conditions and soils.

How to Plant

Plant in any good garden soil with average drainage. If the soil is poor, you may improve it with some organic matter, but an overly rich soil will produce rank growth (and plants more likely to need staking). Plant at the level the plants were growing previously. Water well and mulch.

Care and Maintenance

Physostegia is an enthusiastic spreader. Divide every 2 or 3 years. Little water or fertilizer is needed and there are no major insect or disease problems. Tall plants may need to be staked. Cut plants back by $^{1}/_{3}$ after flowering to encourage another flush of blooms. In late summer or early fall, cut back the plants close to the ground.

Additional Information

The name "obedient plant" comes from the curious ability of the individual flowers to stay in position when pushed gently from side to side. Children and adults alike find this fascinating. The flower spikes make outstanding additions to cut-flower arrangements.

Additional Cultivars or Species

The following cultivars are available: 'Summer Snow' is a less vigorous white form; 'Vivid' produces darker-pink flowers on a more compact plant; 'Variegata' has striking dark-green leaves boldly outlined in white and lavender-pink flowers.

Purple Loosestrife

Lythrum salicaria

Other Name: Lythrum
Zones: 8 and 9
Size: 3 to 4 feet
Type: Dormant in winter
Flowers: Spikes of pinkish-purple flowers
Bloom Period: Summer

Light Requirement:

Many perennials need excellent drainage to do well, but purple loosestrife is at home anywhere—from the average garden bed to a bog—and can even be used in the aquatic garden. Lythrum is tall and graceful and has stems about three feet tall with dark-green, narrow, lance-shaped leaves. Foot-long spikes of pink, purple, or magenta flowers grow from the tips from early summer until fall. Undemanding and easy to grow, the plant is a welcome addition to the background of the garden.

When to Plant

Transplant in fall or early spring. Plant container-grown plants as soon as they are available at local nurseries in the spring.

Where to Plant

Plant in full sun at the back of beds and borders. Lythrum will grow in dry or moist soils. It makes an effective, but not overwhelming, accent plant. Container plants can be placed in aquatic gardens or planted in the ground in moist soil around a water garden.

How to Plant

Plant loosestrife at the same level it was growing in its container or previous location. Water thoroughly and mulch the area. A well-prepared bed where organic matter has been incorporated into the soil will encourage the plants to be more vigorous and grow taller. Purple loosestrife may be planted in a container using heavy garden soil, then placed in an aquatic garden. The water level should be no more than a few inches above the rim of the pot.

Care and Maintenance

Despite its height, lythrum rarely needs staking unless planted in rich soil. Leaf-eating beetles are an occasional problem and can be controlled with Sevin. When flower spikes fade, trim back the stalks to encourage lateral shoots and continued flowering. Cut the plant back to the ground for the winter. Although this is a large perennial, it is well behaved and does not spread.

Additional Information

In some states, purple loosestrife has become a pest and is banned. Named cultivars rarely set seed, and seedlings are not a problem in Louisiana gardens.

Additional Cultivars or Species

Choose named cultivars such as 'Rose Queen', with its tall rosy-pink flower spikes; 'Firecandle', a bright rose-red; and dark-red 'The Beacon'. Cultivars of *L. virgatum* are highly recommended, especially when there is a concern about self-seeding and spreading; this species is much less likely to self-seed. Two cultivars are 'Morden's Gleam', with pink-purple spikes, and 'Robert', a compact 2-foot-tall plant with bright-pink spikes.

Red-Hot Poker

Kniphofia hybrids

Zones: 8 and 9
Size: 2 to 4 feet in bloom
Type: Evergreen or deciduous
Flowers: Spikes of yellow, orange, red, or creamy white on tall, strong stems
Bloom Period: Summer

Light Requirement:

Red-hot poker has the look of a desert plant, but it thrives in our moist climate when drainage is good. The flower spikes are comprised of tubular flowers densely arranged on the upper portion of a strong stalk. It is common for the open flowers to be one color, usually yellow, and the flower buds toward the tip another, usually red. The shading of red to yellow is reminiscent of a poker left in the fire until red-hot. The foliage is long, grass-like, coarse, and tends to sprawl. Red-hot poker is striking in the perennial border where the strong, upright flower stalks provide contrast to more refined perennials.

When to Plant

Fall is an excellent time to plant, but nurseries generally stock these plants in the spring. Plant as soon as they become available.

Where to Plant

Red-hot poker plants need full sun and very good drainage. Poorly drained soils, especially in winter, will rot the roots. In New Orleans, where drainage is often less than ideal, raised beds have generally proven more successful.

How to Plant

Improve the soil area by incorporating a 2-inch layer of fine pine bark (best for improved drainage) or compost and 8-8-8 (at a rate of $^1/_3$ cup per square yard). Use $^1/_4$ cup of 15-5-10 if your soil is high in phosphorus. Plant red-hot poker plants at the same level or slightly higher than they were growing in their containers. Water thoroughly and mulch to prevent weeds and to conserve soil moisture.

Care and Maintenance

Fertilize in March or April with one of the fertilizers and rates noted in the How to Plant section. Trim off flower stalks when the flowers have all faded. Cut the foliage to the ground in early winter. Kniphofia is not susceptible to any major insect or disease problems when growing conditions are favorable. Although division is needed infrequently, you may propagate by division of mature clumps in fall.

Additional Information

Without crowding the clump, surround red-hot poker plants with other interesting perennials. The untidy foliage is rather unattractive. The flowers make dramatic, long-lasting additions to flower arrangements.

Additional Cultivars or Species

K. uvaria has many cultivars and is the species most often mentioned. Some listed cultivars include 'Little Maid', with creamy-white flowers on 2-foot stalks; 'Royal Standard', with red to yellow flowers on 3-foot stalks; and 'Wrexham Buttercup', with yellow-green flower spikes. Some cultivars bloom in winter and are best used in very mild areas.

Rose Mallow

Hibiscus moscheutos

Other Name: Hardy Hibiscus
Zones: 8 and 9
Size: 2 to 4 feet
Type: Dormant in winter
Flowers: Huge, round; white, pink, or red
Bloom Period: Summer

Light Requirement:

There are few sights more impressive than a rose mallow in bloom. The sheer size of the flowers is enough to make an observer stop and look twice. Imagine flowers the size of a dinner plate, resembling soft, delicate crepe, in shades of pink, crimson, rose, or white on a compact shrub. Imagine that it is so easy to grow, anyone can experience success. Rose mallow is often called hardy hibiscus to distinguish it from the tender tropical hibiscus to which it is related. Native species that resemble the rose mallow can be found in damp areas along the Louisiana highways.

When to Plant

Container-grown plants can be planted as soon as they become available in spring or early summer. Rose mallow plants are easily grown from seeds planted in pots in March or April; later, seedlings should be transferred to the garden.

Where to Plant

Full sun encourages growth of the most flowers on the stockiest plant. Excellent drainage is not important to these plants—they were developed from wildflowers grown in damp, poorly drained areas.

How to Plant

Plant in good garden soil at the same level plants were growing in their containers. If the soil is poor, add organic matter and a light sprinkling of general-purpose fertilizer. Seeds are readily available from mail-order sources. They can be started in pots indoors in February or outside in late March or April. Plants grown from seed will bloom the first year.

Care and Maintenance

Provide adequate water during hot, dry weather. Fertilize in spring when new growth appears and again in June or July. In the early fall, when the plant prepares to enter dormancy, the foliage will begin to look tired and flowering will stop. When the foliage turns brown, cut the plants back to within a few inches of the ground. In mid-spring, new shoots will emerge from the base of the stems and rapidly grow into an extravagantly blooming plant by early summer.

Additional Information

The major pest problem for rose mallow is the whitefly. These tiny white insects leave their larvae on the backs of the leaves, suck the sap from the plant, and can be extremely damaging. Control is difficult, but good results are reported from using light oil sprays.

Additional Cultivars or Species

The most popular cultivars are 'Frisbee' and 'Southern Bell', both growing 4 to 5 feet and producing flowers 10 inches across, and 'Disco Bell', a more dwarf cultivar growing only about 2 feet, but with flowers as large as other cultivars. *H. mutabilis*, the Confederate rose, produces 5-inch double flowers in the fall that open white, turn pink, then turn dark rose. Large plants can reach 10 feet or more. *H. coccineus*, the Texas star hibiscus, is a wildflower with single, red, star- shaped flowers 5 inches across; it produces blooms all summer.

Salvia

Salvia spp. and hybrids

Zones: 8 and 9
Size: 1 to 6 feet, depending on type
Type: Evergreen, subject to winter injury
Flowers: Red, purple, blue, pink, magenta, yellow, white, and others
Bloom Period: Spring through fall

Light Requirement:

After growing annual salvia (*Salvia splendens*) for decades, Louisiana gardeners are beginning to discover the tremendous diversity of outstanding garden plants in this genus. Most are native to the southwestern United States and Mexico, and adapt well to Louisiana growing conditions. Gardeners are still learning about the hardiness of salvias. Sun, good drainage, and winter mulch are increasing gardeners' confidence in growing salvia as a perennial.

When to Plant

Plant container-grown plants April through August. A selection is available at most local nurseries. Planting in the spring or early summer is preferred.

Where to Plant

Choose well-drained locations to avoid root rot. If drainage is poor, use raised beds. Full sun to part sun will produce stocky growth and heavy flowering. Salvias are excellent for bedding, mixed beds, containers, and in the front, middle, or back of borders. There is a variety and color for every location.

How to Plant

Prepare the bed by turning the soil to a depth of 8 to 10 inches. Spread a 2-inch layer of fine pine bark or compost over the bed, sprinkle with 8-8-8 (at a rate of $^1/_3$ cup per square yard), and blend with the soil. Use 15-5-10 if your soil is high in phosphorus. Plant salvias at or slightly above the level they were growing in their containers. Water well and mulch.

Care and Maintenance

Fertilize in March and July with the fertilizers and rates recommended in the How to Plant section. Trim faded flower spikes regularly to keep plants attractive and to encourage continued blooming. Salvias can be trimmed back as needed. A late-summer trim produces a shorter, bushier plant. Cut plants to the ground if they freeze in winter.

Additional Information

Salvias make excellent additions to butterfly and hummingbird gardens.

Additional Cultivars or Species

Salvia coccinea is one of the easiest salvias to grow. It produces loose spikes of red, pink, peach, or white on 2- to 3-foot-tall plants, and self-seeds readily. 'Lady in Red' is one of its best cultivars. *S. farinacea*, or mealy-cup sage, is compact with purple-blue, lavender, white, or bicolor spikes. Excellent cultivars include 'Victoria', blue; 'Argent', white; and 'Strata', blue-and-white bicolor. Each of these cultivars is compact and performs well in borders. Autumn sage, *S. greggii*, is a shrub-like plant with small leaves and loose spikes blooming pink to cherry-red. It grows about 2 feet tall. *S. leucantha*, Mexican bush sage, is taller (3 to 5 feet) and produces long spikes of fuzzy purple-and-white flowers that are especially heavy in fall. The underside of the narrow leaves and stems is silvery. A choice cultivar is *S.* 'Indigo Spires'. The indigo-blue spikes are quite long on this attractive 3-foot plant. *S. madrensis* is known as "forsythia sage" for its unique yellow tubular flowers in fall. The cultivar is large, growing to 5 or 6 feet, and has dark-green, quilted foliage.

Shrimp Plant

Justicia brandegeana

Other Name: *Beloperone guttata*
Zone: 9
Size: 2 to 3 feet
Type: Evergreen
Flowers: White, tubular, with reddish-brown bracts
Bloom Period: All summer

Light Requirement:

Common names frequently describe some unique aspect of a plant. Shrimp plant earned its name by way of its unusual flower spike. The spike is about three inches long and is clothed in reddish- or pinkish-brown bracts, out of which peek white tubular flowers. With just a little imagination, you may see a shrimp in this structure. The plant is shrubby and brings a different color to the flower garden. Its popularity comes not only from its unusual flowers, but also from its long bloom period (from spring until late fall). Shrimp plant is often visited by hummingbirds.

When to Plant

Plant in late spring after all danger of frost is past, or throughout the summer. Early planting will allow the plant to become well established before its first winter and increase chances of survival.

Where to Plant

Several hours of morning sun, afternoon shade, and good drainage are optimum conditions for shrimp plants. Though excellent drainage is not crucial, avoid areas that are regularly soggy.

How to Plant

Plant container-grown plants in well-prepared beds at the same level they were growing previously. Water thoroughly and mulch to control weeds and conserve soil moisture.

Care and Maintenance

Fertilize in April and again in July with a general-purpose fertilizer. Water during hot, dry periods, especially if wilting occurs. Trim shrimp plants as needed during the summer to keep them shapely and bushy. Cuttings root easily; a gardener can add more plants or share with friends. Keep plants well mulched with 8 to 12 inches of pine straw during the winter. When winter freezes kill back the top, cut it to the ground. Pull back the mulch in late March or early April.

Additional Information

The hardiness of shrimp plant in northern Louisiana is questionable. As is true of many perennials, it will freeze to the ground in winter. In southern Louisiana, where the shrimp plant is quite popular, it has returned reliably even after temperatures dipped to 11 degrees Fahrenheit and stayed below-freezing for 2 days or more (even the northern part of the state rarely faces worse cold).

Additional Cultivars or Species

J. brandegeana 'Yellow Queen' has chartreuse bracts. There are several unnamed color variations that are occasionally passed from gardener to gardener.

Spider Plant

Chlorophytum comosum 'Variegatum'

Zone: 9
Size: 12 inches
Type: Evergreen
Flowers: Small, white flowers at the ends of long, curving stems; not significant
Bloom Period: Summer

Light Requirement:

More often thought of as houseplants or container plants, spider plants have shown themselves to be remarkably tough and hardy. Often surviving temperatures in the low teens, they can easily make it through an average northern Louisiana winter, and are very reliable in the southern part of the state. A spider plant looks a lot like a variegated liriope, but it grows faster and more vigorously and its variegation is brighter. Its long, thin, pointed leaves are edged in pure white. Long flower scapes are produced periodically, bearing small white flowers. Small plants form on them later; they may be left on to bend to the ground and root, or the runners may be trimmed off.

When to Plant

Plant in spring after danger of frost is past. Spider plants can be planted throughout the summer, but perform better if planted early so they can become established before the first winter in the ground.

Where to Plant

Use spider plants in areas that get 4 hours or less of direct sun. Moist soils rich in organic matter encourage vigorous growth.

How to Plant

Set plants in beds with good garden soil. If the soil is poor, mix in generous amounts of compost, rotten manure, or peat moss and a sprinkling of general-purpose fertilizer. Spider plants are undemanding and will thrive with little care from the gardener.

Care and Maintenance

Plants will sustain some damage to their foliage when temperatures are in the low twenties, but the roots regenerate in spring. Keep plants well mulched in the winter to protect the thick fleshy roots. Prune any freeze damage as it occurs.

Additional Information

The brightly variegated leaves enliven shady areas, and the long, narrow foliage offers nice texture. Clumps increase in size over time and can be divided in spring. Propagation most often occurs by allowing offsets to root around the original plant.

Additional Cultivars or Species

C. comosum 'Vittatum' has a white stripe down the center of each leaf; 'Picturatum' has a yellow stripe down the center of each leaf.

Spiderwort

Tradescantia × andersoniana

Zones: 8 and 9
Size: 2 feet
Type: Dormant in winter
Flowers: Deep sky-blue
Bloom Period: Early summer

Light Requirement:

Native spiderwort grows throughout Louisiana and is often spotted along highways in spring and early summer. The garden spiderwort is a hybrid of the native species that grows larger and has larger flowers. It is as tough as its native cousin and grows happily in full sun to part shade in moist to well-drained areas. Each plant forms a clump of long, narrow leaves that strongly resemble daylilies. The intensely blue, three-petal flowers are produced over a long period, but production slows, then stops, as the weather becomes hot.

When to Plant

Plant in fall or spring. Plants are usually available in area nurseries in spring; purchase them then so you can enjoy a lengthy bloom season.

Where to Plant

Spiderworts will grow in full sun if they are kept moist. They also thrive in more shaded locations if they receive at least 4 to 6 hours of direct sun.

How to Plant

Plant in any good garden soil with average drainage, or one that remains moist. If the soil is poor, add organic matter. An overly rich soil will produce rank growth and plants that require staking. Plant at the same level as plants were previously growing. Water thoroughly and mulch.

Care and Maintenance

Success is almost assured with spiderworts. Fertilizer is optional unless the soil is exceptionally poor. Water during hot, dry spells while in bloom. Once flowering is over, cut the plants back hard. Occasionally they will produce a few more flowers, but they usually rest for the remainder of the summer.

Additional Information

Flower stems grow above the foliage and bear clusters of numerous buds. A few of the buds open every day in spring and continue through early summer. While the weather is mild, the flowers stay open most of the day. As the heat intensifies, the flowers close by noon, and by midsummer the plants enter a more dormant state. Plant spiderworts among other plants that are more active throughout the summer to avoid gaps when fading occurs

Additional Cultivars or Species

Cultivars provide a number of colors in addition to the more common blue: 'Carmine Glow', magenta; 'Innocence', white; 'Isis', deep blue; 'Osprey', large white and blue flowers; 'Red Cloud', rosy-red; 'Zwanenburg Blue', rich blue; and 'Pauline', orchid pink.

Stokes Aster

Stokesia laevis

Zones: 8 and 9
Size: 18 to 24 inches
Type: Dormant in winter
Flowers: Powder blue
Bloom Period: Summer

Light Requirement:

It is gratifying to realize that a number of our finest perennials were developed from native species. Colonies of blooming stokesia can be found from South Carolina to Louisiana. This is a lovely plant, producing attractive dark-green, leathery, lance-shaped leaves that form a low mound. In June, taller stems appear bearing numerous lavender-blue, three-inch flowers that resemble double daisies.

When to Plant

This hardy perennial may be planted in fall or spring. Blooming plants grown in gallon containers may be planted later in early summer.

Where to Plant

Full to part sun is needed for full flower production. In the wild, stokesia grows in rather damp locations, but a site with average drainage is preferred in the garden.

How to Plant

Stokesia look best when planted in a group. Plant container-grown plants at the same level they were growing previously. Improve the bed by adding 2 inches of fine pine bark or compost and a light sprinkling of 8-8-8 (at a rate of 1/3 cup per square yard) or 15-5-10 (at a rate of 1/4 cup per square yard). Water thoroughly and mulch.

Care and Maintenance

When bloom is finished, cut the stalk level with the plant's foliage. Fertilize established plants in March and again in July using the fertilizers and rates noted in the How to Plant section. Keep beds well mulched to control weeds and conserve soil moisture. Water during hot, dry weather, especially during midsummer when the plants are in bloom.

Additional Information

The blue of stokesia blooms is a welcome addition to the bed or border. The large and showy flowers combine well in almost any color scheme. With favorable growing conditions, stokesia are long-lived and form sturdy clumps. They may be divided fall through early spring if desired.

Additional Cultivars or Species

'Blue Danube' has a large, soft-blue bloom; 'Silver Moon' is creamy-white; 'Blue Moon' is hyacinth-blue. 'Wyoming' has the darkest blue flowers available.

Texas Blue Star

Amsonia tabernaemontana

Zones: 8 and 9
Size: 2 feet
Type: Dormant in winter
Flowers: Light blue stars in clusters
Bloom Period: Late spring

Light Requirement:

True-blue flowers are often hard to find, but the pale-blue clusters of Texas blue star have no hint of lavender and are a beautiful addition to the late-spring flower garden. They combine well with the yellows and whites of late narcissus or the pinks and roses of azaleas. Texas blue star is tough, long-lived, and relatively care-free. Two-foot stems emerge from the ground clothed in long, attractive, narrow-pointed leaves that resemble willow leaves. The flower clusters produced at the tips show up nicely against the foliage.

When to Plant

Plant in fall or early spring when plants become available in nurseries. Larger blooming plants may be planted later.

Where to Plant

Choose a sunny location with average drainage. Texas blue star grows naturally in moist sites but can adapt to a variety of growing conditions. It can also be grown in hot and dry areas if watered regularly.

How to Plant

Plant Texas blue star at or slightly above the level it was growing in its container. Water well and mulch. A well-prepared bed with added organic matter encourages vigorous growth. Spread 2 inches of fine pine bark or compost over the bed, sprinkle with 1/3 cup of 8-8-8 per square yard (15-5-10 if soil is high in phosphorus), and mix well.

Care and Maintenance

When flowering is finished, cut back stems to within 6 to 8 inches of the ground to create a fuller plant. There are no major insect or disease problems. If soil is poor, fertilize established clumps in March. Overfertilizing causes floppy growth. Clumps should be cut back to the ground when dormant and divided if desired.

Additional Information

Some foliage becomes an attractive yellow in the fall.

Additional Cultivars or Species

Amsonia tabernaemontana var. *salicifolia*, the willowleaf blue star, produces narrower foliage and has a relaxed growth habit. The flowers are blue with white throats. *A. ciliata*, the downy star flower, is occasionally available; it has very narrow leaves and clusters of light-blue flowers.

Veronica

Veronica spicata

Other Name: Speedwell
Zones: 8 and 9
Size: 12 to 24 inches, depending on cultivar
Type: Dormant in winter
Flowers: Spikes of deep blue, lavender-blue, pink, or white
Bloom Period: Summer

Light Requirement:

Veronica is a tough perennial whose bluish-purple blooms add a cool note to the flower garden during the heat of June and July. The upright spikes make an excellent contrast to the rounded forms of many other perennials. Plants have dark-green two-inch leaves that are slightly shiny and quite attractive. The small densely packed flowers on the spike taper to sharp points. The flowers open gradually from the bottom up, followed by small, round, green seedpods.

When to Plant

Plant container-grown plants in fall through early spring.

Where to Plant

Veronicas require full sun and excellent drainage.

How to Plant

Careful bed preparation will produce vigorous, heavy-flowering plants. Cultivate the soil to a depth of 8 to 10 inches. Spread a 2-inch layer of fine pine bark or compost over the bed, sprinkle with $1/3$ cup of 8-8-8 per square yard (15-5-10 if your soil is high in phosphorus), and mix in well. Place the plant with the crown at or slightly higher than in the container. Water thoroughly and mulch.

Care and Maintenance

Fertilize in March and again in June with the fertilizers and rates referred to in the How to Plant section. Prune off faded flower spikes to extend the blooming period. When a plant has finished flowering, cut it back by half. Occasionally, a few more flowers are produced in late summer. When the top growth fades in late summer and fall, cut back to the new growth at its base. Water plants generously during hot, dry periods. Maintain mulch to prevent weed competition and conserve soil moisture.

Additional Information

This species is native to Europe and honors St. Veronica. The common name "speedwell" derives from the many medicinal uses of the species in this genus.

Additional Cultivars or Species

'Blue Fox' and 'Blue Spires' are blue cultivars; 'Icicle' is white; and 'Red Fox' is rose pink. 'Sunny Border Blue' is an excellent hybrid.

Yarrow

Achillea millefolium

Zones: 8 and 9
Size: 14 to 26 inches in bloom
Type: Evergreen in mild winter areas
Flowers: Flat clusters of white, pale yellow, rosy-red or pink
Bloom Period: Early summer

Light Requirement:

Yarrow is a popular garden perennial because it is tough, adaptable, attractive, and blooms beautifully in early summer. What more could you ask? The very fine foliage is fern-like, but unlike ferns, yarrow thrives in hot, dry difficult areas that many other plants would find stressful. Suitable for use as a groundcover, the foliage generally stays under 12 inches. The flowers are produced on tall stalks that rise well above the foliage and occur in flat clusters of white. New colors have been bred in recent years and the range now includes rosy-red, pink, soft yellow, salmon, light orange, and mauve. Utterly reliable and long-lived, yarrow is an excellent choice for Louisiana gardeners.

When to Plant

Plant this hardy perennial in fall or early spring. Blooming container-grown plants may be planted later.

Where to Plant

Yarrow adapts to a variety of growing conditions but prefers a sunny well-drained area. It rarely tolerates wet, shady areas. Use yarrow in beds or borders among middle-height plants. The plants are taller when blooming, although the foliage remains low.

How to Plant

Plant container-grown plants in well-prepared beds at the same level they were growing in their containers. Water thoroughly and mulch to control weeds and to conserve soil moisture.

Care and Maintenance

Trim back flower stalks when flowers begin to fade. Fertilize in March and again in June with 1/3 cup of 8-8-8 per square yard (use

1/4 cup of 15-5-10 if the soil is high in phosphorus). Yarrow may be evergreen during mild winters. Trim back the foliage if browned by winter freezes. Spider mites are an occasional problem and can be controlled with insecticidal soap or a light oil spray.

Additional Information

The foliage is aromatic, and when dried, can be used in potpourris and moth bags. Cut the flower heads when fully developed and dry in a cool place. Clumps of yarrow spread rather slowly, but occasional division is suggested to keep them neat and in place.

Additional Cultivars or Species

Popular 'Cerise Queen' has cherry-pink flowers; 'White Beauty' produces white flowers. A new hybrid cultivar that has been very successful in Louisiana is called 'Summer Pastels'; its plants come in a wide range of colors and are often available at local nurseries. If you can't find it at a nursery, you can easily grow it from seeds available from seed catalogs. It blooms the first year from spring-planted seeds.

Perennials offer a certain permanency to the flower garden, and provide abundant color and and beauty in return for the care they require.

The Gardener who plans reaps the Greatest Reward

COOL SPRINGS PRESS

Bookmark—fold and remove here

The Louisiana Gardener's Guide

Photographic gallery of featured plants

Alyssum
Lobularia maritima

Calendula
Calendula officinalis

Celosia
Celosia cristata

Coleus
Coleusb x hybridus

Cosmos
Cosmos bipinnatus

Dianthus
Dianthus chinensis

Globe Amaranth
Gomphrena globosa

Impatiens
Impatiens wallerana

Lisianthus
Eustoma grandiflorum

Marigold
Tagetes erecta

Melampodium
Melampodium paludosum

Narrow-Leaf Zinnia
Zinnia angustifolia

ANNUALS

Ornamental Cabbage and Kale
Brassica oleracea forms

Pansy
Violab x wittrockiana

Periwinkle
Catharanthus roseus

Petunia
Petunia x hybrida

Salvia
Salvia splendens

Snapdragon
Antirrhinum majus

Sunflower
Helianthus annuus

Wax Begonia
Begonia x semperflorens-cultorum

Wishbone Flower
Torenia fournieri

Zinnia
Zinnia elegans

BULBS

Amaryllis
Hippeastrum spp. and hybrids

Bearded Iris
Iris x germanica

BULBS

Butterfly Ginger
Hedychium coronarium

Caladium
Caladium x hortulanum

Canna
Canna x generalis

Crinum
Crinum species

Dutch Iris
Iris x hollandica

Gladiolus
Gladiolus x hortulanus

Louisiana Iris
Iris spp. and hybrids

Madonna Lily
Lilium candidum

Narcissus
Narcissus jonquilla

Snowflakes
Leucojum aestivum

Spider Lily
Lycoris radiata

FERNS

Autumn Fern
Dryopteris erythrosora

FERNS

Holly Fern
Cyrtomium falcatum

Maidenhair Fern
Adiantum capillus-veneris

Sword Fern
Nephrolepsis exaltata

Wood Fern
Thelypteris kunthii

GROUNDCOVERS

Asian Jasmine
Trachelospermum asiaticum

Aspidistra
Aspidistra elatior

Creeping Lily Turf
Liriope spicata

English Ivy
Hedera helix

Japanese Ardisia
Ardisia japonica

ORNAMENTAL GRASSES

Monkey Grass
Ophiopogon japonicus

Strawberry Geranium
Saxifraga stolonifera

Giant Reed Grass
Arundo donax

ORNAMENTAL GRASSES

Pampas Grass
Cortaderia selloana

Variegated Acorus
Acorus gramineus 'Variegatus'

Variegated Japanese Sedge
Carex morrowii 'Variegata'

Variegated Japanese Silver Grass
Miscanthus sinensis 'Variegata'

Zebra Grass
Miscanthus sinensis 'Zebrinus'

PALMS

Cabbage Palm
Sabal palmetto

Canary Island Date Palm
Phoenix canariensis

Chinese Fan Palm
Livistona chinensis

Dwarf Palmetto
Sabal minor

Mediterranean Fan Palm
Chamaerops humilis

Needle Palm
Rhapidophyllum hystrix

Windmill Palm
Trachycarpus fortunei

Artemisia
Artemisia ludoviciana

Blue Phlox
Phlox divaricata

Chrysanthemum
Dendranthema x *morifolium*

Comfrey
Symphytum officinale

Daylily
Hemerocallis hybrids

Hosta
Hosta spp.

Lantana
Lantana camara

Liriope
Liriope muscari

Mist Flower
Eupatorium coelestinum

Obedient Plant
Physostegia virginiana

Purple Loosestrife
Lythrum salicaria

Red-Hot Poker
Kniphofia hybrids

PERENNIALS

Rose Mallow
Hibiscus moscheutos

Salvia
Salvia coccinea 'Lady in Red'

Shrimp Plant
Justicia brandegeana

Spider Plant
Chlorophytum comosum 'Variegatum'

Spiderwort
Tradescantia x *andersoniana*

Stokes Aster
Stokesia laevis

Texas Blue Star
Amsonia tabernaemontana

Veronica
Veronica spicata

Yarrow
Achillea millefolium

PERENNIAL VINES

Carolina Jessamine
Gelsemium sempervirens

Chinese Wisteria
Wisteria sinensis

Clematis
Clematis spp.

PERENNIAL VINES

Coral Honeysuckle
Lonicera sempervirens

Five-Leaf Akebia
Akebia quinata

Rosa de Montana
Antigonon leptopus

ROSES

Trumpet Vine
Campsis radicans

Virginia Creeper
Parthenocissus quinquefolia

Climbing Rose
Rosa x hybrida

Floribunda Rose
Rosa x *hybrida*

Grandiflora Rose
Rosa x *hybrida*

Hybrid Tea Rose
Rosa x *hybrida*

SHRUBS

Lady Bank's Rose
Rosa banksiae

Aucuba
Aucuba japonica

Azalea
Rhododendron spp.

Banana Shrub
Michelia figo

Butterfly Bush
Buddleia alternifolia

Camellia
Camellia japonica

Chinese Holly
Ilex cornuta

Chinese Mahonia
Mahonia fortunei

Cleyera
Ternstroemia gymnanthera

Dwarf Yaupon
Ilex vomitoria 'Nana'

Fatsia
Fatsia japonica

Flowering Quince
Chaenomeles speciosa

French Mulberry
Callicarpa americana

Garden Hydrangea
Hydrangea macrophylla

Gardenia
Gardenia jasminoides

Glossy Abelia
Abelia x grandiflora

Indian Hawthorn
Raphiolepis indica

Japanese Viburnum
Viburnum japonicum

Japanese Yew
Podocarpus macrophyllus

Mock Orange
Philadelphus coronarius

Nandina
Nandina domestica

Oakleaf Hydrangea
Hydrangea quercifolia

Oleander
Nerium oleander

Pineapple Guava
Feijoa sellowiana

Pittosporum
Pittosporum tobira

Pyracantha
Pyracantha coccinea

Sasanqua
Camellia sasanqua

SHRUBS

Sweet Olive
Osmanthus fragrans

Vanhoutte Spirea
Spiraea x vanhouttei

Virginia Willow
Itea virginica

Wax-Leaf Ligustrum
Ligustrum japonicum

TREES

American Holly
Ilex opaca

Bald Cypress
Taxodium distichum

Bradford Flowering Pear
Pyrus calleryana 'Bradford'

Canaert Red Cedar
Juniperus virginiana 'Canaertii'

Chinese Parasol Tree
Firmiana simplex

Crape Myrtle
Lagerstroemia indica

Deodar Cedar
Cedrus deodara

Flowering Dogwood
Cornus florida

Ginkgo
Ginkgo biloba

Grancy Graybeard
Chionanthus virginicus

Green Ash
Fraxinus pennsylvanica

Japanese Maple
Acer palmatum

Lacebark Elm
Ulmus parvifolia

Loquat
Eriobotrya japonica

Oriental Magnolia
Magnolia x *soulangiana*

Pistachio
Pistacia chinensis

Redbud
Cercis canadensis

Shumard Oak
Quercus shumardii

Silver Bell
Halesia diptera

Southern Live Oak
Quercus virginiana

TREES

Southern Magnolia
Magnolia grandiflora

Swamp Red Maple
Acer rubrum 'Drummondii'

Sweet Gum
Liquidambar styraciflua

Taiwan Flowering Cherry
Prunus campanulata

Vitex
Vitex agnus-castus

Willow Oak
Quercus phellos

TROPICALS

Angel's Trumpet
Brugmansia arborea

Bird-of-Paradise
Strelitzia reginae

Common Banana
Musa x paradisiaca

Firespike
Odontonema strictum

Fountain Plant
Russelia equisetiformis

Mexican Heather
Cuphea hyssopifolia

Night-Blooming Jessamine
Cestrum nocturnum

Split-Leaf Philodendron
Philodendron selloum

Thryallis
Galphimia glauca

Yesterday - Today - and - Tomorrow
Brunfelsia australis

Beebalm
Monarda fistulosa

Black-eyed Susan
Rudbeckia hirta

Blazing Star
Liatris spp.

Butterfly Weed
Asclepias tuberosa

California Poppy
Eschscholzia californica

Cardinal Flower
Lobelia cardinalis

Coral Bean
Erythrina herbacea

Coreopsis
Coreopsis tinctoria

Evening Primrose
Oenothera speciosa

Indian Blanket
Gaillardia pulchella

Purple Coneflower
Echinacea purpurea

Picture, if you can, a balcony draped with a vine . . . in full bloom during its season. This typifies the elegance and charm of living in the South.

CHAPTER SEVEN

Perennial Vines

WHEN PLANNING OR RENOVATING A LANDSCAPE, gardeners too often overlook perennial vines. Many gardeners are not familiar with woody vines (and most of the perennial types are quite woody), while others fear to plant them due to "horror stories" about how difficult they can be to handle. It is true that some species are quite vigorous and can get out of hand if not controlled with good techniques.

One of the most common offenders is the Chinese wisteria. When speaking of this vine, I commonly tell people that when they plant a specimen, they should be prepared to defend their property against its aggressive habits. The Chinese wisteria is also a super attractant of bees of various kinds, so persons allergic to bee stings should probably never plant it. Yet whether grown as a free-standing plant or trained to a sturdy support, this vine's spring display of purple or white flowers makes a strong, pleasing focal point.

A walk through a Louisiana woodland or special places such as the Kisatchie National Forest in the north-central part of the state will allow you to see that woody perennial vines are very much at home in the warm, moist climate of our southern state. So many of them have ornamental value, from their flowers to their foliage of interesting texture. Because a great number are capable of exceedingly fast growth rates, they can provide a show of beauty in a relatively short time if given the proper support. They can develop into an effective screen to block an objectionable off-site view or to shield private areas within a single landscape. In urban areas where space is so very limited, their screening abilities are truly appreciated. Picture, if you can, a balcony or deck railing draped with a vine that is intertwined with the structural elements of that feature and in full bloom during its season. This typifies the elegance and charm of living in the South.

While a gardener who is planting a woody perennial vine for the first time may incline toward the more sedate types that rarely pose a containment problem, there is no need to fear the more rambunctious species. If a more aggressive type offers a quality that is not available in less vigorous vines, go ahead and plant the ones that will meet your requirements. Never mix annual vines with perennial vines in an attempt to get faster color or cover. The annual vines will eventually dominate, and they can crowd out the perennial types. It is comforting to know that if a poor choice is made or if a particular vine is beginning to get out of control, there are widely available herbicides that will suppress or kill unwanted vines without harming surrounding plants. When using any such herbicides, be sure to follow label directions.

As is true of other types of plants, some of the perennial vines are hardy in south Louisiana but not in north Louisiana. The bougainvillea vine, for example, is commonly planted in the ground in New Orleans where it adorns buildings, fences, and gardens. In north Louisiana, it must be grown in containers, garden rooms, or hobby greenhouses that will give protection during winter's low temperatures. It can be used as a hanging basket plant. Put it in places where colorful plants are needed but where heat and full-sun exposure might literally cook most other plants. Under such circumstances, its vine-like qualities are less apparent and its brilliant profusion of flowers becomes its dominant character.

Only a few of the perennial vines will be presented in this book; there are many others from which to choose for landscape use. Based upon growth habits, there are three distinct types of vines. Twining vines such as Chinese wisteria twine or wrap themselves around their support, whether trellis or tree, as they grow. Self-clinging vines like Virginia Creeper have either aerial rootlets or adhesive tendrils that enable them to attach themselves to vertical surfaces, often brick walls or board fences. A third type of vine is one such as clematis or grapes that has tendrils or similar appendages which "grasp" the members of the support structure. When selecting vines, remember to consider the uses to which they will be put.

Carolina Jessamine

Gelsemium sempervirens

Zones: 8 and 9
Type: Evergreen
Flowers: Yellow
Bloom Period: Early spring

Light Requirement:

Carolina jessamine is a rapid-growing twining vine with wide adaptation. Rather dense in landscape settings, it grows in a more open manner in wooded areas. Its profusion of fragrant yellow flowers early in the spring frequently complements some of the spring-flowering bulbs. Although considered evergreen, the vine will lose some leaves during severe winters, especially in the northern part of Louisiana. Unpruned vines tend to become top-heavy and may have to be pruned drastically to return them to a better form. Jessamine may be propagated both vegetatively and by seed. Its shiny medium-to-fine foliage is attractive year round. Gardeners with children or pets need to be aware that all parts of the vine are considered poisonous. The Carolina jessamine is the State Flower of South Carolina.

When to Plant

Plant in late fall or early winter for a chance of bloom the following spring. With proper care, plants may be installed in the landscape nearly any time, but it's best to avoid hot summer months when possible.

Where to Plant

Full-sun or semi-shade locations tend to maximize bloom production. Mailbox posts, yardlight poles, and trellises are favorite spots. Carolina jessamine adapts to a wide variety of soil types and can be planted near trees.

How to Plant

Set out a container-grown plant in a prepared hole so that the top of the rootball is at about the same level as the surrounding ground. Use a similar technique for seedlings or rooted plants moved from near a mother plant. We suggest incorporating a small amount of slow-release fertilizer into the soil being returned to the planting hole. Mulch the newly planted vine to keep moisture supplies more constant. Plant mature seed relatively shallow.

Care and Maintenance

Fertilize established vines with a general-purpose fertilizer such as 12-12-12. (Very small amounts are needed.) The late-winter season before new growth occurs is the best time for fertilizing. A slow-release fertilizer (also applied in late winter) is an excellent alternative. To maintain desirable form and density, thin vines annually after flowering. This practice also encourages a better show of flowers.

Additional Information

Pay close attention to watering when this vine is growing on live trees in droughty soils. Major pest problems are infrequent, but a jessamine canopy often is chosen as a home by wasps. Allergic persons should beware! This vine can be kept pruned to a 3-foot height and used as a groundcover on steep slopes . . . but this is an uncommon use in our state.

Additional Cultivars or Species

The swamp jessamine, *G. rankinii,* blooms in the fall and handles wet sites better than its relative. South Carolina gardeners report a selection called 'Pale Yellow'. 'Plena' and 'Pride of Augusta' are double-flowered cultivars.

Chinese Wisteria

Wisteria sinensis

Zones: 8 and 9
Type: Deciduous
Flowers: Grape-like, violet-blue flower clusters
Bloom Period: Spring

Light Requirement:

This popular Chinese native is widely grown in Louisiana. Capable of attaining both large size and old age, its spring profusion of flowers makes a striking accent in any landscape. This rapidly growing plant may be grown as a vine on a support or trained as a free-standing specimen, but regardless of form, constant containment will be required to control its aggressive habit. It is best not to grow the wisteria on a live tree. Since bees are attracted to its blooms in such great numbers, persons with bee allergies would be unwise to plant a wisteria unless planning to view the blossoms from a distance.

When to Plant

Wisteria should be planted in the late fall/early winter period but may be planted at other times of the year if given sufficient care.

Where to Plant

Full sun to partial shade is best. A loose, fertile, moist soil accelerates rate of growth, but wisteria will adapt to a variety of soil types. Plant near existing sturdy supports or build one to best display the vine. Avoid planting near live trees.

How to Plant

While seed may be planted, direct-seeding usually delays blooming for 5 or more years. It is better to choose a plant grown from cuttings, preferably a specimen with one or more flowers present. Use minimal or no fertilizer to favor the flowering phase of development and to avoid wasting time in soil preparation.

Care and Maintenance

From the very beginning, constantly and carefully prune and train the vine to conform to the desired shape. Removing any unwanted long streamers, shortening secondary stems, and rubbing or pulling off buds and new shoots provide control of form. The vines may at first need to be tied to their supports with soft, strong cords or cloth. Remove these ties later to prevent girdling of the secured stems. A free-standing tree-like specimen must not be allowed to develop any side branches anywhere along its trunk. Dormant-season pruning is suggested for major canopy alteration, as the structural elements of the vine will be more clearly seen and the flowering process will be enhanced. But because blooms occur only on year-old wood, some of this must remain after pruning. Vines showing poor vigor may be lightly fertilized just after blooming, but it's generally best not to fertilize at all.

Additional Information

Mature vines that grow rampantly but fail to flower may sometimes be made to blossom by moderately severe root pruning. A nursery-worn pot-bound plant typically flowers sooner than younger, more vigorous plants and may be a "best buy."

Additional Cultivars or Species

'Carolina', 'Cooke's Special', 'Alba', and 'Jako' are available in the trade. The latter two are white-flowered cultivars. 'Ivory Tower' is a white cultivar of *W. floribunda*, and there is also a pink-flowered variety in this species. Related species are Japanese wisteria (*W. floribunda*), silky wisteria (*W. brachybotrys*), and American wisteria (*W. frutescens*).

Clematis

Clematis spp.

Zones: 8 and 9
Type: Deciduous
Flowers: Large flowers in several colors including purple, red, and white
Bloom Period: Spring, summer, and fall

Light Requirement:

A native of eastern Asia, the clematis vines enjoy high popularity throughout the state. Their large flowers, available in several colors, are very showy, yet the vine is non-aggressive and is a good choice for use in limited spaces or on small supports such as mailbox posts. It is important to protect the vines from wind and to guard the roots from extreme cold or heat with a thick, loose mulch. As the vines are not well equipped to climb, they must be tied to their support in the early stages of development. Some species of clematis bloom on old wood, some on new wood. With a good mix of clematis vines that flower in the spring, the summer, and the fall, a relatively long season of color is possible from this plant alone.

When to Plant

Healthy container-grown plants may be planted any time, but favor the late-winter and early-spring months when weather stress isn't as great.

Where to Plant

Try to locate plants where they can receive full sun during mornings but can escape the cruel heat of midday and late afternoon. A southern exposure is preferred. Plant clematis in fertile, well-drained, alkaline soil.

How to Plant

Construct raised beds or mounds for dependable drainage, and enrich with organic materials like compost or rotted sawdust. Mix in a liming material such as agricultural lime or dolomitic lime to create an alkaline condition and to improve soil structure, especially in acid soil areas where clay is abundant. One to two cups per plant, depending on soil type, is usually adequate. Blend into the soil a small amount of slow-release fertilizer as well, following label directions. Complete the procedure by placing a deep, loose mulch around the plant to keep the roots cool and moist. Finally, water to moisten the entire mound or bed.

Care and Maintenance

Use a slow-release fertilizer 2 or 3 times during the growing season, with the first application scheduled for late winter and the second for early to midsummer. A third application may be desirable in the southern part of the state. Another method is to use soluble fertilizers monthly during the growing season until a couple of months before significantly cold temperatures arrive. A 1:1:1 ratio food such as 20-20-20, if used properly, should do a good job. Check for a lime requirement every 2 to 3 years and adjust soil as needed. The flowering habit will dictate when to prune. Vines that bloom in the spring flower on old wood; prune them about a month after bloom period. Cultivars that bloom in the summer or fall flower on current-season's growth; prune either in late fall or late winter (late winter is probably best).

Additional Information

Handle vines carefully when pruning; they are somewhat fragile. Check off-colored foliage for insects and disease. For an uunusual table decoration, sear the stem at the base of a flower to seal it and float the flower in a bowl of water. Flat stepping stones placed close to the base of these plants helps keep the soil cooler and provides a better environment for the roots.

Additional Cultivars or Species

The purple hybrid *Jackmanii* is popular. Some of its crosses are white and red. *Henryi* is a large white variety with dark stamens. There are many, many other varieties and cultivars of this vine, and they offer a wide range of flower colors. Consult other references for a more complete listing. Related species are autumn clematis, sweet autumn clematis, native clematis, Japanese clematis, (*C. paniculata*), and evergreen clematis, (*C. armandii*).

Coral Honeysuckle

Lonicera sempervirens

Other Name: Trumpet Honeysuckle
Zones: 8 and 9
Type: Evergreen to semi-evergreen
Flowers: Reddish-orange, yellow centers, unscented
Bloom Period: Late spring into summer

Light Requirement:

The coral honeysuckle is much less invasive than many ornamental vines, and may be grown on a trellis or other suitable support, or allowed to develop into a bush-like shrub. Its clusters of two-inch, tubular red-orange-yellow flowers are borne in abundance from late spring into summer, with even a few scattered blossoms occurring in the fall. The unscented flowers are followed by 1/4-inch red fruits much loved by birds. This moderate-growing, easy-to-manage vine is a favorite of butterflies and hummingbirds.

When to Plant

Coral honeysuckle may be planted any time, but is most commonly planted in the spring when plants being offered for sale are in bloom. The best planting period is November through February.

Where to Plant

Plant in full sun to maximize flowering, though plants will grow in partial shade. Coral honeysuckle prefers slightly alkaline soils.

How to Plant

Loosen the roots of a container-grown plant before placing into a well-prepared hole. Use a cup of thoroughly rotted hardwood sawdust mixed into the hole with a small amount of a slow-release fertilizer. Partially fill the hole with original soil, water, then finish filling the hole with additional backfill. Plants may also be started from seed. Since this plant is a vine, an easy way to get a new plant is to push a small length of the vine into the soil about a foot to a foot and a half from the tip and hold it in that position with a weight like a brick. Slightly injuring the vine at that point may hasten root formation. When the vine is well rooted, sever it close to the rooted area on the "mother side" of plant and move the "new" plant to the desired location.

Care and Maintenance

Fertilize sparingly in late winter with a slow-release plant food or with a "garden-variety" fertilizer such as 12-12-12. Pinch back or prune vine tips after flowering to control size and form. Pests are not a major problem with coral honeysuckle, but if aphids (plant lice) do become a problem, use an appropriate insecticide such as orthene 75S or Malathion, following label directions—unless you have a concern about using materials of this type. Heavy water pressure will blast off some of the aphid population.

Additional Information

Too much water can favor vegetative growth over flowering, so keep plants on the dry side before blooming season.

Additional Cultivars or Species

A yellow form of *L. sempervirens* is 'Sulphurea'. 'Superba' has bright scarlet blooms, 'Magnifica' features large red flowers, and two later-blooming cultivars are 'Leo' and 'Alabama Crimson'. 'Dropmore Scarlet' and 'Goldflame' are two hybrid honeysuckles that are coral honeysuckle look-a-likes. Unlike the common coral honeysuckle, 'Goldflame' has a rather pleasant scent.

Five-Leaf Akebia

Akebia quinata

Zones: 8 and 9
Size: Grows to about 25 feet
Type: Evergreen in south Louisiana, semi-evergreen in north Louisiana
Flowers: Fragrant, dark-purple flowers
Bloom Period: April

Light Requirement:

Fast-growing evergreen vines are always useful for covering arches, arbors, and pergolas, and akebia is an outstanding choice for any of those purposes. Relatively unknown in Louisiana, this twining vine deserves to be planted much more often. The slightly glossy, dark-green foliage is particularly beautiful. Each leaf is divided into five two-inch-long leaflets that give the vine its common name as well as its specific epithet. The dusky purple flowers appear in numerous clusters among the foliage in April and continue to appear sporadically through the summer. Their color is not particularly showy, but they are, nonetheless, noticeable and attractive. Each flower has five cupped petals. The sweet fragrance they produce permeates the air around the vine but is not overpowering. The five-leaf akebia establishes quickly and its rate of growth is rapid after the first year.

When to Plant

Like most hardy, woody plant materials, October through March is the best time to plant five-leaf akebia, allowing them to become established during the cool, moist weather of winter. Container-grown plants can be planted through the summer but will require more care during establishment.

Where to Plant

Plant in full sun to part sun, as vines in too much shade will not bloom well. Avoid damp, poorly drained locations. The vine should be planted close to the structure on which it will climb, and may need a little help to get it started.

How to Plant

Make sure vines are planted at the same level they were growing in their containers. To cover a fence, space vines 8 to 10 feet apart. The soil where the vine is planted may be improved by incorporating organic matter into the area, but if the soil is good, this is optional.

Care and Maintenance

Five-leaf akebia is not susceptible to any major insect or disease problems. Scale has occasionally been observed and can be controlled with 2 or 3 applications of an oil spray, spaced 10 days apart. Follow label directions carefully. Once the vine is established, supplemental watering is rarely necessary. Prune the vine occasionally as needed during the summer for control and to train it appropriately.

Additional Information

Since five-leaf akebia blooms on new growth, you may prune the vines in winter if needed. The flower clusters hang downward, so the vine is particularly effective when used to cover an arbor with a sitting area underneath it. The edible fruit is seldom produced in cultivation. Five-leaf akebia is occasionally used as a groundcover, but the edges of the area it covers must be edged regularly to keep it in bounds.

Other Species or Cultivars

Akebia quinata 'Alba' has white flowers that show up beautifully against its dark foliage.

Rosa de Montana

Antigonon leptopus

Other Names: Coral Vine, Rose of Montana
Zones: 8 and 9
Size: 30 to 40 feet
Type: Dies back in winter
Flowers: Coral pink
Bloom Period: Late summer through fall

Light Requirement:

Rosa de Montana is a fairly common vine in the southern part of the state, where it has been popular for generations. This native of Mexico will die down to the ground in winter, but reliably returns from the roots, even in north Louisiana. Once it wakes up in the spring, growth is very rapid, and by the time the summer gets hot, it will provide shade in situations where it is trained for that use. The rosy pink flowers occur in delicate sprays among the light-green foliage. Flowering begins in earnest in late summer, becoming more prolific in fall and continuing until first frost. It is care-free, reliable, and exquisitely beautiful in bloom.

When to Plant

Plant container-grown vines or transplanted seedlings in spring (after danger of frost) through early summer.

Where to Plant

Rosa de Montana vines are rugged and do not demand special treatment. A location that receives plenty of sun will produce the heaviest flowering, but the vines will do well in part sun to part shade. Avoid poorly drained or wet sites.

How to Plant

Plant container-grown vines or seedlings at the same level they were growing previously.

CARE AND MAINTENANCE

This vine is virtually care-free. Prune occasionally, if necessary, during the summer to control and train as desired, and cut back the top growth when it has been killed by frost. This vine is generally not fertilized, as it will tend to produce rampant growth with less flowering.

ADDITIONAL INFORMATION

Rose de Montana will self-seed in some situations. The seedlings are generally not bothersome and can be transplanted to other areas of the landscape, shared with friends, or pulled up and discarded.

ADDITIONAL CULTIVARS OR SPECIES

Antigonon leptopus 'Alba' is a lovely white form.

Trumpet Vine

Campsis radicans

Other Name: Trumpet Creeper
Zones: 8 and 9
Type: Deciduous
Flowers: Bright orange-scarlet flowers, trumpet-shaped
Bloom Period: Summer into fall

Light Requirement:

The trumpet vine is a vigorous native vine found throughout the entire South, including all of Louisiana. This prolific bloomer commonly adorns fences, utility poles, and abandoned buildings in rural areas of the state where its brightly colored flowers draw the attention of passing motorists. Since it is so frequently seen in the wild, it tends to command less interest from gardeners as a landscape plant—but its invasive nature may also be a factor in this lack of interest. When selected for landscape use, it must be given a sturdy support, for in a short time it will become a very heavy, robust plant. Those who enjoy hummingbirds and who have space for this low-care vine should give some thought to planting it if only for the purpose of attracting these busy little birds.

When to Plant

The dormant season (November through February in much of the state) is the best period for planting, with the end of this stretch probably being the ideal time to set out a trumpet vine.

Where to Plant

Full sun is needed to realize full bloom potential; use a partly shaded spot if you must. If there's a bare fence around that could use a touch of color, consider this location for a trumpet vine. This fast-growing vine is drought resistant.

How to Plant

Trumpet vines may be started from seed, from cuttings, or from container-grown plants. Most gardeners will choose the last. Set out young plants at the same depth they were growing in their containers. Backfill with soil from the planting hole, which should be twice as wide as the rootball. To encourage rapid root development without risking chemical burn, mix a small amount of slow-release fertilizer and a small handful of an organic material into the soil being returned to the hole.

Care and Maintenance

Trumpet vine is an easy-care plant that requires little attention except occasional pruning to confine to desired spaces. Do any required pruning in late winter. A slow-release fertilizer in late winter will promote a heavier summer bloom. NPK levels in such plant foods should be in the mid-to-upper teens.

Additional Information

Roots invading shrub areas and flower beds must be dug up and removed. Cutting deep roots is a temporary relief measure, as suckers will form at the cut ends. The vine is self-clinging.

Additional Cultivars or Species

'Madame Galen' has a display of brightly colored reddish-orange flowers. 'Flava' is a yellow-flowered selection. 'Jekyll' is an evergreen cultivar discovered by Dr. Mike Dirr in a Georgia location. It has orange-to-red blossoms and should do well in Louisiana. A related plant is *C. tagliabuana*, a hybrid between *C. radicans* and *C. grandiflora* (Chinese trumpet creeper).

Virginia Creeper

Parthenocissus quinquefolia

Other Name: Woodbine
Zones: 8 and 9
Type: Deciduous
Flowers: Insignificant; black berries in fall (poisonous)

Light Requirement:

Virginia creeper gives the Louisiana gardener the opportunity to use a versatile native vine that can be grown with little effort. This rapidly growing vine clings to walls, fences, and trees with no help from people, and forms a somewhat open canopy that reveals structural elements of the landscape. It should not be used to cloak wooden supports unless they are made of treated lumber. Properly used, Virginia creeper provides a transitional element between major landscape plant and non-plant materials. A palmate five-leaflet leaf distinguishes it from the despised three-leaflet poison ivy that is often its bedfellow. It is free of pests, drought resistant, grows in almost any kind of soil, and is at home in either sun or shade . . . what more can be asked of a plant? Before the onset of dormancy in the late fall, the foliage assumes a dull red to bright red color (depending upon variety and environmental conditions). Because it is readily available in the wild, you may not always find Virginia creeper at a nursery in your area.

When to Plant

Virginia creeper is best planted in the dormant season (November through February in most of state).

Where to Plant

This drought-resistant vine may be planted nearly anywhere you wish, but it is frequently used as a groundcover for shady areas where there is a limited choice of plant materials. It helps prevent erosion on slopes that are too steep to mow.

How to Plant

Since these plants are likely to occupy a site for a long time, prepare a good planting bed based upon a reliable soil test. Incorporate some organic substances during bed preparation, and use slow-release fertilizers according to label instructions. Plants may be set out bareroot in the dormant season and watered in. Base planting density on quantity of plants available, as there may be no commercial source where you live; sparse plantings should fill an allocated space within a reasonable amount of time.

Care and Maintenance

Should vines show poor vigor, use a little fertilizer in late winter. Either a "garden variety" such as 12-12-12 (used at the rate of 1 cup per 40 or 50 square feet of planted area) or a good slow-release product will work well. Although considered pest-free, scale insects will occasionally appear on the stems. Treat with a dormant oil (non-toxic) when temperatures range between 40 and 85 degrees Fahrenheit. Two applications of the oil, 10 days apart, are required to kill these insects.

Additional Information

Frequent mowing of established vines creates a dense canopy of foliage for an attractive groundcover. Control vines on windowed walls lest views from the windows become blocked by vine encroachment. As vines will invade nearby shrubs and flowerbeds, prune as needed to achieve containment. Supervise small children closely in the fall when the fruits of the plant are present. The fruits are poisonous!

Additional Cultivars or Species

P. tricuspidata (Boston ivy) does better in cooler climates than in the Bayou State, but it may work on a north-facing wall, especially in the northern parishes. It is more sensitive to sun than the Virginia creeper. It also has larger leaves and is more attractive. The cultivar 'Engelmannii' has smaller leaves and makes a denser canopy. 'Beverly Brooks', 'Green Showers', 'Lowii', and 'Veitchii' are selections of Boston ivy.

CHAPTER EIGHT

Roses

PERHAPS NO OTHER NAME IN THE PLANT WORLD conjures up as many pleasant thoughts as the name "rose." The roses that we remember with fond memories are those that have excited us with their brilliant hues in a spectrum of color that rivals the rainbow. Memorable roses have filled our nostrils with a fragrance too wonderful to completely describe, whether we sniffed from a short distance or buried our noses in a many-petaled flower. It is estimated that more than 60 million families in the United States have one or more roses growing somewhere in their gardens or landscapes. A plant that popular, in spite of its need to be protected from the wrath of winter in the Northern states and from pests over a long season in the Southern states, must be very special indeed. It is commonly referred to as the "Queen of Flowers" and not too long ago was proclaimed the national flower of the United States by an act of Federal Congress.

As a gardener and resident of Louisiana, you may wish to grow a single plant or a whole garden of roses. The number of plants chosen will more than likely be determined by a complex of personal and environmental factors. Some of the information you need in order to grow roses successfully can be found in this chapter. There are also many books on the specialized subject of rose culture, there are knowledgeable rosarians all over the state who can help you, and there are many professionals in the Louisiana Cooperative Extension Service who have considerable expertise on this subject. If you live in or visit the northwest part of the state, you will have access to the American Rose Center. This is the headquarters of the 25,000-member American Rose Society, where rose information is "stockpiled" and many beautiful roses are on display.

Rose Selection

Your first decision will probably be which kind of rose to grow. Which do you like best? Hybrid teas? Grandifloras? Floribundas? Climbers? Miniatures? How many roses can you care for? Gardeners with plenty of space, time, and money can grow many roses of several kinds, but where one of these resources is limited, a gardener may be forced to make a choice.

Choosing Varieties

After deciding on the color(s) and type(s) of rose that you wish to grow, consult the "Handbook for Selecting Roses," a pocket-sized booklet that is updated annually and is available from the American Rose Center for a nominal charge. Rose varieties from those introduced years ago up to the most recent introductions are rated by competent rosarians in locations throughout the country. The scores are averaged; the scale is 1 to 10, with 10 being perfect. For greater certainty of satisfactory performance, buy a rose that has a rating of 8.5 or higher.

Buy Good-Quality Plants

The saying "you get what you pay for" is quite applicable to roses. Always buy the best, and the best is a Grade No. 1 plant. Grade No. $1^1/_2$ plants are not quite as good, but they are acceptable. It is not advisable to buy a Grade No. 2 plant. The highest-grade plants typically have from three to five thumb-sized canes, are between 1 and $1^1/_2$ feet tall, have no major physical injuries, and show no evidence of insect or disease problems.

Bed Preparation

The location of the rose or rose bed is another decision that will have to be made early in the game. Find a site that can offer full sun and a well-drained soil. If such is not available, try to find a place that has a minimum of six hours of sun each day.

For rose plants to continue to have good health and vigor over an extended period of several years, it is essential that a suitable bed be properly constructed for them. This project can be started at a gardener's convenience, but the months of November and December are ideal times for the task. Unless the cost is just too high, build a raised bed, for in this way you can be assured that your roses will have the good drainage which is of vital importance.

Retaining walls, though not mandatory, will help hold the soil in place and maintain the preferred bed depth. Such walls may be made of materials such as bricks, weathered railroad crossties, or landscape timbers. Gravel, coarse sand, or other porous material may be placed as deep as 4 inches thick at the base of the bed in order to provide better-than-average drainage. Then fill the bed with a good-quality sandy loam soil that's been enriched with substantial organic matter. One often-used mixture is 5 parts soil, 4 parts organic substance, and one part sharp sand, combined on the basis of volume measure, not weight. Total bed depth to the original soil surface should be around 1 1/2 to 2 feet. At this point, collect a representative sample of the soil and have it tested. The LSU soil-testing lab will process your soil sample for only $5.00. Take your sample to your nearest County Extension office along with your check. You should receive a report in about three weeks, and you can mix in the suggested nutrients and/or other amendments. Afterwards, let the soil settle until it's time to plant your roses.

Planting Procedures

Dig a hole about twice the width and depth of the rootball on container plants, or of the root spread on bareroot plants. Incorporate a mixture of half sharp sand and half peat moss, plus a modest amount of an appropriate slow-release fertilizer into the soil removed from the hole. Use this mixture to make a cone of soil in the middle of the hole. The height of the cone should place the plant at a depth that allows its graft union to be an inch or so above the soil line of the surrounding ground. The rose's root system should drape naturally over the cone, and any damaged or overly long roots should be trimmed off. While holding the plant carefully in position, fill the hole with the improved soil mix until most of the roots are covered. Fill the remaining space with water or starter solution, then let it drain completely. After firming the soil with moderate pressure, finish filling the hole with the mix, leaving only a shallow basin around the base of the plant. Firm the surface of the soil once more and cover with an organic mulch.

Roses Must Have Water

Although relatively sensitive to waterlogged soils, roses require plenty of moisture in order to grow properly. The soil mix used in the bed or on the planting site must not only be able to drain in a fairly rapid manner, but must also be somewhat moisture-retentive. Watering techniques vary widely and often depend on how great an interest the gardener has in the plants and how much expense the gardener is willing to bear. Dragging a garden hose along the bed is the least expensive method but time-consuming. Overhead sprinkler irrigation is not desirable as wet foliage on roses will often cause major disease problems. Two methods are considered by most rose growers to be the ideal ways to provide the necessary moisture: drip irrigation lines can be run under the mulch and placed strategically near the bases of individual rose plants; and/or small sprinkler heads that pop up and spray out water parallel to the soil surface only inches above the mulch. While timers can be used on such systems, it's best to water only when you think the plants need a drink.

Mulches

While it's possible to grow roses without the use of a mulch, most successful rose growers use relatively thick mulches around all of their plants—for the very same reasons that mulches are used with other plants. Pine straw is the number-one mulching material for roses in Louisiana, probably because it is so plentiful statewide. There are a number of other natural materials that make satisfactory mulches. Find out what materials you can obtain locally.

Maintenance

You cannot fear chemicals if you're going to grow roses. In the warm, humid climate of Louisiana there are countless pests that are as fond of roses as you are. But the pests do much more than just admire them; they eat them or use them to sustain their own lives. Several kinds of insects, several types of diseases, and marauding deer may attack roses. To protect the plants from insects and diseases, a variety of insecticides and fungicides must be used with considerable frequency. Our specific pest control recommendations follow under the "Care and Maintenance" section included in each plant entry. Roses also need good nutrition to perform their best. It seems that there are as many ways to fertilize roses as there are people growing these rewarding plants. Our specific recommendations concerning fertilization follow under the "Care and Maintenance" section included in each plant entry.

Climbing Rose

Rosa × hybrida

Other Names: Rambling Roses, Ramblers
Zones: 8 and 9
Size: Up to 20 feet tall
Type: Deciduous
Flowers: Variety, including pink, white, red, and orange
Bloom Period: Depends on type (spring to early summer)

Light Requirement:

You'll surely have to search far and wide to find a plant that can offer as much as this rose. Few plants can produce a visual impact as unforgettable as that of a climbing rose when it buries its support in an avalanche of blossoms. Roses with this "specialized" growth habit are divided into two groups based upon flowering characteristics. One of these groups is composed of roses that bloom only in the spring in one mass show of flowers. This normally occurs in late spring to early summer in the northern part of the state, but is usually two or three weeks earlier in the southern areas. Most of the natural climbers are in this category. The other group is made up of varieties that have a big show of flowers as well as sporadic blossoms into the summer and fall months. Most of this group is composed of sports (mutations) of bush-type cultivars including hybrid teas, grandifloras, floribundas, polyanthas, and miniatures. But regardless of their group affiliation, all of the climbing roses need a long period of establishment (usually one or two full years) during which time they should not be pruned except for minor repair and training cuts. Climbers that bloom only once a season should be pruned right at the end of the flowering cycle; older canes that lack vigor should be removed to favor the more productive wood. The other climbers that bloom over a long period should be pruned in late winter along with bush roses. Again, remove the older wood and thin out weak stems. Since flowers are borne on secondary growth, cut these laterals back to within two to four buds of the main canes.

When to Plant

Plant in late winter as a first choice, but the spring months are a good second choice.

Where to Plant

Plant where the roses have full sun, a well-drained soil, and some type of structure to climb on. An area of high visibility is suggested.

How to Plant

See the introduction to this chapter.

Care and Maintenance

Fertilize in late winter with no more than 4 ounces of an all-purpose fertilizer per mature plant, placing it in a broad band 6 inches away from the plant; or use a rose specialty fertilizer or controlled-release material according to label instructions. For repeat bloomers, a second fertilization is recommended in late summer. Use small amounts of high-nitrogen materials at 6-week intervals between these times. Provide drip or low-profile sprinkler irrigation to maintain a reasonable moisture level in the soil; otherwise, deep-water 2 or 3 times a week. Pest control is essential—use recommended materials on a weekly basis. Specific products are suggested in other places in this chapter.

Additional Information

It may be necessary to tie the long main canes to their support. Secure with soft, strong ties, and don't allow the canes to rub the support. Training major canes to a horizontal position may increase their flowering.

Additional Cultivars or Species

Among the natural climbers are the old red varieties 'Blaze' and 'Don Juan'. 'Altissimo' and 'Dublin Bay' make the "high-rated" list. 'New Dawn' is a high-rated pink climber. 'America' (orange-blend) and 'Golden Showers' are AARS (All America Rose Selections). Among sport-type climbers are 'C1. Chrysler Imperial' (red), 'C1. Queen Elizabeth' (pink), and 'C1. Double Delight' (white). There are many other cultivars.

Floribunda Rose

Rosa × hybrida

Zones: 8 and 9
Size: 2 to 4 feet tall
Type: Deciduous
Flowers: Wide variety, including pink, white, yellow, and red
Bloom Period: April through October

Light Requirement:

Gardeners who want plants that produce masses of color need look no farther than the class of roses known as floribundas. Flat-topped clusters of medium to small flowers literally cover the whole plant and present a color extravaganza. Developed from combinations of hybrid teas and polyanthas, these smaller plants possess much vigor, probably a trait that is inherited from *R. multiflora,* a grandparent on the polyantha side of the family. The flowers in the class can be any of several colors, much like the hybrid tea roses. While not well suited for use as a cut flower, these roses are great to use as borders, barriers, or informal hedges. If the *ARS Handbook for Selecting Roses* is any indication, the floribundas must be popular, for breeders have turned out several highly rated varieties in the last few years.

When to Plant

For best results, plant in the latter part of the dormant season. If you fudge a little into the early spring months, there shouldn't be any major problems.

Where to Plant

Plant anywhere in the landscape that you need lots of color or a barrier, but be sure the sites chosen are in full sun and have well-drained soils.

How to Plant

Planting techniques are fully presented in the chapter introduction.

Care and Maintenance

It may be that a little less care is required for this plant due to its tough nature, but fertilizing, spraying for pests, watering, and pruning needs are similar to those of other classes of roses. Pests are somewhat less of a problem for floribundas than for most other roses. Check the care instructions for grandiflora roses if you wish to have more details about caring for these plants.

Additional Cultivars or Species

Several of these cultivars have made the AARS (All America Rose Selection) list, including the relatively famous 'Europeana'. Those varieties making the ARS (American Rose Society) 1997 handbook for high-rated roses include 'Europeana', 'Lavaglut', 'Showbiz', 'Stad den Helder', and 'Travemunde' (all red); 'Gene Boerner', 'Poulsen's Pearl', and 'Sexy Rexy' (pink); 'Sunsprite' (yellow); 'Bridal White', 'Iceberg', 'Margaret Merril', and 'Nicole' (white); 'Escapade' (mauve); 'Hannah Gordon', 'Priscilla Burton', and 'Tootsie' (blends); 'Dicky' (orange-pink); and 'Playtime' and 'Royal Occasion' (orange-red).

Grandiflora Rose

Rosa × hybrida

Zones: 8 and 9
Size: 3 to 10 feet tall
Type: Deciduous
Flowers: Wide variety, including yellow, red, pink, and white
Bloom Period: April through October

Light Requirement:

Some of the grandiflora roses have resulted from crosses between hybrid tea roses and floribunda roses. This ancestry has given them some of the better qualities of both parents and they are consequently a bit more adapted for use as a landscape plant than are hybrid tea roses and make a better cut flower than the floribundas. Although single blossoms may approach the size of hybrid tea flowers, many stems will have multiple blooms that are of smaller size. Not all grandifloras are the result of crossing two classes of roses, however. It is thought that some of the named varieties of grandiflora roses are merely vigorous descendants of hybrid tea roses. Several colors of flowers are available in this class of roses which may still be one of the smallest classes.

When to Plant

Plant these kinds of roses in the latter part of the dormant season for easiest establishment, but early spring months are suitable, particularly if the temperatures remain moderate.

Where to Plant

Plant in beds where good drainage is assured and where there is at least 8 hours of full sun.

How to Plant

Planting procedure was thoroughly presented in this chapter's introduction.

Care and Maintenance

Fertilize in late winter and again in late summer with an all-purpose fertilizer, using no more than 4 ounces per plant. Spread the material in a broad band that's about 6 inches away from the main stem or trunk. Between these times, give plants a light feeding of a high nitrogen fertilizer or a complete fertilizer every 4 to 6 weeks. A specialty rose food or a slow-release fertilizer may be used if preferred, but be sure to follow label directions for such materials. Maintain good soil moisture levels throughout the growing season, but don't overwater. There are some good irrigation systems that take the work out of this regular task. Pest problems on roses are far too numerous to ignore, and a good weekly spray program using recommended pesticides is essential. Contact your county agent or other local expert for the latest information. The pruning of bush roses is best done in late winter (February) and again in late summer (August). In the late-winter period, retain no more than 7 major canes (preferably of thumb-size or larger), and cut these back to a height of 12 to 18 inches, depending on the vigor of the plant. In late summer, follow the same guidelines, but cut back only to a 30- to 36-inch height. All other growth should be removed. Where cuts are made on canes to be kept, make the cut about $^{1}/_{4}$ inch above a bud or eye that faces away from the center of the plant. The angle of the cut should parallel that of the bud below it. When harvesting blooms for decorative use, cut the stem just above a 5-leaflet leaf, long enough to serve your purpose.

Additional Information

These multipurpose plants can serve as a source of cut flowers, as a component of a landscape design, as background for other plant species, and as very effective sharp-thorned barrier plants.

Additional Cultivars or Species

Only two cultivars are currently listed among the high-rated roses in the ARS (American Rose Society) Rose Handbook. These are 'Arizona', an orange blend, and 'Gold Medal', a medium-yellow rose. Other notable cultivars are 'Shreveport' (an orange-blend which does well in Shreveport, but not as well in other places), 'Love' (red), 'Aquarius' (pink), 'Camelot' (pink), 'Pink Parfait' (pink), 'Queen Elizabeth' (pink), 'Tournament of Roses' (pink), 'Solitude' (orange-blend), and 'White Lightnin' (white).

Hybrid Tea Rose

Rosa × hybrida

Zones: 8 and 9
Size: 3 to 10 feet tall
Type: Deciduous
Flowers: Wide variety, including pink, white, red, yellow, and orange
Bloom Period: April through October
Light Requirement:

Of all kinds of roses, this is the one that commonly steals the show with its large to very large blossoms (usually one to the stem), its host of colors, and its nearly perfect flower form (when it receives the proper culture). Whenever someone says "rose," this is the one that most people picture in their minds. Is it surprising, then, that the hybrid teas as a class out-sell all other types of roses combined? As a result of this immense popularity, rose breeders have put lots of effort over the past several years into developing and producing hybrid tea varieties of roses in what seems to be an almost unending stream. Thanks to their skills, patience, and persistence, modern-day gardeners have a tremendous selection of hybrid tea roses from which to choose. Regardless of your rose preferences, it would be a rare experience to not find a hybrid tea that meets your needs.

When to Plant

Favor the later part of the dormant season for planting hybrid tea roses. Installations made in the cooler spring months are generally satisfactory as well.

Where to Plant

Plant these beauties in a bed that offers a well-drained soil and full sunlight. If possible, locate them where they can be easily seen by all who enjoy roses or in a frequently used part of the landscape.

How to Plant

Planting information may be found in the chapter introduction.

Care and Maintenance

Fertilize with an all-purpose fertilizer, a rose specialty plant food, or a controlled-release fertilizer in late winter as suggested in chapter introduction. Use watering practices that will keep the soil sufficiently moist during the entire growing season. Drip irrigation systems in good working order are efficient and waste little water. Besides, they don't wet the rose foliage (wetting of foliage makes conditions for disease all too favorable). Pest control is an absolute necessity. Most experienced gardeners discover that weekly applications of insecticides and fungicides are required to keep their roses healthy. Several of these were mentioned in the introduction. A new fungicide on the horizon looks very promising for disease prevention and has reportedly given 30-day control of blackspot in experimental trials. It does not presently have a label for roses. Spider mites, a common pest of roses, can be controlled with M-PEDE, Talstar 10 WP, Avid, and Kelthane. Always follow label directions when using any chemical products. The pruning of bush roses is best done in late winter (February) and again in late summer (August). Follow pruning guidelines given for grandiflora roses.

Additional Information

According to one reference, 'La France' was the first hybrid tea cultivar, introduced in 1867.

Additional Cultivars or Species

'Chrysler Imperial' and 'Mr. Lincoln' are two older popular red varieties. According to the American Rose Society (ARS), 'Dublin', 'Kardinal', 'Olympiad', and 'Mr. Lincoln' are currently the high-rated roses among red hybrid teas. The other high-rated hybrid teas are 'Dainty Bess', 'Elizabeth Taylor', and 'Marijke Koopman' (pink); 'Pristine' (white); 'Elina' (yellow); 'Silver Star' (mauve); 'Touch of Class' (orange-pink); 'Double Delight', 'First Prize', 'Irish Elegance', 'Kathleen Mills', 'Louise Estes', 'Silver Jubilee' and 'Southern Lady' (blends).

Lady Banks Rose

Rosa banksiae

Zones: 8 and 9
Size: Potential mature size, 20 feet
Type: Evergreen
Flowers: Yellow and white
Bloom Period: Spring

Light Requirement:

During most winters in Louisiana, Lady Banks roses tend to remain evergreen, though they are generally listed as semi-evergreen. True to their kindred, they must have full sun to produce the impressive array of blossoms that are borne in clusters on their nearly thornless canes and stems. Although the relatively small flowers would not create much of an individual impact, the abundant clusters they form in the spring make a mass of color that can easily dominate the landscape. There are both yellow- and white-flowered cultivars of the Lady Banks rose. Unlike most of the other roses, this rose usually adapts easily to environmental conditions and seems to have very few pest problems. While this Chinese native is somewhat vine-like in structure, it sends up tall canes with a graceful arching habit that intensifies the beauty of the plant. For even greater beauty, provide attractive supports (trellises, fences, etc.) so that it can better display its multitude of flowers. Once established, the plant exhibits great vigor and commonly must be pruned at intervals during the growing season to confine its spread to the prescribed area.

When to Plant

A gardener can install this plant at almost any time that's convenient. If you have a choice, give preference to the cooler months of the year when environmental stress is lowest.

Where to Plant

Plant the Lady Banks rose in full sun in a well-drained soil. Bloom reduction can be significant in partial shade.

How to Plant

Make a planting hole twice as wide and a bit deeper than the size of the rootball. Combine with the soil removed from the hole some organic material such as finely-ground pine bark, along with some controlled-release fertilizer. Place some of this improved material in the bottom of the hole and use the rest of it to make a mound in the center of the hole. The roots of the plant should be carefully pulled free of the rootball and allowed to drape over the mound in a natural configuration. If the rootball is tightly packed, the plant may have to be handled more like a conventional shrub. Either way, hold the plant in the desired position with the crown at or just above the surrounding ground surface and partially fill the hole with the improved backfill. After gently pressing the soil down between the roots, fill the remaining space with water or starter solution and let it all soak in. Then finish filling the hole with the backfill, leaving only a shallow basin around the plant. Mulch the ground, then apply plenty of water to settle the soil and eliminate internal air pockets.

Care and Maintenance

Due to this plant's vigor, some gardeners choose not to fertilize it at all. Others fertilize in late winter. Use materials like 15-5-10 or 12-12-12, depending on the soil fertility. About 1/2 cup per square yard of soil surface under the plant should be sufficient. Prune large plants heavily just after bloom and keep plant size in check by clipping the plant at several intervals during the growing season. Watering will be required only when extended drought conditions prevail. Pests are rare in most of the state.

Additional Information

For more color impact, grow plants on sturdy supports.

Additional Cultivars or Species

Four cultivars are listed. These are the 'Lutea' (double yellow flowers), 'Alba-Plena' or 'White Banksia' (double white), 'Normalis' (single white), and 'Lutescens' (single yellow).

CHAPTER NINE

Shrubs

SHRUBS CAN BE DEFINED AS WOODY, MULTISTEMMED PLANTS that mature at less than 20 feet in height—but such a definition gives no hint of the importance and versatility of this class of ornamental plants. Visualize a home surrounded by a sparse, struggling turf and maybe a shade tree or two. Is this a pretty picture? Could this be a cool environment during the heat of summer or a warm space in the cold of winter? Is this a pleasant place for everyday living? The obvious answer is, "No!"

Shrubs can help significantly to change that scene. But you can't take just any old shrub and put it just any old place and expect it to have a resounding impact. First, you must make a wise choice of plants. Residents of Louisiana are extremely lucky because they have so many different kinds of plants from which to choose. Louisiana's climate varies from moderately temperate in the northern part of the state to subtropical in the southernmost areas. In some parts of the state, gardeners have opportunities to plant both subtropical species and temperate-zone species in the same landscape. Of course the subtropical plants are at greater risk of cold damage when planted in the northernmost parishes, and the distinctly temperate-climate plants may not perform to their highest potential in the southern part of the state. But for some gardeners, this situation is a challenge—and they love it.

A plant pathologist I know once said that Louisiana is one big disease from border to border; a knowing entomologist might chime in that the state is also a Garden of Eden for bugs and related creatures. Louisiana's warm, humid climate does foster many more pest problems than those normally found in cooler and drier sections of the country. When selecting shrubs, look for those that are resistant to some of the diseases. Shrubs generally have their share of insect problems as well. Borers, leaf eaters, scales, white flies, thrips . . . you name it and it is somewhere in the state, dining on a shrub. In order for your shrubs to remain vigorous and attractive, these pests must be dealt with quickly and effectively. Fortunately, there are both chemical and non-chemical ways to achieve control of many of these problems before a shrub is lost.

When ordering a plant from a catalog which claims its final size will be, for example, 12 feet tall, don't be surprised to find the plant can reach a height of 15 to 18 feet in Louisiana conditions. (Note in the individual plant profiles that listed sizes indicate plant height, first, followed by plant width.) New gardeners sometimes pay no attention to plants' predicted size at maturity. They only realize the importance of mature plant size when the "little" plants they bought to plant on either side of the front walk begin to interlock branches—forcing people to use a new pathway.

Just like trees, shrubs for landscape use can be evergreen (or semi-evergreen) or deciduous. Deciduous species in bloom provide that burst of color we associate with special periods or seasons (such as spring). Evergreen shrubs with their winter foliage are useful for year-round screens and barriers.

Shrubs must be selected, in part, on the basis of their light requirements and their soil preferences. Only a few can survive for long periods in deep shade, and even the species that have some degree of shade tolerance tend to do better in light, high shade such as the filtered shade found beneath tall pine trees. Since there are so many soil types across the state, the gardener should make an evaluation of the soil in the area to be developed before selecting shrubs. If there seem to be drastic soil differences within a single landscape, performing several soil tests may be well worth the cost. The kind of information these tests provide can prevent costly mistakes. While there are a few shrubs that tolerate poorly drained soil, the majority struggle in places where there is low soil oxygen or where water stands for days after a rain. When landscapes contain such areas, it is of vital importance to regrade for improved drainage or to construct raised beds in which to grow the shrubs.

To provide more interest and vitality in a landscape, plan for a good selection of time-tested shrubs and combine them with some of the newer introductions which display a variety of forms, foliage textures, flowers, and branch structures.

Aucuba

Aucuba japonica

Other Names: Gold Dust Aucuba, Variegated Japanese Aucuba (both 'Variegata' cultivar)
Zones: 8 and 9
Size: Expected mature size, 6 x 4 feet
Type: Evergreen

Light Requirement:

This native of Japan and the Himalayas is one of the few of our available shrubs that will grow and compete in relatively heavy shade. While the regular green forms are sold in various nurseries, the variegated forms are far more popular and probably account for the majority of sales. These plants have very coarse, thick, leathery leaves that are attached to green stems which arise from the crown. The variegated forms have various patterns of yellow splotches, streaks, small dots, and yellow edges. Sometimes fungus disease and/or spider mites and mealybugs can be a problem, but all are controllable with the proper selection of chemicals. For best performance, it may be necessary to improve the soil with organic substances or sharp sand for better aeration and drainage. These plants make good tub specimens since they can be planted in a tailor-made soil mix and placed in a shady site where planting in the ground may not be feasible.

When to Plant

Container-grown plants may be planted at any time. Those planted in the summer months may require slightly more attention until they are well established.

Where to Plant

Plant aucuba only in shady areas. If possible, choose northern exposures where it is cooler, as the plant's performance diminishes as it moves south. Avoid placing the plant in direct sun, or it may burn. Aucuba performs best in organically rich, moist, but well-drained soil. This is an excellent plant to grow in a large container.

How to Plant

Surround the plant's roots with a generous amount of high-grade soil mix in an oversized hole. Include a small amount of slow-release fertilizer in the mix. Add water and soil mix in increments until the hole is filled and the plant is at the same level it was growing in its original container.

Care and Maintenance

Fertilize in late winter with a balanced fertilizer such as 8-8-8 at the rate of about 4 ounces (1/2 cup) for good-sized plants—proportionally less for smaller plants. Scatter fertilizer in a broad band around the base of the plant and water or scratch into the soil surface—or use a slow-release fertilizer as prescribed on the label. Thin and shape plant by removing older canes at ground level in the late winter. If disease or insects threaten, identify the problem and use materials or methods of your choice for control. Otherwise, consult with your county agent or other local experts for the most up-to-date information, since chemicals and recommendations change frequently.

Additional Information

The aucuba is a dioecious species—meaning that the male and female flowers are on separate plants. When both sexes of plants are planted close together, the female may produce colorful clusters of red berries.

Additional Cultivars or Species

Green cultivars include 'Longifolia', 'Serratifolia', 'Viridis', and 'Nana', a dwarf form. Two of these are females. Variegated selections are 'Variegata' (the most common one is known also as 'Gold Dust'), 'Crotonifolia' (male), 'Fructu Albo', 'Picturata' (possibly the worst choice for the New Orleans area), 'Sulphur', and 'Mr. Goldstrike'.

Azalea

Rhododendron spp.

Zones: 8 and 9
Size: Expected mature size, 8 x 8 feet
Type: *R. indicum*, evergreen; other species evergreen or deciduous
Flower Color: Red, white, pink and purple
Bloom Period: Massive spring bloom

Light Requirement:

The Indian azaleas are among the most popular shrubs both in Louisiana and throughout the entire south. Their massive, mid-spring blooming period draws visitors from beyond the region and prompts local people to take leisurely drives through mature neighborhoods where very large plants of this species adorn one landscape after another. Indian azaleas are a featured plant in various public and private gardens throughout the state. They bear flowers of good size, and the flowers cover the plant to create a mound of living color. Numerous varieties and cultivars provide a wide range of mostly pastel colors, but white-flowered varieties are also common. They usually grow in the dappled shade of tall pines; hardwood trees offer too much competition for them. Moist, organically-rich soil sets the stage for the plant's best performance; good drainage is practically a requirement for survival. Pests are many in number, but controllable. Every home owner ought to include one of these wonderful plants somewhere in the landscape.

When to Plant

The dormant season is best, but container-grown plants may be planted successfully at any time. A much higher level of care is required if plants are set out during summer heat.

Where to Plant

Plant where both you and passers-by can enjoy the plants in full bloom. Select a site that is well drained and lightly shaded. Azaleas need moist, acid soil for best bloom performance.

How to Plant

Dig a generously sized hole that is twice the width of and slightly deeper than the rootball. Line the hole with a good soil mix enriched with a slow-release fertilizer. Slash the roots vertically in three or four places and place the rootball near the top of the hole. Embed the rootball firmly in the hole with additional soil mix. Plant in a raised bed if there is a question of poor drainage; always make sure that an inch or two of the rootball shows above the top of the ground. Mulch with a suitable organic material and water thoroughly.

Care and Maintenance

Fertilize plants shortly after flowering with an azalea food formulated for plants in acid soil; follow label directions for application. Repeat in early September, but at one-half the label rate. Azaleas need frequent watering; using drip irrigation tubes to supply water is a good idea. Both insect and disease pests love azaleas, but most can be controlled with good techniques and the right materials. Orthene 75S is excellent for lace bugs, and Maneb works well as a preventative for leaf gall—but it is usually a good idea to get some help from experts in dealing with pest problems. Be sure to follow label directions when applying products. When substantial pruning is necessary, do this just after blooming. Late-summer pruning removes flower buds for the next spring's crop of flowers.

Additional Information

Smaller-growing, large-flowered azaleas that bloom in both spring and fall are rapidly becoming more widely available.

Additional Cultivars or Species

Kurume hybrids, Robin Hill hybrids, and the *R. austrinum* (Florida azalea) offer some outstanding choices for landscape plants. Hundreds of other azaleas will also grow satisfactorily in Louisiana. Rhododendrons and azaleas together constitute a massive group of plants with varieties numbering in the thousands. For years the most popular species in Louisiana has been the Indian azaleas, *R. indicum*.

Banana Shrub

Michelia figo

Other Name: Magnolia fuscata (botanical name used as common name), Michelia fuscata
Zones: 8 and 9
Size: Mature size, 15 x 10 feet
Type: Evergreen
Flowers: Very fragrant, banana-scented blossoms
Bloom Period: Spring

Light Requirement:

You will want to plant a banana shrub if you enjoy fragrance in the garden. Planted on sites where air movement is slow or where surrounding plants or structures shield it from wind currents, its flowers produce a fragrance that permeates the air and is unmatched by most other flowers. Happy in fertile soil that is moist, moderately acidic, and well-drained, banana shrub is a great evergreen shrub to have in a Southern garden. But if you plant it in an unfavorable environment—especially in an alkaline, poorly drained soil—expect the plant to have some problems, such as iron chlorosis, and a thin canopy of foliage. This relatively slow-growing shrub can be damaged by low, teen-level temperatures, but I've seen good-sized plants in the northernmost parishes survive rather severe winters with little or no injury. Banana shrub makes a striking specimen plant.

When to Plant

Select one of the dormant-season months as first choice. Healthy container-grown specimens may be planted in the warmer months, but more care is required. Steer clear of the months of extreme heat.

Where to Plant

A site with a well-drained soil is a must. Plant near a protected patio or in a courtyard, giving preference to spots offering partial shade. In northern areas, choose a site on the south side of structures or dense stands of large plants.

How to Plant

Plant on a mound of soil if poor drainage is suspected. Dig a hole twice the width of and slightly deeper than the rootball. Add a good-quality soil mix (enriched with a slow-release fertilizer) and place the plant in the hole. The top of the rootball should be nearly level with the surrounding soil surface. Continue adding mix until it covers at least half of the rootball. Then add water or a starter solution. When water has soaked completely into the ground, add more mix until only a shallow depression surrounds the base of the plant. Make a mini-levee around this depression and apply mulch to ensure a more even supply of moisture. Finish the planting with a thorough watering.

Care and Maintenance

Use a balanced fertilizer such as 8-8-8 in late winter, at the rate of 1 cup for mature plants—proportionally less for smaller plants. Spread fertilizer evenly around the base of the plant in a broad band and scratch it into the surface of the soil. If you prefer, use a slow-release fertilizer instead; follow label directions. Prune as needed to adjust form and density just after flowering. Water as often as necessary to maintain a reasonably moist soil, but do not overwater. In extremely hot weather you may need to water as often as every 10 to 14 days. Banana shrub is usually not bothered by pests.

Additional Information

An old, neglected specimen can be converted into a nice tree form by removing several of the bottom limbs and reshaping the canopy of top branches.

Additional Cultivars or Species

M. champaca and *M. doltsopa* are listed in some of the references but may not be available in our state. *M.* × *foggii* includes selections with larger flowers and leaves. 'Maude', 'Allspice', and 'Jack Fog' are included in this group. One recognized cultivar of *M. figo* is 'Port Wine', which has maroon flowers.

Butterfly Bush

Buddleia alternifolia

Other Name: Fountain Buddleia
Zones: 8 and 9
Size: Mature size, 10 x 8 feet
Type: Deciduous
Flowers: Purple flower clusters; other colors becoming available
Bloom Period: Long summer bloom period

Light Requirement:

This old Chinese native has been used for many years in Southern gardens, but performance decreases when there is insufficient cold. Butterfly bush does very well in northern Louisiana. This plant is attractive—its gracefully arched branches are tipped with purple tapering flower clusters that decorate the bush for most of the summer. Butterfly bush is not picky about where it grows (it tolerates sun or partial shade and all but poorly drained soils), and it has few pests. It is a fast-growing, easy-to-maintain species—but the main reason that gardeners buy and plant this shrub is its ability to attract both butterflies and hummingbirds in great numbers.

When to Plant

For greater ease and certainty of establishment, select one of the cool dormant-season months for planting this shrub. Container-grown specimens may be planted at any time, but they will require far more care if you plant them in hotter weather.

Where to Plant

Plant the butterfly bush wherever you wish, except in deep shade or sites with poorly drained soil. Keep in mind that you will want to watch the visiting butterflies (and hummingbirds), so select a site where the bush is highly visible.

How to Plant

Dig a hole at least twice as wide as and slightly deeper than the rootball. Add a good soil mix to the bottom of the hole and firm to a thickness that will allow the plant to continue growing at its previous level. Make shallow, vertical cuts into tightly bound roots before placing the plant. Fill around the roots with additional soil mix (enriched with a slow-release fertilizer) until it covers at least half of the rootball; then add water or a starter solution and let it soak completely into the ground. Finish filling the hole with soil until there is only a shallow depression surrounding the base of the plant. Build a mini-levee around the depression to facilitate watering, and cover the whole area with an organic mulch. Finish with a thorough watering.

Care and Maintenance

Use either a slow-release fertilizer or an all-purpose fertilizer in late winter to prepare the plant for the growing season. If you use fertilizer such as 12-12-12, plan for 1/4 pound for each square yard of soil surface the plant covers, and distribute it evenly around and under the shrub. If feasible, scratch the fertilizer into the top of the soil. Prune out older, less productive canes from the center of the plant during this same period. Extra watering will probably only be required during the hottest, driest months, so plan to soak soil to a 4-inch depth about every 3 weeks during those stress periods. Pests are relatively rare, so don't worry about them until definite problems appear.

Additional Information

With skillful pruning and training, the butterfly bush can be made to resemble a small single- or multistemmed tree.

Additional Cultivars or Species

Several cultivars of *B. davidii,* which give a much wider range of flower colors, are becoming more readily available in area nurseries and garden centers. Some of the more popular ones are 'Black Knight' (blue-black), 'Border Beauty' (crimson to purple), 'Charming' (rose-pink), 'Royal Red' (red), and 'White Bouquet' (white). 'Argentea' is a widely planted cultivar of *B. alternifolia.*

Camellia

Camellia japonica

Zones: 8 and 9
Size: Expected mature size, 15 x 10 feet
Type: Evergreen
Flowers: Large, showy red, pink, white
Bloom Period: Late fall to early spring depending on zone

Light Requirement:

This relatively slow-growing native of China and Japan has been a favorite in the Southern states ever since its introduction. Camellia's glossy leaves and vast array of bloom sizes, shapes, and colors have made it popular throughout Louisiana. Camellias planted outdoors in northern Louisiana often experience flower-bud damage during the winter. While these plants have problems with the alkaline soil of southern Louisiana, they are still widely planted—and for good reason. Groupings of these shrubs in full bloom under scattered tall pines makes a lasting impression. Many pests injure this species, but most can be controlled. Camellias are well suited for tub culture as specimen plants, and considerable numbers are grown in greenhouses for winter protection. Since it is important to keep the roots relatively cool, thick mulches are needed year-round.

When to Plant

The dormant season is ideal. Since these plants bloom during the cool months, you can see the flower color on container plants. Planting at other times carries more risk.

Where to Plant

Camellias perform best when they grow in the filtered shade of tall pines. A semi-shaded spot on a patio or terrace is perfect for a tub specimen.

How to Plant

Dig a hole twice the width of and slightly deeper than the rootball. Add some slow-release fertilizer to a good-quality soil mix, and pack several inches of the mix into the hole. Firm, and add more mix until the top of the rootball is slightly higher than the surrounding ground when the base of the ball is resting on the mix at the bottom of the hole. When the soil mix covers at least half of the root-ball, stop and fill the hole with water or a starter solution. After the water has soaked into the ground, finish filling the hole with soil until there is only a shallow depression surrounding the base of the plant. Make a mini-levee around the depression and then apply a thick mulch of organic materials. Finish with a thorough watering.

Care and Maintenance

Fertilize with an azalea-camellia food at label rates in late winter just before new growth is initiated. A light feeding in the early fall may also be beneficial, but use half the suggested label rates. Prune as needed in the period just before spring growth to control plant density and form or to remove dead, diseased, or insect-riddled parts. Well-timed applications of broad-spectrum fungicides may help prevent some of the fungus problems; many gardeners use dimethoate for controlling scale insects. For the most up-to-date information, consult your county agent or other local expert. To meet camellia's high water demands, consider using drip irrigation lines under the mulch. Maintain thick mulches at all times.

Additional Information

Trim off bottom limbs of old plants to convert to a tree form. Float blossoms in a bowl of water as a table decoration.

Additional Cultivars or Species

C. sasanqua is the other principal species that is widely planted in the state. It will be covered as a separate entry later. There are dozens of the *C. japonica* that do well in Louisiana. Check with your local nurseries and garden centers for those most popular in your area.

Chinese Holly

Ilex cornuta

Zones: 8 and 9
Size: Expected mature size, 10 x 8 feet
Type: Evergreen
Flowers: Small white in spring
Bloom Period: Berries in winter on female plants

Light Requirement:

This holly is another Chinese native that has found a home in Louisiana. Chinese holly grows in a wide range of soils, but likes fertile, acid soils best . . . especially those with a clay subsoil. The stiff, glossy leaves are equipped with sharp spines which make them attractive, but which also command respect. Should there be a need for a barrier against unwanted intruders, this plant deserves your consideration. Female plants are attractive when loaded with their red berries and make nice specimen plants; unless a male holly is nearby to furnish pollen, however, there will be no berries. While Chinese hollies should be planted in full sun for best performance, they will grow in a light shade. The berries of female plants attract wildlife, and both sexes are often chosen by birds as safe places to build their nests. Since Chinese hollies are very tolerant of drought, heat, and cold, they make good landscape plants anywhere in the state. Their main weakness is their susceptibility to the scale insects that coat the bottom sides of their leaves.

When to Plant

The dormant season should be your first choice for planting. Container-grown plants may be planted at other times, however, as long as you give them extra care.

Where to Plant

Put specimen plants in a full-sun, highly visible spot. Place plants that will serve as screens or barriers in rows where they can fulfill your intended purpose.

How to Plant

Dig a hole at least twice the width of and slightly deeper than the rootball. Cover the bottom of the hole a few inches deep with a good-quality soil mix fortified with a slow-release fertilizer; press to firm. Place the rootball on the surface of the packed mix and adjust the amount so that the plant may continue to grow at its previous level. Put more mix in the hole until it covers at least half of the rootball, then add water to fill the space. When the water has soaked completely into the ground, continue adding soil until just a shallow depression remains at the base of the plant. Mulch lightly and water.

Care and Maintenance

Use dormant oils to control scale insects; apply during periods of moderate temperature, and direct spray at bottoms of leaves. Prune annually to limit size and maintain desired form. Do this in the late winter after the berries are gone, but before the inconspicuous flowers appear. Take your cue from the female plants. Exercise caution when pruning, as contact with the spine-tipped leaves can be painful. Fertilize plants in late winter by spreading an all-purpose plant food such as 8-8-8 under the branches at the rate of 1 to 2 cups per mature specimen—proportionally less for smaller plants. Slow-release fertilizers are also excellent, but more costly. Rain usually provides enough water, but a good soaking every 3 or 4 weeks may be needed during the summer heat.

Additional Information

Set plants 4 to 6 feet apart in rows for screening or barriers. Make sure there are one or two male plants so that female plants can produce berries; 'Burfordii' cultivar is an exception. Berried branches are an excellent substitute for American holly for decorating at Christmas. Wear heavy clothing and leather gloves when pruning.

Additional Cultivars or Species

Several cultivars and hybrids of *I. cornuta* perform well in Louisiana. Some of these are 'Burfordii', 'Carissa', 'D'Or', 'Dazzler', 'Nellie R. Stevens', and 'Rotunda', a dwarf form. Related species include Japanese holly (*I. crenata*) and yaupon (*I. vomitoria*).

Chinese Mahonia

Mahonia fortunei

Zones: 8 and 9
Size: Expected mature size, 4 x 4 feet
Type: Evergreen
Flowers: Yellow flowers, unimpressive
Bloom Period: Late winter

Light Requirement:

Chinese mahonia is another native of China that is appreciated in the South for its ability to grow in shade. Give it a shady spot with well-drained soil of at least average fertility, and it will grow for you without very much care. While a bit tender where winters are more severe, it should do well over much of the state. The shrub's slow rate of growth means that only limited pruning will ever be necessary. The almost complete absence of pests means Chinese mahonia remains attractive without large expenditures for pesticides. Although the flowers it produces are nice, they are not considered a major feature of this plant.

When to Plant

The cool months of the dormant season are best for planting this shrub. There is latitude for planting at other times of the year, however, because Chinese mahonia is typically planted on shady sites. Expect to provide a bit more care if you choose a warmer time to plant.

Where to Plant

Although this species of mahonia tolerates a little more sun than do most of its relatives, select sites that provide some degree of shade. In more northern areas, seek shaded places that are protected from north and northwest winter winds.

How to Plant

Dig a hole twice as wide and slightly deeper than the rootball. Add a slow-release fertilizer to an enriched soil mix, cover the bottom of the hole, and firm. The mix should be deep enough so that, when the rootball is placed on top of it, the crown of the plant remains at the same level it was previously growing. Add more improved mix until it covers at least half of the rootball, and fill the hole with water or a starter solution. When the water has soaked completely into the ground, fill the hole almost to the top, leaving only a shallow depression to facilitate watering. Build a mini-levee around the depression and then cover the soil with a suitable mulch. A final watering will complete the installation.

Care and Maintenance

After plants are well-established, distribute 2 to 3 ounces (about 1/2 cup) of fertilizer under the branches in late winter. A balanced product such as 8-8-8 or 12-12-12 should work well—or use a slow-release fertilizer according to label directions. Following establishment, size, shape, and density can be controlled by pruning out the more mature canes in the center of the plant in late winter. Water only as often as needed to maintain a reasonable level of soil moisture—which should be infrequently, except during the torrid conditions of summer. Don't be concerned with pest problems until they begin to affect the health or appearance of your plant; pests of this plant are few.

Additional Information

Although many of the other mahonias may grow slightly larger, most are more cold hardy and therefore often a better choice for the colder parts of the state. A characteristic common in various degrees to all mahonias is spine-tipped, leathery leaves.

Additional Cultivars or Species

The Oregon holly grape, *M. aquifolium*, is a closely related species that contains several desirable cultivars. Some of these are 'Compacta' (dwarf), 'Moseri', 'Orange Flame', and 'Vicarii'. Leatherleaf mahonia, *M. bealei*, produces attractive yellow flowers that become grape-like clusters of blue berries . . . and the birds love them.

Cleyera

Ternstroemia gymnanthera

Other Names: Japan Ternstroemia;
Cleyera japonica
Zones: 8 and 9
Size: Expected mature size, 10 x 6 feet
Type: Evergreen
Flowers: Small, fragrant off-white flowers
Bloom Period: Spring to early summer

Light Requirement:

The cleyera—an import from southeast Asia and Japan—is enjoying increased popularity in Louisiana due to its many favorable qualities. It grows very well in either full sun or partial shade and in most soils as long as they are well drained and somewhat acidic. While its small, off-white flowers are borne in abundance and have a nice fragrance, they are usually considered of secondary importance to the relatively thick, dark-green to bronze foliage which has a distinctive metallic appearance. This shrub's fairly slow growth and lack of any major pest problems makes it a low-maintenance choice . . . the very thing for which many weekend gardeners are searching. Due to its mature height, its density of foliage, and its tolerance of pruning, it is well qualified for screening purposes. In short, it is a highly versatile plant that usually lives up to its billing.

When to Plant

Choose the cool months of the dormant season whenever possible. Container-grown plants can be installed successfully at other times of the year, but more care is generally required—especially on full-sun sites.

Where to Plant

Plant the cleyera almost anywhere except in poorly drained soil or in dense shade. It is attractive as a specimen plant; if you use it this way, place it in a highly visible position. Planted in rows, it makes an effective screen. It can also be used to separate use areas within a landscape.

How to Plant

Dig a hole slightly deeper than and twice the width of the rootball. Cover the bottom of the hole with a few inches of a good soil mix fortified with a slow-release fertilizer and firm. Set the plant's root mass on the packed mix and adjust the depth so that the plant can grow at its previous level. Continue to add soil mix until it covers at least half of the rootball. Fill the hole with water or a starter solution and let it drain into the ground. Finish filling the hole with soil until only a slight depression is left around the base of the plant to facilitate watering. Construct a mini-levee around the depression, then mulch and water the whole zone.

Care and Maintenance

Fertilize in late winter with a slow-release fertilizer, an azalea-camellia plant food, or an all-purpose material such as 8-8-8 or 12-12-12. Follow directions for applying the first two or use up to 1 cup per mature plant of the latter; spread under the plant's branches. Water every 3 to 4 weeks in the absence of rain; increase the frequency under torrid summer conditions. After flowering, prune as needed to shape and groom plant or to train for a specific purpose. Pinch off tips of new growth for increased density. Pests are rarely a factor.

Additional Information

Cleyera is suitable as a tub specimen, for poolside plantings, and for adding more variety to a mature, moderately shaded landscape. If you care for the prunings properly, they keep well and may be used as the foliage component in floral designs.

Additional Cultivars or Species

The cultivar 'Variegata' has foliage that is green and white.

Dwarf Yaupon

Ilex vomitoria 'Nana'

Zones: 8 and 9
Size: 2 x 3 feet
Type: Evergreen

Light Requirement:

Dwarf yaupon is perhaps one of the most care-free plants that can be installed in a landscape. It performs well in full sun or partial shade and in both acid and alkaline soils—this latter quality sets it aside from practically all the other hollies. Hot or cold, wet or dry . . . this plant is a survivor. Pests are few, with a leaf miner causing only very minor problems. While dwarf yaupon's average size is relatively small, "dwarf" is a misleading term. Under good conditions, the plant can grow six feet tall with a spread of up to eight feet. Reported maximum size in the New Orleans area, however, is only four feet. Since it handles pruning with ease, dwarf yaupon can be maintained at any size you desire. If a low hedge is needed, this plant is an excellent choice.

When to Plant

Time of planting is not critical, especially with good container stock, but the lower stress conditions of the dormant season are preferable.

Where to Plant

Locate this plant wherever it is needed or will look good, as it tolerates almost any environment. Avoid deep-shade areas.

How to Plant

Dig a hole that is at least twice the width of and slightly deeper than the rootball. Enrich the soil (or a soil mix) with slow-release fertilizer; return several inches of soil to the bottom of the hole and press to firm. Position the rootball and then adjust the depth of the planting by adding or removing backfill. When the plant is at the same level it was previously growing, surround the rootball with additional soil until at least half of the roots are covered. Fill the hole with water or a starter solution. As soon as the water has soaked completely into the ground, fill the hole nearly to ground level with more soil, leaving only a shallow depression around the base of the plant to catch water. Mulch lightly and water.

Care and Maintenance

Fertilize in late winter with an all-purpose fertilizer such as 12-12-12 or 8-8-8; spread about $^{1}/_{2}$ cup evenly under the plant. Orthene 75S, Diazinon, or a product of your choice should take care of any leaf miner problems. Late winter pruning (if needed) just before the onset of new growth is recommended. Pruning at other times for specific purposes is fine. Although there is usually enough rain to meet the minimum water requirement, provide water during extended dry spells, especially during periods of summer heat stress.

Additional Information

This plant bears no fruit. It is attractive when maintained as an individual, low-mounded plant in groupings of several plants. Properly sheared, it can present a formal look.

Additional Cultivars or Species

'Stokes Dwarf' and 'Schillings Dwarf' are other dwarf selections of *I. vomitoria* that have a smaller mature size than 'Nana'.

Fatsia

Fatsia japonica

Other Names: Japanese Aralia; *Aralia sieboldii* and *A. japonica*
Zones: 8 and 9
Size: Expected mature size, 5 x 4 feet
Type: Evergreen
Flowers: Off-white
Bloom Period: Late fall

Light Requirement:

The fatsia's very large, nearly foot-and-a-half-wide leaves present a tropical look that is hard to find in a temperate zone setting. It is a good shade plant that thrives in south Louisiana, but it also grows satisfactorily in protected locations in the northern tier of parishes. Provided with a moist, acidic, well-drained, organically rich soil, the fatsia should perform beyond expectations. This plant does have one major problem. It is quite susceptible to damage from a number of insects that, if not controlled, can kill it. In the final analysis, the fatsia's merits far outweigh its problems, so if you wish to create an exotic look in some part of your landscape, be sure to include this plant in your plans.

When to Plant

Plant containerized plants at any time of the year, but favor the late winter and spring seasons. Hot-weather plantings nearly always require extra care.

Where to Plant

Plant in shady, protected locations to minimize winter injury. Tub culture is possible; if you grow it this way, fatsia can become a houseplant during the winter months if it gets enough direct sunlight. Fatsia makes an excellent poolside plant.

How to Plant

Dig a hole twice the width of and slightly deeper than the rootball. Cover the bottom of the hole with a few inches of a good-quality soil mix (enriched with a slow-release fertilizer), and press until firm. Place the roots of the plant on top of the mix and adjust the level so that the plant can continue to grow at the same depth. Fill in more soil mix until it covers at least the lower half of the rootball. Add water or a starter solution to the hole and let it soak completely into the ground. Then fill the hole almost to the top, leaving just a slight trench to facilitate watering. Surround this trench with a mini-levee, cover root area with an organic mulch, and complete the installation with a thorough watering.

Care and Maintenance

Fertilize these plants in late winter with an all-purpose plant food such as 8-8-8; distribute no more than $1/2$ cup around the base of the plant in a wide band, and carefully blend the material with the soil surface. You can also use a slow-release product; follow label instructions. Keep plants well watered on a regular basis, at least every 10 to 14 days. Prune lightly each year to stimulate new growth, remove insect and other damage, encourage open density, and maintain a nice form. Use dormant oils, miticides, and other suitable materials to control scale insects, mealybugs, aphids, and spider mites. If you are uncomfortable using pesticides, seek advice about how to handle particular problems from your county agent or other local expert.

Additional Information

Leaf scorch can be serious where there is insufficient shade. Make major cuts on old plants to invigorate them.

Additional Cultivars or Species

The cultivar 'Moseri' makes a lower, more compact form, but it is difficult to find. 'Variegata' has leaves with white or yellow edges.

Flowering Quince

Chaenomeles speciosa

Zones: 8 and 9
Size: 8 x 6 feet
Type: Deciduous
Flowers: White and pastel flowers; yellow fruits
Bloom Period: Early spring

Light Requirement:

The flowering quince came to the United States from Asia and is grown nationwide. In Louisiana it is best suited to the cooler, less humid parts of the state because of a leaf disease that results in premature defoliation. Otherwise, few pests find flowering quince an attractive host. Many gardeners choose to plant flowering quince—with its refreshing flowers of white or pastel hues—because it is often the first plant to usher in the spring season. Since flowers form on the new wood that develops after pruning, you can prune at intervals until midsummer; this will give you different sizes of flowering stems the following spring. You don't have to worry about cold damage to this plant; the species grows at latitudes far above those which run through Louisiana. While flowering quince is not especially choosy about where it grows it doesn't like poorly drained soil. It makes a good hedge or barrier plant with its dense mass of stems and its contingent of thorns. The fruits of this plant are edible, and sometimes made into jelly. Harvest after they turn yellowish-green or yellow in the fall. Fruit will be few in number, however, unless several plants are present for cross-pollination.

When to Plant

Select a dormant-season month as first choice, but the few weeks shortly before or after this period will work as well. Container stock may be planted during warmer times, but more care is required.

Where to Plant

Plant where a hedge or screen is needed—or anywhere else you wish, as long as the plant will not be growing in deep shade and the soil drains reasonably well.

How to Plant

Dig a generously sized hole twice the width of and slightly deeper than the rootball. Enrich the soil with a slow-release fertilizer and return a small amount to the bottom of the hole; press to firm. Position the rootball and then adjust the depth of the planting by adding or removing backfill. When the plant is at the same level it was previously growing, surround the rootball with additional soil until at least half of the roots are covered. Fill the hole with water or a starter solution. As soon as the water has soaked completely into the ground, fill the hole nearly to ground level with more soil, leaving only a shallow depression around the base of the plant to catch water. Apply mulch around the plant and water.

Care and Maintenance

Fertilize in late winter with an all-purpose fertilizer such as 8-8-8; spread under branches at the rate of 1/2 cup per square yard of ground surface. Prune after flowering to maintain size and form by cutting out selected stems of old wood near ground level. Prune at intervals through spring and early summer to generate more flowering stems for the next spring's show. Extra watering is rarely needed.

Additional Information

Prune branches in heavy bud and put them in a vase of water to help create a spring-like atmosphere. The buds will open and lend a note of cheer on a dreary winter day.

Additional Cultivars or Species

C. japonica is a well-known species that is better suited to a colder climate than Louisiana. As this is a relatively old species, there are a host of cultivars. Some of these are 'Apple Blossom', 'Cameo', 'Snow', 'Texas Scarlet', and 'Simonii'.

French Mulberry

Callicarpa americana

Other Name: American Beautyberry
Zones: 8 and 9
Size: Expected mature size, 8 x 6 feet
Type: Deciduous
Flowers: Inconspicuous (there are clusters of purple berries)
Bloom Period: Berries in late summer and early winter

Light Requirement:

The French mulberry is a Southern native often found growing in or at the edge of wooded areas. Although its flowers are small and somewhat inconspicuous, they are followed by clusters of pea-sized, purple berries spaced at intervals along the stems (the berries grow only on new wood). Some improved cultivars or varieties of other species have white berries. The native species is very hardy in our state and requires no special protection in the winter. This species isn't at all picky about where it grows, but it does seem to favor acid soil. Those searching for a low-maintenance plant would be pleased with the French mulberry. It has few, if any, pest problems, and wildlife fanciers will delight in the birds it attracts. Although considered a short-lived plant—possibly no more than a dozen years—it is easily propagated from its own seed. It may be difficult to find at nurseries, though it is fairly easy to find its relatives.

When to Plant

Nursery stock grown in containers may be set out at any time. Plants installed in the landscape during summer heat stress will require more care, however, than those planted during the dormant season.

Where to Plant

Berry production is often heavier in full sun. Light shade at the edge of other mass plantings is also an excellent place—especially if the location allows you to watch the birds dine on the mulberry's fruits.

How to Plant

Dig a hole twice as wide and slightly deeper than the rootball; prune or slash roots if the plant is root-bound. Improve soil removed from the hole with a slow-release fertilizer and cover the bottom of the hole with several inches of it before placing the plant in the hole. Adjust the amount of soil at the bottom so that the plant can continue growing at the same level it was growing previously. Fill in around the roots with soil until half or more of the root system is covered; then fill the hole with water. After the water has soaked completely into the ground, finish filling the hole with soil. Leave a shallow depression around the base of the plant to facilitate watering. Mulch well and water.

Care and Maintenance

Little care is required. For more vigor and accelerated growth, fertilize in late winter with an all-purpose fertilizer such as 8-8-8; spread about 1/2 cup in a broad band under the plant. For fully mature specimens, increase the amount to no more than 1 cup. Prune only to control size and form; pruning must be done in late winter before flowering, or there will be no berries in the fall. Rain generally supplies all of the water a plant requires. If severe wilting does occur, give the plant a drink. Pest control is rarely, if ever, necessary.

Additional Information

Don't be alarmed if the yellow fall leaves hit the ground quite some time before cold weather arrives. This is just the plant's way of showing off its beautiful fruit. Incidentally, the bare, berry-laden branches are attractive items that can be used in arrangements.

Additional Cultivars or Species

The native species variety, 'Lactea', bears white berries. 'Profusion' is a heavy-fruiting variety of *C. bodinieri* that bears lilac-colored fruit. Both 'Albifructus' (*C. dichotoma*) and 'Leucocarpa' (*C. japonica*) are white-fruited types. Related species include Bodinier beautyberry, *C. bodinieri*; purple beautyberry, *C. dichotoma*; Japanese beautyberry, *C. japonica*.

Garden Hydrangea

Hydrangea macrophylla

Other Names: Common Hydrangea; *H. hortensia, H. opuloides, H. otaksa*
Zones: 8 and 9
Size: Expected mature size, 4 x 4 feet
Type: Deciduous
Flowers: Color varies—blue or pink, depending on soil acidity
Bloom Period: Early to midsummer

Light Requirement:

The garden hydrangea performs satisfactorily in Louisiana, but it really prefers a cooler climate. Nevertheless, it remains relatively popular and is planted statewide. While garden hydrangea will bloom in moderate shade, a sunnier site gives better results. Specimens planted on northern exposures always seem to do a little better than average, so save a spot in such a location if you wish to have the greatest success with this species. One interesting characteristic of this plant is its ability to change flower color. In strongly acid soil, flowers are blue . . . sometimes intensely blue. Sweeten the soil with enough lime and flower color will change to pink. During the transition, flowers may be almost purple. Garden hydrangea's shallow root system is often inadequate in summer heat, so watering is important. Diseases and insects are seldom a concern, though these can be a problem in the more humid areas.

When to Plant

Select the dormant season to plant garden hydrangeas. Avoid the summer months altogether.

Where to Plant

Because of its shallow roots, garden hydrangea should be planted in moist, fertile, well-drained soil. Some light shade and a northern exposure are also prime ingredients for the successful cultivation of garden hydrangea this far south.

How to Plant

Dig a hole at least twice the width of and slightly deeper than the rootball. Cover the bottom of the hole a few inches deep with a good-quality soil mix fortified with a slow-release fertilizer; press to firm. Place the rootball on the surface of the packed mix and adjust the amount of soil so that the plant may continue to grow at its previous level. Put more mix in the hole around roots until half or more of the rootball is covered, then add water to fill the space. When the water has soaked completely into the ground, continue adding mix until just a shallow depression remains at the base of the plant. Build a mini-levee around the depression, apply a mulch, and water.

Care and Maintenance

Fertilize in late winter with an all-purpose plant food such as 12-12-12; use $^{1}/_{2}$ cup per square yard of bed surface. Spread fertilizer evenly under the bush and cover with a light mulch. For blue flower color, use $^{1}/_{4}$ cup of aluminum sulfate periodically until the desired hue is reached. For pink flowers, add lime in small increments to make the soil alkaline—this may take up to 2 years. Proper pruning techniques are important. Prune out taller stems to maintain a good form and to stimulate newer, more productive canes. Always leave some of the taller terminals. Pruning must be done immediately after the main bloom cycle in order to not sacrifice the next year's flowers. The wise gardener would do well to place some drip irrigation lines under these plants so that the frequent summer watering required will be less trouble.

Additional Information

Garden hydrangea makes nice dried arrangements. Cut long stems on the large flower "balls" as they begin to dry; hang them upside down in an airy place to finish drying.

Additional Cultivars or Species

H. quercifolia, the oakleaf hydrangea, will be discussed independently. Cultivars of *H. macrophylla* that may be of interest are 'Forever Pink', 'Goliath', 'Pia' (always pink), and 'Sister Therese'. A subspecies contains a cultivar known as 'Preziosa' that initially has pink flowers; when temperatures begin to cool, the flowers become more deeply colored.

Gardenia

Gardenia jasminoides

Other Name: Cape Jasmine
Zones: 8 and 9
Size: Expected mature size, 6 x 5 feet
Type: Evergreen
Flowers: Large, fragrant, creamy-white flowers
Bloom Period: Early summer

Light Requirement:

Gardenias are native to China but are very much at home in Louisiana. With proper care, their large, evergreen, glossy leaves can be attractive throughout the year—but there's a catch. Several insects call this plant home and many of them deposit a substance called "honeydew" on the foliage—a sticky coating that becomes the base upon which sooty mold fungus forms. Although the fungus does not enter the leaf, it blocks sunlight and makes the plant look unhealthy. The gardenia blooms in early summer and may have sporadic flowering for several weeks. Gardenia blossoms are nicely sized (three to four inches in diameter), creamy-white in color, and so fragrant that you may think you are in a perfume factory when you are near a blooming plant. Not surprisingly, gardenias are popular corsage flowers. Unfortunately, these flowers have only a brief period of beauty because insects such as thrips quickly turn the flowers brown. Gardenias perform exceptionally well in fertile, moist, acidic, well-drained soils generously supplied with humus; they also require well-lit conditions. Effective insect control is important. Iron chlorosis, a nutritional deficiency, must sometimes be addressed.

When to Plant

Gardenias are best planted in the dormant season, but they may be planted at other times of the year if you are willing to give them more care.

Where to Plant

Choose either full-sun or semi-shaded spots, but make sure that soil conditions are favorable. Whiskey barrel halves or other sizable containers are good for tub culture, and specimens can be used to decorate patios, decks, etc.

How to Plant

Dig a hole twice the width of and slightly deeper than the rootball. Cover the bottom of the hole with a few inches of a good-quality soil mix fortified with a slow-release fertilizer and press to firm. Set rootball on packed mix and adjust the amount of soil to allow plant to continue growing at its previous level. Place additional mix around rootball until half or more of it is covered. Fill the hole with water and allow it to soak completely into the ground. Finish filling the hole with soil until just a shallow depression remains around base of plant, apply a thick mulch, and water thoroughly.

Care and Maintenance

An azalea-camellia food is a desirable fertilizer choice, but you may also choose a slow-release fertilizer or an all-purpose fertilizer such as 12-12-12. Apply fertilizer in late winter using label instructions. Apply all-purpose materials at the rate of 4 ounces per square yard of ground covered by the plant. Some gardeners claim benefits from additional monthly applications of liquid plant foods during the growing season. Special iron fertilizers may be needed if iron chlorosis becomes a problem. Supply water frequently with a drip irrigation unit. Pruning is best done just after the major bloom in early to midsummer. Use dormant or superior oils for scale insects; when applied following label directions, Orthene 75S and Talstar usually work well for most other insects. Diseases are seldom a concern.

Additional Information

Remove spent flowers regularly as they detract from the appearance of the plant.

Additional Cultivars or Species

Nice cultivars of *G. jasminoides* worthy of planting include 'August Beauty', 'Chuck Hayes', 'First Love', 'Mystery', and 'Veitchii'. 'Radicans' is a low, sprawling form with much smaller leaves and flowers.

Glossy Abelia

Abelia × grandiflora

Zones: 8 and 9
Size: Mature size, about 6 feet by 6 feet (height x width)
Type: Semi-evergreen
Bloom Period: Flowers for much of growing season

Light Requirement:

Glossy abelias are shrubs that have been on the scene for many years, but they are not appreciated and used as often as they should be in Louisiana. Their long period of blossoming covers much of the summer season and provides almost uninterrupted color to fill in the gaps between the bloom cycles of other plant species. While the plant's little bell-shaped flowers could not be termed spectacular, its show of color may have little competition at times during the summer. This semi-evergreen plant has few pests and thus is considered a low-maintenance shrub. Due to its expected mature size and the fact that it can be shaped into a tight, dense form, glossy abelia is a very good choice for a screening plant or for use as a noise barrier. Several dwarf cultivars make this species a quite versatile shrub.

When to Plant

If there is a choice, pick a dormant-season month for planting. Container plants may be set out at any time, but more care is required in summer.

Where to Plant

For best flowering, select a full-sun location where possible. Dwarf cultivars are useful as bed borders for larger plants or to line drives. Glossy abelia adapts to a wide variety of soil types.

How to Plant

Dig a hole that is somewhat deeper than and twice as wide as the plant's root system. Place 3 or 4 inches of an improved commercial soil mix in the bottom of the hole and press until quite firm. You will have added enough when the top of the rootball is near the surface of the surrounding ground while the bottom rests on the firmed soil mix. Use more mix to bring the level up to mid-way on the rootball, then add water or a starter solution to thoroughly moisten the contents of the hole. The hole may then be filled with additional mix. Leave a shallow depression around the plant and create a mini-levee around this depression to facilitate watering. Application of an organic mulch around the plant and a final thorough watering should complete the job. In multiple plantings, space full-sized cultivars 5 or 6 feet apart, dwarfs 2 to 3 feet apart.

Care and Maintenance

Fertilize with a balanced fertilizer such as 8-8-8 in late winter; use 3 to 4 ounces (1/3 to 1/2 cup) in a broad band around each plant after plants are well-established. A tablespoon or so of a high-nitrogen material such as ammonium nitrate may be spread evenly under branches in midsummer to increase plant vigor. Near the end of the dormant season, prune out about 1/3 of the old canes and any dead wood at ground level to remove unsightly parts and to encourage new stems. Wet soil to a 3- or 4-inch depth every 7 to 10 days during periods of heat stress or no rain.

Additional Information

If plants growing in alkaline soil show signs of iron chlorosis, treat the soil with an iron fertilizer and add a little sulfur to the soil during the cool season.

Additional Cultivars or Species

A. chinensis is similar to *A. grandiflora*. Dwarf cultivars of glossy abelia include 'Chreech's Dwarf', 'Edward Goucher', 'Prostrate', and 'Sherwoodii'. 'Francis Mason' is a cultivar that has yellow-variegated foliage.

Indian Hawthorn

Raphiolepis indica

Other Names: India Hawthorn, Raphiolepis
Zones: 8 and 9
Size: Expected mature size, 5 x 4 feet (dwarfs smaller)
Type: Evergreen
Flowers: Small, white or pink
Bloom Period: Massive spring bloom

Light Requirement:

Over the past two decades, Indian hawthorns (some references say "India" hawthorns) have become one of the most widely planted evergreens in Louisiana. Their massive bloom of small pink or white flowers resembles the bloom style of azaleas and occurs at about the same time each spring. While they are often used as a substitute for azaleas in alkaline soil areas, they grow well in any well-drained soil that is fertile and reasonably moist. Most varieties and cultivars make plants of medium size, but several dwarf cultivars are also available. Whenever a plant gets too large or needs an adjustment of form, it may be pruned to achieve the gardener's goal. Pruning is best accomplished just after blossom time. Particularly in the most humid parts of the state, disease and insect pests inflict serious damage. Gardeners in the New Orleans area commonly report major problems with fungal leaf spot, root rot, fire blight, scale insects, and aphids. Pests seem much less serious in the drier parts of the state where primarily the leaf spot fungus renders plants unhealthy and unattractive. It is wise to choose cultivars with great care if you reside in a more humid section of Louisiana, for some definitely do better than others under those stressful conditions.

When to Plant

Choose a dormant-season month if possible, but planting into the early summer is generally successful. Hotter conditions mean greater care will be necessary.

Where to Plant

Full-sun sites with well-drained soil are ideal.

How to Plant

Dig a hole twice the width of and slightly deeper than the rootball. Cover the bottom of the hole with a few inches of soil mix fortified with a slow-release fertilizer; press to firm. Set the plant in the hole and adjust the depth by adding or removing small amounts of soil mix until the plant is at the correct depth and can continue growing at its former level. Put in more mix until half or more of the rootball is covered. Then fill the space above with water and let it soak completely into the ground. Continue to add mix until only a shallow depression surrounds the base of the plant; mulch and water. A mini-levee may be built around the depression to facilitate watering if necessary.

Care and Maintenance

Fertilize after flowering with an all-purpose fertilizer such as 12-12-12; spread evenly under branches at the rate of 1/2 cup per square yard of ground. Prune for form and/or size control after blossoms have faded. Deep-water every 2 to 3 weeks during heat stress, but don't wet the foliage. Gardeners in humid areas will generally find that the frequent use of pesticides is necessary. Choose products with which you've had success or consult your county agent or another knowledgeable person for the best product for your specific problem.

Additional Information

Good air circulation, full sun, and irrigation that doesn't wet the foliage help reduce diseases. Because of their salt-spray tolerance, these plants are suitable for coastal use.

Additional Cultivars or Species

Yeddo hawthorn, *R. umbellata,* has rounded leaves, but is quite similar to *R. indica*. Popular cultivars of the latter include 'Ballerina'*, 'Jack Evans'*, 'Enchantress'*, 'Springtime', 'Clara', 'Janice'*, and 'Majestic Beauty'. Note: The cultivars marked with an asterisk (*) have a poor performance record in New Orleans. 'Snow', 'Clara', and 'Alba' have proven more dependable in that region.

Japanese Viburnum

Viburnum japonicum

Other Names: Wax Leaf Viburnum, *Viburnum macrophyllum*
Zones: 8 and 9
Size: 12 x 8 feet
Type: Evergreen
Flowers: Off-white clusters (red fruits)
Bloom Period: Spring

Light Requirement:

As the common name indicates, this is a Japanese native. Its mature size, rapid growth, and evergreen nature make it a great choice for use as a screening plant or hedge. And its relative freedom from most pest problems doesn't hurt its popularity with the practical gardener. Thrips seem to be its worst insect enemy, but diseases are uncommon—especially in the less-humid areas of Louisiana. Like most plants, it does best where there is plenty of light and the soil is fertile, well-drained, and kept reasonably moist. Flowers of the plant are borne in clusters and are an off-white color. These may be followed by red fruits in the fall—attractive, but generally just scattered over the plant. I would have to rate the flowers and fruits of secondary importance to the nice, shiny, coarse leaves. Don't be surprised if you see it tagged *V. macrophyllum,* as this botanical name is still occasionally used in the trade.

When to Plant

Although healthy container plants may be set out at any time of the year, broadleaf evergreens like the Japanese viburnum fare best when planted sometime during the dormant season. This allows them to get established before the stress of summer heat arrives. The warmer the temperatures at planting time, the more extra care will be necessary.

Where to Plant

Choose full- to part-sun locations on well-drained sites. Placement may also depend upon intended use (i.e., to screen out unpleasant views, objects, or structures).

How to Plant

Dig a hole that is at least twice the width of and slightly deeper than the rootball. Enrich the soil (or a soil mix) with a slow-release fertilizer and return a small amount to the bottom of the hole; press to firm. Position the rootball and then adjust the depth of the planting by adding or removing backfill. When the plant is at the same level it was previously growing, surround the rootball with additional soil until one-half to three-quarters of the roots are covered. Fill the hole with water or a starter solution. As soon as the water has soaked completely into the ground, fill the hole nearly to ground level with more soil, leaving only a shallow depression around the base of the plant to catch water. Apply a suitable mulch and then water thoroughly.

Care and Maintenance

Fertilize in late winter with 2 cups of 12-12-12 or similar fertilizer for full-size plants (proportionally less for smaller specimens); spread evenly under the branches. Prune only as needed to maintain desirable form and density or to remove damaged parts. This, too, is a late-winter chore or one to be done just after flowering. Some fruit loss can be expected. If thrips attack, spray with Orthene 75S or another material of your choice. Water sufficiently often to maintain reasonably moist soil.

Additional Information

Large plants may be pruned into tree form if desired.

Additional Cultivars or Species

The hybrids 'Chippewa' and 'Huron' are more cold hardy than the species but may not be available in the state. There are many other species of viburnums and numerous cultivars within those species. Selections from *V. odoratissimum*, *V. suspensum*, and *V. tinus* seem to do well in the drier areas of the state. Unlike *V. japonicum*, these species are bothered with several pest problems in the humid regions.

Japanese Yew

Podocarpus macrophyllus

Other Names: Southern Yew, Yew Pine
Zones: 8 and 9
Size: 15 x 5 feet
Type: Evergreen
Flowers: Yellow for male; green for female
Bloom Period: Spring

Light Requirement:

The Japanese yew is an Asian import that has been well-received by Louisiana gardeners. While somewhat exacting in its soil requirements, it has a lot to offer because it can be used in a variety of ways. It is an ideal plant for use as a topiary or espalier, and it makes an excellent tub specimen—both indoors and out. Pest pressure in the drier areas of the state is either low or non-existent. In the more humid regions, the Japanese yew is bothered by a particular aphid and a leafspot disease. It should never be planted in heavy clay or poorly drained soil because of root rot and stunting possibilities. If you need a dense, dark-green plant for a tight space—and can provide all the required environmental conditions—this plant should definitely be a candidate.

When to Plant

Plant the Japanese yew during the dormant season, if at all possible. Planting at other times of the year will require somewhat more care. Avoid planting in the hot summer months.

Where to Plant

A site that offers well-drained, sandy-loam soil and partial shade is the best choice for this plant. Use it on an eastern or southern wall as an espalier or as a topiary for a focal point—or plant it in a tub or other large container for use on a patio or porch.

How to Plant

Dig a hole that is twice the depth and 3 times the width of the rootball. Enrich the soil (or a soil mix) with organic material and a slow-release fertilizer; return several inches of soil to the bottom of the hole and press to firm. Position the rootball and then adjust the depth of the planting by adding or removing backfill. When the plant is at the same level it was previously growing, surround the rootball with additional soil until at least half of the roots are covered. Fill the hole with water or a starter solution. As soon as the water has soaked completely into the ground, fill the hole nearly to ground level with more soil, leaving only a shallow depression around the base of the plant to catch water. Mulch the ground around the plant and water thoroughly.

Care and Maintenance

Fertilize in late winter with an all-purpose fertilizer (both 12-12-12 and 8-8-8 are suitable); spread 1/3 cup evenly over each square yard of surface area covered by the plant—or use a slow-release product, following label directions. Should you have pest problems, treat with materials of your choice or seek the advice of your county agent or other local expert. Prune and clip to develop or maintain chosen form during most of the year (except July, August, and September). Provide water as often as necessary to maintain a reasonable level of soil moisture. Typically, little watering is required during the winter and spring months, but frequent watering may be dictated by summer weather. When irrigating, wet soil to a depth of 4 inches.

Additional Information

Although a relative, the Japanese yew is not a true yew. Plants are dioecious. Mature plants are easily converted to tree form. True yews (*Taxus* species) are not commonly planted in Louisiana because they do not like our hot climate.

Additional Cultivars or Species

P. m. 'Maki' has extra-slow growth and a smaller mature size. 'Prostrata' is a very low-growing variety.

Mock Orange

Philadelphus coronarius

Other Name: Sweet Mock Orange
Zones: 8 and 9
Size: 10 x 6 feet
Type: Deciduous
Flowers: Off-white, usually fragrant flowers
Bloom Period: Late spring

Light Requirement:

Of European and Asian descent, the mock orange is found not just in Louisiana, but across the nation—which is a good clue to its hardiness. The mock orange grows relatively fast in most soils and in either full sun or partial shade. While a couple of pests may pay it a call in the humid climate of south Louisiana, this long-lived shrub is relatively pest-free in the drier areas of the state. Gardeners searching for a low-maintenance plant should be quite happy with the mock orange. An added bonus is its creamy or off-white flowers of 1½- to two-inch size. Several cultivars have a rather nice fragrance and may be single, semi-double, or double. Yet another interesting feature is the orange bark that naturally peels off the plant's stems. Since the single-flowered types usually have four petals and bear a strong resemblance to the blossoms of a flowering dogwood, at least one species, *P. grandiflora*, is often called the "English Dogwood."

When to Plant

Plant mock oranges any time during the dormant season. Container stock may be set out at other times of the year, but more care is required for successful establishment during hot periods.

Where to Plant

Avoid planting in poorly drained soil, but plant almost anywhere else except deep shade. They are suitable for background plants, screening plants, and for a variety of other uses.

How to Plant

Dig a hole twice as large as the rootball. Use soil or soil mixes (either should be enriched with a slow-release fertilizer) to fill around roots after the plant is adjusted in the hole to grow at its previous level.

Pack soil firmly around roots to minimize sinking as soil settles. When roots are at least half-covered with soil, fill the empty hole space with water and let it soak completely into the soil; this aids in the settling process. Leave a shallow depression around the base of the plant to collect water over the root system. A mini-levee around the depression can improve effectiveness in holding water and may be an asset if planting during the hot months.

Care and Maintenance

In late winter use 1/2 to 1 cup of an all-purpose fertilizer (such as 8-8-8 or 12-12-12) for mature plants—or use a slow-release fertilizer as directed on label. Spread evenly under branches. Prune out older portions of a plant just after flowering to control size and induce development of productive stems. Old plants may be cut back to ground level for complete rejuvenation. Although problems with leaf miners and a fungal leaf spot disease have been observed in the more humid climate of south Louisiana, the plant is almost pest-free in most parts of the state. Use wide-spectrum pesticides for control or seek advice from a county agent or other local expert regarding the use of more specific materials.

Additional Information

This plant's bloom period is commonly later than many other shrubs which, in effect, extends the spring-flowering season.

Additional Cultivars or Species

Varieties that have been satisfactory in the southern part of the state include 'Primuliflorus', 'Deutziflorus', 'Nanus', and 'Duplex'. The last three are dwarfs. 'Aureus' has yellow foliage, turning yellow-green in summer. One well-known selection of *P. lemoinei* is 'Enchantment'.

Nandina

Nandina domestica

Other Names: Heavenly Bamboo, Sacred Bamboo
Zones: 8 and 9
Size: 6 x 4 feet
Type: Evergreen
Flowers: Small white flowers that become grape-like clusters of red berries
Bloom Period: Late spring

Light Requirement:

The nandina is a tough import from the Orient. It is very comfortable living in Louisiana—even in the often oppressive humidity of New Orleans. It is an extremely low-maintenance plant—there is only one annual chore and sometimes even that doesn't get done: it is the suggested annual pruning to control size, density, and (to a small extent) form. So, busy gardeners, take note. When planted in full sun or light shade, nandina produces an abundance of almost cone-shaped flower heads that are followed in the winter season by grape-like clusters of bright-red berries . . . very eye catching. Deeper shade will curb flowering to some degree, but the plant will still be attractive. Although performance may be slightly improved in a fertile, moist soil with good drainage, the shrub does a remarkable job of delivering beauty no matter what the circumstances. Nandina is virtually pest-free.

When to Plant

Container stock can be planted at any time. It is best to avoid planting during the heat stress of summer, however.

Where to Plant

Plant nandina anywhere you desire. Just remember—heavy shade reduces flower production, and that means fewer of those clusters of pretty red shiny berries in the winter months when color is at a premium. Nandina makes an attractive container planting.

How to Plant

Dig a hole substantially larger than the rootball. Try to set the plant at the same level it was growing previously and fill in around roots with an improved soil mix. When soil mix covers at least half of the rootball, fill the empty space above with water and let that soak completely into the soil. Finish filling the hole, leaving only a shallow depression around the base of the plant to concentrate water when rain falls. If soil is very sandy, mix in a small amount of an organic material (particularly if you are not using a potting mix for the planting process). Mulch around the plant and water.

Care and Maintenance

Minimum fertilization is needed; apply in late winter. Try using a slow-release product as directed by label instructions. When plants reach the height you desire, begin a program of removing one-third of the tallest canes at their base each year in late winter. If possible, choose canes scattered throughout the crown. Normally there is sufficient rain to meet the needs of this species; should drought conditions persist, occasionally give the plants a deep soaking.

Additional Information

A tub specimen of nandina can help intensify an Oriental appearance where a Japanese flair is desired in the landscape.

Additional Cultivars or Species

Cultivars worthy of consideration include 'Gulf Stream', 'Compacta', 'Alba' (white berries), and 'Moyers Red' (suitable only to north Louisiana). Desirable dwarf cultivars are 'Harbour Dwarf', 'Nana', and 'Pygmaea'.

Oakleaf Hydrangea

Hydrangea quercifolia

Zones: 8 and 9
Size: Expected mature size, 8 x 5 feet
Type: Deciduous
Flowers: Large, elongated clusters of white
Bloom Period: Late spring; early summer

Light Requirement:

Unlike its relative, the garden hydrangea (which hails from the Orient), the oakleaf hydrangea is a native of the southeastern United States. It has many of the same cultural requirements as the garden hydrangea: it likes well-drained, acid soil that is reasonably fertile; it does best in light to moderate shade; and it needs plenty of water when conditions are dry. The only major problem it seems to have is a root rot that is caused by a fungal organism. While the flower heads are large (similar to the garden hydrangea), and appear at the tips of the previous season's stems, they are much more elongated compared to the more rounded, ball-shaped flower heads of the common garden hydrangea. Additional features of this species are its exfoliating bark and dark fall leaves that take on red and purple tones. These leaves look like over-sized oak leaves.

When to Plant

The dormant season is the best planting time; late fall and mid-spring are second best. Avoid summer plantings.

Where to Plant

Plant in partially shaded areas with fertile, well-drained soil.

How to Plant

Dig a hole twice the width of and slightly deeper than the rootball. Cover the bottom of the hole with a few inches of a good soil mix enriched with a slow-release fertilizer; press to firm. Place the rootball on the surface of the mix and adjust the depth by adding or removing small quantities of the mix until the plant is set at its previous level. Begin filling around the roots and continue until half or more of the roots are covered. Then add enough water to fill the space above the roots. When water has soaked completely into the ground, continue to add mix until only a shallow depression surrounds the base of the plant. Build a mini-levee around the depression, apply a mulch, and water.

Care and Maintenance

Fertilize in late winter with an all-purpose plant food such as 12-12-12. Spread it evenly under the plant and cover with a light mulch. Use $^1/_2$ cup per square yard of bed surface—or use a slow-release fertilizer according to label directions. Prune after flowering to maintain a nice form and to stimulate new growth. A few flowers may be left to dry on the plant; harvest them later for decorative uses. Hydrangeas need a lot of water; to make watering easier, place drip irrigation lines under the plants and cover with a natural mulch (which the plants need anyway). Turn the system on frequently to keep soil reasonably moist, but don't overwater. Pest problems are few.

Additional Information

Avoid planting this species in heavy clay soil, for the plant will do poorly or die in that situation. Plants that receive some amount of morning sun tend to flower more freely. The oakleaf hydrangea makes a nice container specimen for use on a shady patio or terrace.

Additional Cultivars or Species

Cultivars of interest include 'Snow Queen', 'Snowflake', 'Harmony', and 'Roanoke'.

Oleander

Nerium oleander

Zones: 8 and 9
Size: 15 x 10 feet
Type: Evergreen
Flowers: Variety, including red, pink, and salmon
Bloom Period: Mid-spring into summer

Light Requirement: Full sun

While this shrub is indigenous to the Mediterranean area, it has adapted to Louisiana's varying climatic conditions admirably. Its one weakness is its inability to handle the cold temperatures of winter; moderate to severe damage to the plant occurs whenever temperatures drop into the mid-teens or lower. Thus, the further north in the state it is planted, the greater the chance of its being injured by winter weather. Although plants may be totally killed by the cold, usually they only die back to the ground surface—leaving viable roots to push up new stems the following spring. Poor soil, a shortage of moisture, air pollution, salt spray . . . you name it and the oleander will hang in there. This is a plant that practically thrives on neglect. Crown gall disease and a few aphids may inflict injury. The species embraces cultivars that provide a relatively wide choice of flower colors; flowers are borne in abundance from mid-spring well into the summer months, with sporadic blooms appearing in to mid and late summer. Flower production will suffer, however, whenever plants are placed in any amount of shade. One fact about oleander should be remembered—every part of the plant is highly poisonous! Keep it and its prunings away from children, pets, and livestock.

When to Plant

Due to its toughness, container stock may be planted at any convenient time. Do try to avoid planting during periods of high summer temperatures; establishment at that time can be a bit more difficult and requires a little more care.

Where to Plant

Plant anywhere there is no shade. It is unwise, however, to plant oleander near any area that is inhabited by livestock.

How to Plant

Dig a hole of greater size than the rootball and cover the bottom of the hole with loose, improved soil; press to firm. Set the plant in the hole and adjust hole depth with additional soil so that the plant can grow at its previous level. Surround the roots with the improved backfill and cover at least half of the rootball; add water to the hole to melt the fill around the roots. After the water has soaked in, continue adding soil until the hole is full, but leave a shallow depression around the base of the plant to catch rain. Mulch the ground surface around the plant and water again.

Care and Maintenance

If increased vigor is desired, use about 1/2 cup of all-purpose fertilizer (8-8-8 is suitable) spread evenly under plant in late winter. Prune away any winter-damaged stems in late winter to stimulate new spring growth. Should that mean cutting the plant off just above the ground, do it! Established plants seldom need any extra water. Pest problems occur infrequently, but take appropriate action if necessary.

Additional Information

In the northern part of the state, plant oleander shrubs on southern exposures to reduce possibility of winter injury. Do not use the wood of this species in *any* capacity associated with food preparation or consumption. If you must burn oleander prunings, stay out of the smoke—it can cause painful irritation.

Additional Cultivars or Species

There are many sizes and flower colors among the various cultivars. Some of the better ones include 'Sister Agnes', 'Mrs. Roeding', 'Hawaii', 'Hardy Red', and 'Sugar Land'. 'Petite Pink' and 'Petite Salmon' are a couple of nice dwarfs. Other cultivars are 'Little Red', 'Casablanca', 'Ruby Lace', and 'Tangier'.

Pineapple Guava

Feijoa sellowiana

Zones: 8 and 9
Size: 8 x 6 feet
Type: Evergreen
Flowers: Partially edible flowers, edible fruit
Bloom Period: Early summer

Light Requirement:

This South American plant has found considerable favor with many Louisiana gardeners. Gardeners in the northern portions of the state have seemed reluctant to plant it—possibly out of the fear that it is incapable of withstanding cold winter weather. That fear seems unfounded—several nice, relatively mature specimens grow in the Shreveport area and these have endured several winter days of mid-teen temperatures. These plants are endowed with some interesting characteristics that capture the attention of most who see them in bloom for the first time. Their inch-and-a-half-wide flowers have a crowded center of bright red stamens that are long and showy. These are surrounded with puffy petals that are white, but appear to have been slightly stained with some purple ink. The thickened petals are edible and can be eaten on the spot, or they may be mixed into salads for a special touch. The attractive flowers are followed by small fruits, also edible, most commonly made into jelly. Fruit set is poor under humid conditions, which makes fruit production far less certain in south Louisiana. Improved fruit set often occurs when more than one plant is present. Turn the handsome, dark-green leaves over and you will see a most attractive silvery surface. While pests do not seem to be a problem for this plant anywhere in the state, poorly drained soil is. Don't try to grow one of this species in poorly drained soil—even if it survives, you will be disappointed with it.

When to Plant

Always choose one of the dormant-season months. Container stock may be planted at other times, but more care is required. Avoid the hot months of summer.

Where to Plant

Full sun and well-drained soil are primary requirements.

How to Plant

Improve soil removed from the planting hole with a slow-release fertilizer and use for backfill. Dig a hole at least twice the width of and slightly deeper than the rootball; cover the bottom of the hole with a few inches of backfill. After placing the plant in the hole, use small amounts of soil to adjust the height of the plant until its placement will allow it to continue growing at its previous level. When additional soil covers half the roots, stop and fill the hole with water or a starter solution. After the water has soaked completely into the ground, resume adding soil until only a shallow depression is left around the base of the plant to catch water. Apply a mulch to the soil around the plant and water well.

Care and Maintenance

Fertilize in late winter with an all-purpose fertilizer such as 12-12-12; spread evenly under the plant at a rate of 1/2 to 1 cup per square yard of ground surface. Prune out selected older stems in late winter to control form and size, as well as to encourage the production of new wood. This action may not be necessary every year. Watering is needed only during extended periods of drought. When watering, soak soil to a minimum depth of 4 inches.

Additional Information

Plants can be converted from bush to tree form. Fruits require a long period to mature.

Additional Cultivars or Species

Improved self-fertile cultivars include 'Beechwood', 'Coolidge', and 'Nazemetz'. 'Pineapple Gem' and 'Trask' are also good fruiting selections.

Pittosporum

Pittosporum tobira

Zones: 8 and 9
Size: 12 x 10 feet
Type: Evergreen
Flowers: Off-white or light yellow, fragrant
Bloom Period: Spring

Light Requirement:

The pittosporum, a plant of southeast Asian origin, has become a rather popular plant in Louisiana over the years. Due to its susceptibility to cold injury, it is a higher-risk choice in the northern parishes—but that doesn't mean it completely escapes that fate in the warmer end of the state either. Gardeners looking for low-maintenance plants should certainly consider this plant—it is almost pest-free, having only stem or trunk rots at mature sizes. Pittosporum's attractive and somewhat unusual foliage is the reason many gardeners wish to include it in their landscape. Although they are often regarded as of secondary importance, the flowers exude a nice, almost orange-blossom-quality fragrance; the plant's dark-green foliage serves as a most suitable background for them. Since plants tend to be a bit wider than they are tall, they can sometimes be used where taller-growing plants would look out of place. Gardeners who can overlook the problem of potential cold damage should not hesitate to incorporate this plant in their landscape plans.

When to Plant

For fewest problems with establishment, select a dormant-season month for installing this plant. Avoid planting during summer heat, but choose any other time of the year if you are willing to give the required care.

Where to Plant

Full-sun locations or sites with partial shade are both satisfactory places for the pittosporum. Just be sure the site chosen can offer well-drained soil. If the soil is reasonably moist and fertile, that's even better. The plant's tolerance for salt spray allows it to be planted near coastal waters.

How to Plant

Dig a hole at least twice the width of and slightly deeper than the rootball. For backfill, use a soil mix or the soil removed from the hole; improve either one you choose with a slow-release fertilizer. Cover the bottom of the hole with a few inches of backfill and press to firm. Next, place the plant in the hole and adjust the depth of the backfill so that the plant may continue to grow at its previous level. When you have covered at least half of the roots with soil, fill the hole with water or a starter solution. After the water has soaked completely into the ground, fill the hole completely with soil (or mix) until only a shallow depression remains around the base of the plant to catch water. Apply mulch and water.

Care and Maintenance

Fertilize in late winter with an all-purpose fertilizer such as 12-12-12, and spread evenly under the branches, using 1/2 cup per square yard of ground surface. Prune after flowering to control form and size or to remove parts damaged by cold temperatures or rot fungi. Water often—particularly during the summer months—to maintain good soil moisture. (This could be a weekly occurrence.) The best approach is to lay drip irrigation lines under plants so that watering can be done quickly and easily. Timed systems may overwater.

Additional Information

Split stems or trunks are evidence of cold damage. Plants in protected locations may experience less cold damage. Cut leafy branches for use in floral arrangements.

Additional Cultivars or Species

'Variegata' is a variegated cultivar; 'Turner's Dwarf' is a dwarf form with similar foliage. 'Nana' and 'Wheeler's Dwarf' are other small forms. Both are more subject to disease.

Pyracantha

Pyracantha coccinea

Other Names: Firethorn, Scarlet Firethorn
Zones: 8 and 9
Size: 12 x 10 feet
Type: Evergreen
Flowers: Small white clusters in spring
Bloom Period: Berries in fall and winter

Light Requirement:

Among the first shrubs to show ripe fruit color in the fall months, the pyracantha is a favorite plant of many Louisiana gardeners. It is far from the perfect plant, however. While it will grow in alkaline soil better than many ornamentals, its form leaves much to be desired and its long, sharp thorns can be painful. Those same thorns, however, make it a good barrier plant. Although it supposedly cannot withstand severe pruning, it is frequently the plant of choice when a bare wall or fence needs to be decorated with an espaliered plant. Birds love its berries, but insects of many kinds love the whole plant. Perhaps this tendency for problems is enhanced by the humid climate of south Louisiana—but pyracantha will have problems wherever it is grown. Unfortunately, the problems are not confined to insects; the plant has its fair share of diseases as well. In its favor, you will probably never lose one of these plants to the cold of winter; it is hardy well north of our borders.

When to Plant

Dormant-season planting is recommended, but container stock may be set out at your convenience. The peak months for heat should be the last choice for a planting period, as much greater care is required for successful establishment during those months.

Where to Plant

Choose a site in full sun, but avoid planting too close to drives and walks because of the prominent thorns that can harm those passing by. Use as an espalier plant on a solid wall or fence.

How to Plant

Dig a generously sized hole to accommodate the rootball. Adjust the depth of the hole so that the plant will be able to grow at the same level it grew previously. Improve the soil from the hole with a slow-release fertilizer and use it for backfill. When you have placed enough soil around the roots to cover at least half of them, fill the hole with water or a starter solution and let it soak completely into the soil. Continue filling the hole with backfill until only a shallow depression is left around the base of the plant to catch water. Mulch and water.

Care and Maintenance

Fertilize in late winter with an all-purpose fertilizer such as 8-8-8; spread it evenly under the plant using 1/2 cup per square yard of ground. Prune in late winter—but don't remove all of the previous year's wood, as this is where the berries are produced. Training-type cuts must be made throughout the growing season to maintain espalier plants. Extra water may be needed during extended dry spells, especially in summer. When watering, soak the ground deeply; frequency will depend upon environmental conditions. Pest problems can be a nightmare. Use pesticides of your choice; better still, consult with your county agent or other local expert about the most effective products available.

Additional Information

Some people have an allergic reaction to the pricks of pyracantha thorns.

Additional Cultivars or Species

The less cold-hardy *P. koidzumii* may be selected for the southern part of the state. 'Santa Cruz' and 'Victory' are two of the best-known varieties. Popular cultivars of *P. coccinea* include 'Kasan', 'Lalandei', 'Lowboy', and 'Pauciflora'.

Sasanqua

Camellia sasanqua

Other Name: Camellia
Zones: 8 and 9
Size: 10 x 8 feet
Type: Evergreen
Flowers: Various colors, including red, pink, and white, fragrant
Bloom Period: Long bloom season in fall and winter

Light Requirement:

The sasanqua is a close relative of *C. japonica,* and has many of the same characteristics. The most notable difference is its smaller flowers, which are produced in abundance. Because sasanqua flowers have less eye appeal, this species is planted far less often in greenhouses and it is not generally chosen for use as a container specimen. Like the *C. japonica,* it has its share of pest problems. Leaf gall occurs frequently and dieback of the plant is not uncommon. Scale insects are regular visitors to the bottom surfaces of the leaves; they must be suffocated with coatings of dormant oil or killed with dimethoate sprays before too many claim squatter's rights. Although reported to be less cold hardy than *C. japonica,* it has a good survival record in northern Louisiana. Gardeners who like camellias and who have suitable growing conditions for them should plan to have a sasanqua or two in their landscape.

When to Plant

The dormant season clearly offers the best conditions for plant establishment. Planting at other times is certainly possible with good, strong container plants—but the risk is greater and more care is required.

Where to Plant

A location that offers light shade should be the top choice for growing sasanquas, but some varieties seem well adapted to full-sun exposure.

How to Plant

Dig a hole twice the width of and slightly deeper than the rootball. Pack several inches of a good-quality soil mix (after adding some slow-release fertilizer) into the hole; press to firm. Set the plant in the hole and add more mix until the top of the rootball is slightly higher than the surrounding ground. When the level of the soil mix covers at least half of the rootball, stop and fill the hole with water or a starter solution. After the water has soaked completely into the ground, finish filling the hole with soil until there is only a shallow depression surrounding the base of the plant. Make a mini-levee around the depression and then apply a thick mulch. Finish the operation with a thorough watering.

Care and Maintenance

In late winter (just before new growth is initiated), fertilize with an azalea-camellia food at label rates. A light feeding in early fall may also be beneficial, but use half the suggested label rates. Prune as needed just before spring growth to control plant density and form or to remove dead, diseased, or insect-riddled parts. Well-timed applications of broad-spectrum fungicides may help prevent some of the fungus problems; many gardeners use dimethoate for controlling scale insects. For the most up-to-date information, consult your county agent or other local expert. To meet high water demands, consider using drip irrigation lines under the mulch. Maintain thick mulches at all times.

Additional Information

Flowers of the sasanqua don't last as long, generally, as those of *C. japonica*. For the most attractive plant, remove those flowers that have begun to discolor as soon as you spot them.

Additional Cultivars or Species

Tea Camellia, *C. sinensis*, has small white flowers that bloom in the early fall. It is sufficiently cold hardy to be planted anywhere in the state. For fragrance, consider the fragrant camellia, *C. lutchuensis*—but you will have to overlook its less-attractive form. Cultivars of the sasanqua that may be of interest are 'Bonanza' (red flowers), 'Jean May' (double pink flowers), 'Mine-no-Yuki' (large, white, peony-type flowers), and 'Shi Shi Gashira' (semi-double, rose red). There are many others.

Sweet Olive

Osmanthus fragrans

Zones: 8 and 9
Size: 20 x 10 feet
Type: Evergreen
Flowers: Small, fragrant
Bloom Period: Fall through spring

Light Requirement:

One whiff of a sweet olive in bloom on a still Louisiana night will be enough to convince most gardeners that this is a plant which belongs in every garden—preferably near a frequently used porch or patio. The evergreen leaves are attractive and partially hide the clusters of tiny white flowers which produce the powerful fragrance. Usually a series of bloom cycles occurs from early fall through spring in south Louisiana; some minor ones appear in north Louisiana during the summer months. If you want to keep sweet olive for a long time, be sure to plant it in well-drained soil that is slightly acidic. Annual fertilization and a steady supply of moisture keep the plant vigorous and productive. Pests are rarely a problem, but cold damage can occur during very cold winters on open sites, particularly in (but not limited to) north Louisiana.

When to Plant

While sturdy container plants may be set out at your convenience, easy and dependable establishment is more certain during the dormant season. Avoid planting during the heat of the summer months.

Where to Plant

Check to make sure the soil at the chosen site is well drained. Location is also an important consideration. Ideally, the plant should be placed relatively close to areas frequented often by the family and its guests.

How to Plant

Choose soil with good internal and external drainage. Dig a hole that is at least twice the width of and slightly deeper than the rootball. Enrich the soil (or a soil mix) with a slow-release fertilizer and return a small amount to the bottom of the hole; press to firm.

Position the rootball and then adjust the depth of the planting by adding or removing backfill. When the plant is at the same level it was previously growing, surround the rootball with additional soil until one-half to three-quarters of the roots are covered. Fill the hole with water or a starter solution. As soon as the water has soaked completely into the ground, fill the hole nearly to ground level with more soil, leaving only a shallow depression around the base of the plant to catch water. Apply a suitable mulch and then water thoroughly.

Care and Maintenance

While an all-purpose fertilizer may be used in late winter to provide the necessary nutrition, as an alternative we suggest using a slow-release fertilizer at the same time to help support the sweet olive's habit of flowering in cycles. Pruning in late winter is recommended to improve form and to control size. More mature plants can become small trees if you remove several of the lower branches. Pests are seldom a problem; don't concern yourself with them unless there is obvious damage or the appearance of the plant is being adversely affected. Water as often as needed to maintain a reasonable level of soil moisture—but be cautious about overwatering.

Additional Information

This versatile plant may be used as a hedge or screen, a small tree, a backdrop, an espalier, or a tub specimen. Pinch off the soft tips of young, vigorous stems to give the plant more body and a starting point for the desired form.

Additional Cultivars or Species

O. fragrans 'Aurantiacus' produces light-orange blossoms with more eye appeal, but reportedly has only a single cycle of flowering in the late spring. In New Orleans, however, it only blooms in October.

Vanhoutte Spirea

Spiraea × vanhouttei

Other Name: Bridal Wreath Spirea	**Light Requirement:**
Zones: 8 and 9	
Size: 6 x 5 feet	
Type: Deciduous	
Flowers: White, in flat clusters	
Bloom Period: Spring	

Vanhoutte spirea, or bridal wreath spirea, is a tough plant that grows about anywhere except on really wet sites; flowering is adversely affected by heavy shade. Flat clusters of white flowers adorn gracefully arching branches to create a special type of beauty to complement other landscape companions. Flowering is more dependable in northern Louisiana, where colder temperatures work their magic on this plant, which is really more at home in colder climates. But even in warmer areas, in most years there will be at least a sporadic bloom that will satisfy all but the few gardeners who demand perfection. Pest pressure will be mostly from diseases; this seems to be directly related to the humid conditions in southern Louisiana. Pest problems are rare in the cooler, dryer areas of the state. Some maintenance pruning to preserve the form and to stimulate new growth is advisable and should be done just after the plant's spring floral display. The Vanhoutte spirea certainly makes a worthy contribution to the color of Louisiana landscapes in the northern parishes, if not in the southern ones.

When to Plant

Set out container specimens at any time except the peak heat of summer.

Where to Plant

Plant singly or in groups with other landscape plants. Encourage flowering by planting in a sunny spot. Avoid low, poorly drained areas.

How to Plant

Dig a generously sized hole twice the width of and slightly deeper than the rootball. Enrich the soil (or a soil mix) with a slow-release fertilizer and return a small amount to the bottom of the hole; press to firm. Position the rootball and then adjust the depth of the planting by adding or removing backfill. When the plant is at the same level it was previously growing, surround the rootball with additional soil until at least half of the roots are covered. Fill the hole with water or a starter solution. As soon as the water has soaked completely into the ground, fill the hole nearly to ground level with more soil, leaving only a shallow depression around the base of the plant to catch water. Add an organic mulch and water thoroughly.

Care and Maintenance

Fertilize in late winter near the end of dormancy. Use about 1 cup of an all-purpose fertilizer (such as 12-12-12) for each mature specimen; spread evenly under the branches. Prune just after flowering to remove old, non-flowering stems and to admit more light to the center of the plant. Always attempt to preserve the striking, fountain-like form. Water at the first sign of wilting when dry conditions prevail. A wide-spectrum fungicide may be all that is necessary should any disease appear; follow label directions.

Additional Information

Make use of flowering branches for fresh spring floral designs. Foliage may assume a purple cast during winter cold.

Additional Cultivars or Species

'Anthony Waterer' is a cultivar of *S.* × *bumalda* ; it has dark pink flowers and a more dwarf form then Vanhoutte. These flowers bloom later in the spring and into early summer. An interesting cultivar of *S. japonica* 'Coccinea', the Red Japanese spirea, is 'Shibori' because it has flowers of three different colors all on the same plant.

Virginia Willow

Itea virginica

Other Name: Virginia Sweetspire
Zones: 8 and 9
Size: 5 x 4 feet
Type: Deciduous
Flowers: Tiny white clusters
Bloom Period: April and May

Light Requirement:

The Virginia willow is a plant that should be considered for greater landscape use. It is a native of the region and one of the few shrubs that actually prefers rather wet soil. There is such a limited number of plants that will tolerate poorly drained soil that any gardener with low, moist areas should take note of this plant. It was one of the earliest plants chosen for the "Louisiana Select" program (a joint effort by the Louisiana Association of Nurserymen and the Louisiana Cooperative Extension Service), which promotes worthy plants that are not well known. This erect (but small) shrub features leaves of medium texture which have a fall color of purplish to bright red; it produces tiny, white flowers in tight clusters along the ends of its stems. These spike-like clusters are held by the plant in a variety of positions, and the flowers deliver their color and fragrance in April and May. Plants spread by means of underground stems to form clump-like colonies; individual plants from such colonies may be transplanted rather easily during the winter. The Virginia willow can be considered a low-maintenance shrub, as it has minor pest problems and may never need pruning.

When to Plant

Dormant-season planting is preferable, but container plants (if you can find some) may be planted a few weeks on either side of that period with reasonable success. Summer plantings require more care for survival.

Where to Plant

Set these plants in either full sun or partial shade. The Virginia willow does well in a location where the soil is fertile and stays wet much of the time.

How to Plant

Dig a hole that is twice the width of and slightly deeper than the rootball. Enrich the soil (or a soil mix) with organic materials and a small amount of slow-release fertilizer; return several inches to the bottom of the hole and press to firm. Position the rootball and then adjust the depth of the planting by adding or removing backfill. When the plant is at the same level it was previously growing, surround the rootball with additional soil until at least half of the roots are covered. Fill the hole with water or a starter solution. As soon as the water has soaked completely into the ground, fill the hole nearly to ground level with more soil, leaving only a shallow depression around the base of the plant to catch water. Apply a suitable mulch and then water thoroughly.

Care and Maintenance

Use a slow-release fertilizer or an all-purpose plant food in late winter to promote good vigor and health (about 1/2 cup of 8-8-8 per mature shrub is sufficient); spread evenly between the soil surface and the mulch. Pruning is seldom necessary and pests generally cause little harm.

Additional Information

Virginia willow is a suitable understory shrub that can survive harsh conditions.

Additional Cultivars or Species

I. chinensis, the Chinese sweetspire, matures at a 4-foot height. *I. japonica* is smaller and features a rich, red foliage in the fall. A selection of *I. virginica*, 'Henry's Garnet', displays 6-inch flower clusters and has garnet-red leaves in the fall. Another selection in this species is 'Saturnalia', which shows red, orange, and purple pigments in the fall foliage.

Wax-leaf Ligustrum

Ligustrum japonicum

Other Names: Japanese Privet, Wax-Leaf Privet
Zones: 8 and 9
Size: 15 x 10 feet
Type: Evergreen
Flowers: Clusters of small, creamy white
Bloom Period: Spring to summer
Light Requirement:

This Oriental introduction is planted statewide for a number of good reasons. It grows rapidly and is tolerant of all soils except those with very poor drainage. It is evergreen, can be pruned to any size and shape, and is an effective hedge plant. It thrives in urban, suburban, and rural settings. Its pest problems can be controlled. It is widely available at nurseries and garden centers . . . and it is usually quite inexpensive. Although its clusters of small black fruit add little to the attractiveness of the plant, they are relished by various birds. Since it can handle both heat and cold with ease, there is little chance of losing it once it is established in your landscape. Gardeners rarely fail with this plant.

When to Plant

Late winter, spring, and early summer are all desirable planting times. Actually, container stock may be planted at any time of the year, but a bit more care is needed to get it established in periods of high temperatures.

Where to Plant

Wax-leaf ligustrum favors full-sun or partial-shade sites, but use this plant anywhere it is needed or wanted.

How to Plant

Dig a hole slightly larger than the rootball. Enrich the soil removed from the hole with a little slow-release fertilizer and use it to fill around and over the rootball once the plant is positioned in the hole. The plant should be set at the same depth it was previously growing. Leave a shallow depression around the base of the plant to catch water. Mulch the soil surface surrounding the plant and soak.

Care and Maintenance

Fertilize and prune in late winter to maintain vigor and form. Use an all-purpose fertilizer (such as 8-8-8) and broadcast it around the base of the plant at rates not exceeding 1 cup per mature specimen—use proportionally less for smaller plants. Hedges and sculptured plants must be clipped at intervals during the growing season to promote greater density and maintain shape or form. Wax-leaf ligustrum will generally need extra water to supplement rain only during extended drought conditions. White flies are typically the worst insect pest, but scales can also move in. Root rot may be an occasional problem, and given Louisiana's high humidity climate, there is always a chance that a leaf spot fungus will show up. Use control measures with which you are comfortable to deal with these pests. Several applications of one or more pesticides may be required. Another approach is to consult with your county agent or other local expert for the most up-to-date information concerning the control of a specific pest.

Additional Information

Minor cold injury can occur on plants not conditioned for winter or when much lower-than-normal temperatures are present for too many hours. Gardeners who are allergic to flower pollen or bees should keep their distance from this plant when it is in bloom.

Additional Cultivars or Species

L. lucidum (glossy privet) is similar to the wax-leaf species, but is more commonly grown in tree form. 'Texanum' is a smaller-growing cultivar of *L. japonicum*. 'Recurvifolium' and 'Rotundifolium' have twisted leaf tips, and 'Howard', 'Frazerieri', 'Silver Star', and 'Aureum' are all variegated in one way or another.

CHAPTER TEN

Trees

TREES ARE VALUABLE AND SHOULD BE VALUED for their contributions that enrich our lives and beautify our surroundings. This is true in Louisiana and anywhere else you choose to live. Those who have traveled in the deserts of this country or other treeless areas of the world are keenly aware of the importance of trees and sincerely appreciate them. Large, old trees of preferred species are literally worth thousands of dollars because they are virtually irreplaceable. Real estate agents know the appeal the presence of trees makes on a residential property and usually increase the asking price for the property accordingly.

But what about gardeners—the ones who are responsible for maintaining their trees or for planting trees in their own landscapes? They, of all people, need to know why trees are necessary in a "complete" landscape. They should have a good understanding about where to use trees, how to plant them correctly, what each species made a candidate for the landscape has to offer and how they can fit in with shrubs, vines, annual and perennial flowers, groundcovers and other plants with which they will be companions. Trees can serve as sources of shade, as an effective screen, for background, for framing a special place in the landscape or even the residence itself. Some trees make perfect specimen plants, attractive in their own rights because of their nearly perfect shapes, or for their spectacular show of blossoms or for several other equally important reasons. And more home owners are discovering what residents of older residential areas with mature trees have known all along, that trees can significantly reduce utility bills. Here in Louisiana, where summers are long and hot, many dollars worth of energy are saved every year because of tree-shaded roofs.

Louisiana spans at least two climatic zones...and some recent works claim three. In the northern sector of the state the temperate zone is present, but this fades into a semi-tropical zone in the midstate region and below while the southernmost portion of Louisiana borders on being nearly tropical. Obviously, then, a very wide range of both hardwoods and softwoods (the latter, mostly various species

Chapter Ten

of pines) can be found growing wild and scores of introduced species grow quite well in the state. With a terrain varying from rolling hills to soggy swamps and coastal marshes, nearly anyone can find a myriad of tree species they like and which will do well for them in their own landscape.

Louisiana gardeners must fully realize at the time of planting the mature size to which a particular species of tree is expected to grow. Then the wise gardener should add about ten or twenty feet to that figure as the state's climate is so favorable to the development of these large plants. The expected width of a tree's crown is just as important and can be a gauge as to how far away from a residence or other structure a tree should be planted.

Although there is a somewhat limited number of evergreen species of trees compared to deciduous types, there is certainly opportunity to use both kinds in the traditional Louisiana landscape. Most of the pines, for example, in time make a high, thin canopy that allows the passage of sufficient light to nourish the highly prized azaleas and camellias that are grown in their shade throughout the state. Evergreens also provide that feeling of permanence to a landscape even though they shed some of their leaves the year around. And of course in this grouping of evergreen trees you will find the Southern Magnolia which bears the state flower—the magnolia blossom. Other than the various pines, few other conifers are suited to Louisiana's climate . . . so forget the idea of bringing in a spruce or fir or hemlock. There is one notable exception to this, however. The Bald Cypress, a conifer, grows well throughout the state. It is Louisiana's state tree and for many, symbolizes the Bayou State.

The dedicated gardener who moves to Louisiana from a harsher region will be delighted at the many species of trees available for use in a landscape. The success attained in growing any of the species of trees will depend on matching the desired trees to the site (both climate and soil) and in the use of correct planting techniques. Due to the high water tables in most of the soils of the state, many species will necessarily have to be planted on mounds created in the landscape, especially if the soil is one of high clay content.

The tree descriptions on the following pages will help acquaint you with several of the diverse species that will grow nicely in Louisiana.

American Holly

Ilex opaca

Zones: 8 and 9
Size: Expected mature size 25 to 30 feet tall, with a 20- to 25-foot spread
Type: Evergreen
Flowers: White, little aesthetic value
Bloom Period: Red berries on female plants in winter

Light Requirement:

The American holly grows nicely all over the state, even in the alkaline soils of the New Orleans area. Its slow growth reduces maintenance, although minor pruning and shaping may be needed to keep it compact and in the desired form. It is ideal as a specimen plant but also makes a good screening plant . . . if you can wait long enough. Male and female flowers (both rather inconspicuous) are borne on separate plants—so if you want the female to bear fruit, a non-fruiting male plant must be planted nearby. These fruits are a favorite of many songbirds, so if you are a bird lover . . . do plant! The holly sheds its spiny leaves throughout the year; this means there is a need for periodic disposal of the leaves, an unpleasant task. Often, gardeners will time pruning chores to coincide with the Christmas season so that berried branches may be used for decorations. If you have a secluded space, you can grow one of these trees for the sole purpose of providing branches for use at Christmas.

When to Plant

Plant this tree only in the dormant period (November through February). Planting at other times will substantially increase the risk of loss.

Where to Plant

Plant trees in full sun or near larger trees that can provide some late-afternoon shade. Plant specimen trees where they can be clearly seen from preferred vantage points.

How to Plant

Choose a small, well-shaped tree; plant it in the ground at the same level it was growing in the container. Dig a hole that is the same depth as, and much wider than, the rootball. Cut bindings on balled-and-burlapped trees, and roll the burlap to the bottom of the ball. Enrich the soil from the planting hole with a slow-release fertilizer, and use it as backfill. After positioning the tree in the hole, cover most of the rootball with the backfill. Quickly fill the hole to the top with water or a starter solution. As soon as the liquid disappears, finish filling the hole with the remaining soil. Spread mulch on the ground around the tree, and water this area.

Care and Maintenance

Fertilize annually in late winter with a slow-release fertilizer—or use a general-purpose material such as 12-12-12 at the rate of 1 pound per inch caliper of the trunk after the second year. Keep the tree's roots covered with an organic mulch, if feasible. Prune in the dormant season (between the berry crop and new flowers) to maintain good form and density; pruning at this time will also protect the next crop of fruit. If you want berried branches for decorating, you may do limited pruning just before Christmas. Apply dormant oils in cool weather to control scale insects; two applications (with a 10-day interval between them) are required. Water every 2 to 3 weeks during hot, dry weather, making certain the soil is wet to a depth of at least 4 inches.

Additional Information

The tree's canopies are more open in shaded situations. Resist pruning lower limbs; allow the tree to branch as close to the ground as possible for the most attractive appearance.

Additional Cultivars or Species

Hundreds of cultivars are listed in the literature. The cultivars vary considerably in performance, structure, and appearance; the regions in which they grow will also affect these qualities. 'Amy', 'Bountiful', 'Calloway', 'Howardii', and 'Miss Helen' are among those that do well in Southern conditions.

Bald Cypress

Taxodium distichum

Other Name: Common Cypress **Zones:** 8 and 9 **Size:** Expected mature size 50 to 60 feet tall, with a 25- to 30-foot spread **Type:** Deciduous	**Light Requirement:**

People who are not Southerners somehow have gotten the idea that bald cypress trees grow only in swamps. It is true that they are among the few trees that can adapt to swamps and poorly drained soils—but they can also grow amazingly well on high sites that are far removed from any standing water. A unique feature of the bald cypress is its "knees," which originate from root tissue. A single tree may have several knees. The exact function of the knees remains something of a mystery, but they appear mainly where trees occupy water sites. Old trees are very resistant to blow-over, even on wet sites. Bald cypress trees laden with Spanish moss are quite picturesque, which may be the reason the species was chosen as the Louisiana State Tree.

When to Plant

The dormant season (primarily November through February) is the preferred time for planting. Small container-grown plants are widely available at nurseries; they generally experience less transplant shock than do the larger specimens. If you collect seedlings from the wild, choose small ones for the same reason.

Where to Plant

For a "typical" setting, select a site near permanent surface water such as a pond, stream, or bayou. Otherwise, incorporate bald cypress in a landscape where it looks natural. A grouping of 3 or 5 can be very attractive.

How to Plant

Young plants should be set at approximately the same level they were growing in their containers or in their natural habitat. Dig a hole 2 to 3 times the diameter of the root system. Enrich the soil from the planting hole with a small amount of slow-release fertilizer; use it to fill the hole until it is about two-thirds full. Add water slowly to "melt" the soil around the roots. When the water has soaked in, finish filling the hole with loose soil. Complete the job by applying a thick, loose mulch around the tree. Water as needed—but don't overwater.

Care and Maintenance

Occasional watering may be required in hot, dry weather. There are only a few insect and disease problems, but deer can be destructive. Should deer become a problem, use protective measures; correctly identify other pests to determine proper treatment for effective control.

Additional Information

The fallen foliage of trees can be used for composting or mulching. Shredded cypress bark is a prized mulching material.

Additional Cultivars or Species

There are only two other trees in Louisiana that could be easily mistaken for the bald cypress. One, a relative, is *T. ascendens*, the pond cypress. It is smaller than the bald cypress, and it has spiraling foliage rather than opposite-ranked leaves. Its columnar form also differs from the more conical shape of younger bald cypress trees. The other—unrelated—species is the dawn redwood, *Metasequoia glyptostroboides*, a native of China. This increasingly popular tree has a form similar to that of the bald cypress; its foliage is nearly identical. It has an opposite-branch arrangement, however, while the bald cypress has an alternate-branch arrangement. Fall foliage of the dawn redwood has a more reddish-gold cast; the leaves of the bald cypress are rust colored. All three of these coniferous species are deciduous. Several new horticultural forms of the bald cypress have been reported. Survey local nurseries for new introductions. 'Monarch of Illinois', 'Pendens', and 'Shawnee Brave' are named cultivars of bald cypress. 'Prairie Sentinel' is a variety of pond cypress.

Bradford Flowering Pear

Pyrus calleryana 'Bradford'

Other Name: Callery Pear
Zones: 8 and 9
Size: Expected mature size 30 to 40 feet tall, with a 20- to 25-foot spread
Type: Deciduous
Flowers: White
Bloom Period: Late winter

Light Requirement:

The Bradford flowering pear is a Louisiana favorite for a number of reasons: its distinctive form, its heavy bloom in late winter, and its multicolored fall foliage that shows hues of purple, yellow, orange, and red. At maturity, the weight of the branches, the poor structural form, and the brittle wood combine to make the tree very susceptible to wind damage. Early pruning and training, however, can help prevent such injury. The Bradford pear makes a good street tree (as well as a good yard tree) thanks to its compactness and tolerance of air pollution. The bacterial disease fire blight has only recently become a widespread serious problem. The Bradford pear still has a lot to offer, but you should look at some of the newer cultivars before you make the decision to buy this still-popular tree.

When to Plant

Plant these trees during the dormant season for best results. Planting at other times requires more care to ensure survival.

Where to Plant

Select a well-drained, full-sun location. Choose a spot where you can conveniently view the tree when it reaches its peak beauty in both the spring and fall. The Bradford pear makes a nice tree to line a drive or edge a street.

How to Plant

Dig a hole about the same depth as the rootball, and twice as wide. If the tree is balled and burlapped, roll back the burlap after placing the tree in the hole. Improve soil from the planting hole with a slow-release fertilizer, and use it for backfill. Partially cover the roots with the backfill, and then add water or a starter solution to "melt" the soil around the roots. After this liquid soaks completely into the ground, continue adding soil until the hole is completely filled. Then mulch around the tree, stake if necessary, and water the area well.

Care and Maintenance

Fertilize just after flowering with a general-purpose fertilizer such as 12-12-12; use $^1/_2$ pound per inch of trunk diameter, and spread it evenly under the tree's branches. Use this smaller amount to avoid an abundance of succulent growth—which is more readily attacked by fire blight. Minimize pruning, but do any necessary major pruning immediately after bloom. You can minimize the devastating impact of fire blight by spraying the tree during bloom with streptomycin sulfate or a copper-based fungicide. Blighted limbs that show up after the bloom period must be pruned off and destroyed. Prune the diseased branches by cutting into healthy wood, one foot away from the closest visible symptom of the disease. Pruning tools should be disinfected for twenty seconds between each cut. If significant natural rain does not fall, wet soil to a depth of 4 inches every 3 to 4 weeks during periods of heat stress.

Additional Information

Flowering may not be as spectacular or reliable in the warmer climate of southern Louisiana as it is in the northern sections of the state.

Additional Cultivars or Species

Two other species, *P. kawakamii* and *P. salicifolia*, are not suggested for use in Louisiana, due to their high susceptibility to fire blight. Cultivars of *P. calleryana* that make good alternates for the Bradford pear include 'Aristocrat', 'Capital', 'Chanticleer', 'Redspire', 'Trinity', and 'Whitehouse'.

Canaert Red Cedar

Juniperus virginiana 'Canaertii'

Other Name: Eastern Red Cedar (the cultivar named above is just one of several)
Zones: 8 and 9
Size: Expected mature size 30 feet tall, with a 15-foot spread
Type: Evergreen
Flowers: Female, inconspicuous
Bloom Period: Spring

Light Requirement:

The Canaert red cedar, an attractive female cultivar of the eastern red cedar, deserves more attention from Louisiana gardeners. In a state where there are so few native species of coniferous evergreen trees, these trees provide variety and interest to almost any landscape. With its exfoliating bark and aromatic foliage, the cedar was once a popular species for Christmas trees. It is valued particularly for its ability to attract wildlife—especially birds, which appreciate its cover and its abundant production of food. In exchange for food and shelter, the birds carry the tree's seed to new locations; bird-deposited seed is chiefly responsible for the many eastern red cedars found along fence rows and at forest edges. According to one legend, the city of Baton Rouge (Louisiana's state capitol) got its name from the red wood of this tree—Baton Rouge means "red stick" in French.

When to Plant

The dormant season (November through February) is the best period. Container plants may be planted at any time, however, as long as they receive adequate care. Avoid planting in the heat of summer.

Where to Plant

Plant in full sun in well-drained, alkaline soil. Cedars make good windbreak trees when several are strategically located in the landscape. Since many kinds of wildlife are attracted to red cedars, consider a location where you can observe the "action."

How to Plant

Most gardeners choose small container-grown plants, since large specimens may not transplant well. Dig a hole the depth of the rootball, and 2 to 3 times its width. Mix a small amount of slow-release fertilizer with the soil from the planting hole. After separating the plant from its container, loosen a few roots; if the tree is root-bound, slash the rootball in 3 or 4 places. With the rootball positioned in the hole, add backfill until about three-fourths of the rootball is covered. Flood the hole with water or a starter solution, and let it soak in. Finish filling the hole with the remaining soil, and mulch the tree. Water frequently, but do not overwater. Staking is probably unnecessary.

Care and Maintenance

Fertilize annually, preferably in February. Use a general-purpose fertilizer (such as 12-12-12) at the rate of 1 pound per inch caliper of trunk after the second year; spread material evenly under the branches. Bagworms are easily controlled with Orthene 75S or Diazinon; you can hand-pick and destroy worms if you prefer not to use chemicals. Spider mites are also a common problem; they may be controlled with Kelthane. Power-washing the tree may help reduce the mite population. Consult with your county agent to identify and control other pests.

Additional Information

Trees may be sheared to increase density and improve form. Some cultivars of red cedar take on a purplish cast in cold weather. In order to minimize the chance of cedar-apple rust galls, don't plant cedars near apples, crabapples, or related plants. When removing old trees from a landscape, convert them into lumber—cedar is a prized wood for making storage chests and lining closets.

Additional Cultivars or Species

There are many other cultivars of the Eastern red cedar besides *J. v.* 'Canaertii'. A few worthy of mention are 'Glauca', 'Burkii', 'Emerald Sentinel', 'Skyrocket', 'Gray Owl', 'Hillii', and 'Compressifolia'.

Chinese Parasol Tree

Firmiana simplex

Other Names: Varnish Tree, *F. platanifolia*
Zones: 8 and 9
Size: Expected mature size 30 to 40 feet tall, with a 10- to 20-foot spread
Type: Deciduous

Light Requirement:

The Chinese parasol tree, a native of China and Japan, is a unique tree that is widely adapted in the state. While poor drainage may eventually kill these trees, they perform well in a wide variety of soil types. Their striking greenish, smooth trunks (topped by a rounded canopy of huge leaves) provide a tropical look. They can be the ideal tree for small spaces such as enclosed courtyards or restricted-space swimming pool areas. In the fall, the dense parasol tree features interesting seedpods and yellow foliage. Older specimens tend to lose some of their attractiveness, but this species deserves to be planted more often.

When to Plant

It is best to plant this species in the dormant season; planting at other times can be successful, however, if enough care is given. Avoid planting during the hot summer months.

Where to Plant

Plant in either full sun or partial shade. Consider this tree for limited-space areas.

How to Plant

Dig a hole, and set the plants at the same depth they were growing in the nursery row or in their containers. Cut bindings on balled-and-burlapped trees, and roll the burlap to the bottom of the rootball. Enrich the soil from the planting hole with a slow-release fertilizer; return it to the hole in small amounts, until three-fourths of the rootball is covered. Flood the hole with water, allowing it to soak completely into the ground. Finish filling the hole with the remainder of the soil. Surround the tree with a good mulch, and water thoroughly after staking. Taller plants need stake support for one year.

Care and Maintenance

Fertilize annually in late winter. A garden-variety fertilizer such as 8-8-8 may be used at the rate of 1 pound per inch caliper of trunk after the second year; spread the fertilizer evenly under the tree. When there is no rain, water every 10 to 14 days during summer heat. Watch for white scale insects on trunk and branches. To kill the scales, treat with dormant or superior oils. You will need to use at least two applications, with a 10-day interval between uses. Remove any stakes used for support after one year.

Additional Information

Thanks to its tall, branchless trunk and a high canopy of foliage, this tree is good for shade in tight spaces. The wood is subject to splitting on older specimens. These trees may be planted in groups with only a 4-foot spacing between them. Unique green trunks and foot-wide leaves make this tree a conversation piece.

Additional Cultivars or Species

No other relatives of this tree are known to be used in the ornamental trade.

Crape Myrtle

Lagerstroemia indica

Zones: 8 and 9
Size: Expected mature size 20 to 25 feet tall, with a 12- to 15-foot spread
Type: Deciduous
Flowers: Several blossom colors
Bloom Period: Long summer bloom

Light Requirement:

Because of its flowers and plant habits, the crape myrtle is often referred to as the "lilac of the South." With proper cultivation, the crape myrtle may bloom as many as four times during a growing season. This plant possesses additional beauty in the form of branches that have a sculptured appearance when bare of foliage. As the exfoliating bark is shed, the smooth inner bark—ranging from light gray to cinnamon brown—provides extra beauty during the dormant season. Newer cultivars are resistant to powdery mildew and leaf spot, diseases that are traditionally common to the crape myrtle. This species is widely appreciated, widely available, and planted throughout the state.

When to Plant

The best time for planting is the dormant period (October through early March). The crape myrtle may be somewhat forgiving when planted in the summer months, however, as it is a bit more drought tolerant than the average tree.

Where to Plant

Plant this species in full sun if you want plenty of flowers. Choose sites that are well drained and that offer a good view of the trees.

How to Plant

Plant good-quality container- or field-grown plants at the level they were previously growing; make sure the roots are loosened or slashed if the tree is pot-bound. Cut bindings on balled-and-burlapped trees, and roll the burlap to the bottom of the ball. Enrich the soil you remove from the planting hole with a slow-release fertilizer, and use it to fill the hole. When you have nearly covered the rootball, flood the hole with water or a starter solution; allow the water to soak into the ground. Finish filling the hole with the remaining soil, and mulch the ground around the tree. Water thoroughly. Staking may be desirable on a larger plant that has a reduced root system. Keep the soil reasonably moist until the plant is well established.

Care and Maintenance

Fertilize with a general-purpose fertilizer such as 12-12-12 in late winter each year—or use a slow-release fertilizer, if you prefer. Prune at the same time. Begin training the tree, either as a single- or multitrunk specimen—during the first year. Three or 5 stem trunks are quite attractive. Periodically remove basal sprouts. As flower clusters fade and dry during the summer, clip them off at their base to hasten the next round of blossoms. Watch for insects that cause sooty mold; spray with Orthene 75S, Diazinon, or another suitable insecticide to control them. Use fungicides to prevent powdery mildew and leaf spot. Sooty mold deposits can be soaked loose from the foliage with warm soapy water; then blast the deposits off the leaves with pressure from a forceful stream of water.

Additional Information

Prune crape myrtles properly to avoid creating large, ugly knots that detract from the plant's appearance.

Additional Cultivars or Species

Numerous cultivars are available. 'Natchez' is a mildew-resistant white cultivar that is very popular. 'Watermelon Red' is an older cultivar that is still widely grown. 'Muskogee' bears a light orchid flower, and 'Potomac' has a clear pink flower. All of these cultivars reach a height of at least 15 feet at maturity.

Deodar Cedar

Cedrus deodara

Zones: 8 and 9
Size: Expected mature size 40 feet tall, with a 20-foot spread
Type: Evergreen

Light Requirement:

The deodar cedar, a beautiful native of the Himalayas, has a pleasing pyramidal form and sweeping branches arranged in tiers, features that make it an ideal specimen tree. To a degree, its short, evergreen, needle-like leaves (feathery, with a silvery to bluish cast) and its pyramidal shape mimic several of the cooler-climate evergreen species. New residents who move to Louisiana from colder areas may be reminded of home by these trees. The deodar cedar is a slow to moderate grower; it will produce moderate-size cones after two years of growth. Despite the fact that mature specimens often exhibit flat tops due to borer injury (or just because of the aging process), this is a tree that gardeners should plant more frequently.

When to Plant

Plant the deodar cedar in the dormant season (November through February). There is more risk associated with planting at other times.

Where to Plant

Plant in full sun. The deodar cedar is adaptable to a wide variety of soil types but needs good internal as well as good external soil drainage. It may perform better in northern Louisiana.

How to Plant

Select a well-drained area or plant on a constructed mound. Dig a hole the same depth as the rootball, and 2 or 3 times wider. Cut bindings on balled-and-burlapped trees, and roll the burlap to the bottom of the ball. After the plant is positioned, add a small amount of slow-release fertilizer to the soil from the planting hole; use it to refill the hole. When backfill covers three-fourths of the rootball, flood the hole with water or a root-stimulator solution; wait until the liquid soaks in before you finish filling the hole. Mulch the ground surface around the tree, and water thoroughly. Until plant is well established, repeat waterings as needed to keep soil reasonably moist—but don't overwater. Stabilizing the tree with a triangle of stakes is recommended; remove the stakes after the first growing season.

Care and Maintenance

Fertilize once a year in late winter. A general-purpose fertilizer such as 12-12-12 may be used at the rate of 1 pound per inch caliper of trunk after the second year. Broadcast plant food evenly under the tree's branches, but move the zone of application further from the trunk as the tree ages. Water as necessary to compensate for a lack of rain. If you detect damaging insects, treat for control. Dursban and Lindane are commonly used to eradicate borers.

Additional Information

Because large plants do not transplant very well without a very large rootball, select small specimens to plant. Provide plenty of space—these trees attain large sizes at maturity; they also need room to show off their attractive form when used as specimen plants. If you want to curb the spread of the tree (and/or make the canopy more dense), prune off half of the new growth on the tree's side branches in late spring.

Additional Cultivars or Species

'Shalimar' is very hardy and suited to the northern parishes. 'Compacta', 'Prostrata', and 'Viridis' are interesting small-tree or shrub forms listed by various bayou state horticulturists. The new foliage of 'Aurea' is initially yellow but turns to a yellowish-green during the growing season. *C. atlantica*, the atlas cedar, is a related species.

Flowering Dogwood

Cornus florida

Zones: 8 and 9
Size: Expected mature size 18 to 20 feet tall, with a 12- to 15-foot spread
Type: Deciduous
Flowers: Pink, red, and white
Bloom Period: Spring

Light Requirement:

The flowering dogwood is one of the most popular small trees in the state. While the native species has the white-bracted flowers, there are both pink and red cultivars. These trees require acidic, well-drained soil; they can be fertilized only sparingly due to their high sensitivity to commercial products. Typically an understory species, they enjoy light afternoon shade, but they can be acclimated to full-sun sites. Dogwoods are not generally well suited to the flood plains of the Mississippi or Red Rivers, due to the predominance of alkaline soils in those areas. Performance in the New Orleans area is also unpredictable and often poor. Pests can be devastating, particularly borers and anthracnose, although the type of anthracnose that has been killing dogwoods in northern areas has not yet been a factor in Louisiana. Since larger dogwoods are difficult to transplant, choose small, nursery-grown stock. Dogwoods are most impressive in full bloom, particularly when planted with azaleas of contrasting colors that blossom at the same time.

When to Plant

Plant container-grown dogwoods from October to March. Planting outside of this period decreases the likelihood of success, and requires more care.

Where to Plant

Plant trees in elevated areas, or create a "turtleback" mound of soil on which to plant them. Select sites with acidic soil that receive shade in the afternoon.

How to Plant

Set the dogwood at the same depth it was growing in the container. Dig a hole the same depth as the rootball, but 3 to 4 times wider. Enrich the soil from the planting hole with a small amount of slow-release fertilizer, and use it for backfill. Amend the loosened soil surrounding the hole with small quantities of both peat moss and sharp sand to increase porosity and water retention; this will improve the spread of the root system. Partially fill the hole with improved soil, and flood with water. Allow the water to soak in, then put the remaining soil in the hole. Finish by surrounding the tree with a thick, loose mulch, and water again.

Care and Maintenance

Use minute amounts of an azalea/camellia fertilizer just after flowering; spread thinly over the outer parts of the root system. Prune, as needed, at the same time. Periodically inspect trees for borers and diseases. Treat with Lindane or a similar product for the insects. For disease factors, spray trees with a fungicide such as maneb, chlorothalonil, or benomyl just before bud-break. Water frequently during the hot months, especially when drought conditions exist.

Additional Information

The dogwood's berries attract wildlife. Berries from pink cultivars produce white-flowered trees. Mulches are very important—particularly if the dogwood is planted in soil that tends to be dry. Dogwoods are not well suited to city environments.

Additional Cultivars or Species

C. kousa chinensis, a native of the Orient, has more disease resistance than our native tree—but it is less attractive. Selections of *C. florida* are 'White Cloud', 'Cloud 9', and 'Bonnie' (outstanding white-flowered trees); 'Cherokee Chief', 'Spring Song', 'Gulf Coast', and 'Rubra' (red or pink flowers); and 'Cherokee Brave' (red flowers), which has some powdery-mildew resistance. The varieties and cultivars named above are but a few of the dogwoods available in the trade. Stellar dogwood (*C. rutgersensis*) and Kousa dogwood (*C. kousa*) are related species.

Ginkgo

Ginkgo biloba

Zones: 8 and 9
Size: Expected mature size 50 to 60 feet tall, with a 25- to 30-foot spread
Type: Deciduous

Light Requirement:

The ginkgo is a unique tree with leather-like, fan-shaped leaves. It is a native of China, and is thought to have been growing somewhere on the planet for millions of years. This is why it is sometimes referred to as "the living fossil." Specimens that are 1,000 years old are known in its native areas—but old trees can be found almost anywhere on earth, thanks to the gingko's adaptability to an extremely wide range of environments. This great tolerance for stressful conditions (including pollution) makes the ginkgo ideal for urban use. The ginkgo was introduced into the United States in the late 1700s, and it has consistently grown in popularity. This tree tends to grow rather slowly on its own; annual applications of fertilizer will speed up the process. It is rare to find any damage to the tree from either insects or diseases. Even ice and wind storms seldom inflict any major damage. Female trees are not desirable because of the strong disagreeable odor of their fruits. The fall foliage is a striking, bright, golden yellow. When the leaves fall, they do so in a short period, making raking them up less of a job.

When to Plant

This species may be planted any time, but always try to favor the dormant period (November through February).

Where to Plant

Full-sun locations are the best places to plant ginkgoes. If you use it as a specimen plant, locate the tree where there is an unobstructed view from either the house or the street . . . or both.

How to Plant

Dig a hole that is as deep as, and 2 to 3 times wider than, the rootball. Cut bindings on balled-and-burlapped trees, and roll the burlap to the bottom of the rootball. Improve the soil from the planting hole with a slow-release fertilizer, and use it for backfill. Place the enriched soil around the rootball until most of the roots are covered, then flood the hole with water or a starter solution. After the liquid soaks in, use the remaining soil to finish filling the hole. Cover the soil surface around the tree with an organic mulch; water and stake for extra support during windy weather.

Care and Maintenance

Ginkgoes require only minimal care. Remove any stakes used at planting after one year. Fertilize in late winter annually to sustain maximum growth rate. After the second year, use 1 pound of fertilizer (such as 12-12-12) for each inch of trunk caliper. Spread the fertilizer over the surface of the ground under the outer two-thirds of branches, and scratch or water it into the soil surface where possible. Water every couple of weeks during hot, dry weather.

Additional Information

Female trees bear plum-sized fruit that smells horrible. Make sure you buy grafted male trees for landscape use. Ginkgoes are excellent choices where air pollution is a problem.

Additional Cultivars or Species

Several cultivars are offered in the trade. These include 'Autumn Gold', 'Fairmount', 'Fastigiata', 'Pendula' (a weeping form), 'Princeton Sentry', and 'Saratoga'. Forms differ somewhat between cultivars.

Grancy Graybeard

Chionanthus virginicus

Other Name: White Fringe Tree
Zones: 8 and 9
Size: Expected mature size 20 to 25 feet tall, with a 12- to 15-foot spread
Type: Deciduous
Flowers: Panicles of gray or white
Bloom Period: Early spring

Light Requirement:

The grancy graybeard is prized in the acidic soil areas of the state for its impressive show of blooms. It can be trained to the form of a small tree, or allowed to develop multiple stems and become more shrub-like. Appearing in profusion in the early spring, the hanging panicles of flowers can give a gray, smoke-like appearance—or they can resemble a white, lacy garment. Because of their longer fringes, male flowers (found on separate trees from the female flowers) are considered more attractive. Where plants of both sexes are present, small blue fruits may be formed on the female plants; these can serve as a source of food for wildlife. In the fall, yellow foliage is an added feature of this native tree. Grancy graybeard is tolerant of air pollution, making it a good tree for city use.

When to Plant

The dormant season (November through February) is the preferred planting time for this species. Planting at other times of the year requires more care for plant survival. Avoid planting during the hottest months.

Where to Plant

Plant in full sun for the best show of blossoms. This tree is also a good choice for use at the edges of mass plantings of larger trees.

How to Plant

This species develops a substantial taproot, so plant younger, smaller specimens of container-grown stock. Seedlings found under female trees transplant fairly easily. Dig a hole the depth of the rootball, and at least twice its width. Make sure that both seedlings and container stock are planted at the same depth they were growing. Improve the soil from the planting hole with a slow-release fertilizer, and use it for backfill. After partially covering the rootball with enriched soil, flood the hole with water and let it soak in. Finish filling the hole with the remaining soil. Mulch around the tree, and water the general area.

Care and Maintenance

Maintain soil fertility by using a light application of an acid-forming fertilizer (such as azalea/camellia food) in late winter every year. Six to 8 ounces should be sufficient for a mature tree; use proportionally less for younger, smaller specimens. Provide water about every 2 weeks in hot, dry weather. When watering, soak the soil to a reasonable depth—at least 4 inches deep.

Additional Information

While the flowers have a trace of fragrance, it is their appearance that makes them an asset. It takes 4 to 6 years for the grancy graybeard to reach sufficient maturity for flowering. Double-dormancy seed requires specific conditions for germination. This tree is excellent to use in a mixed grouping of plants. Borers may attack stressed trees, so watch for this problem; control with Lindane or a method of your choice. This species may be difficult to find in the trade.

Additional Cultivars or Species

The Chinese fringe tree, *C. retusus*, has smaller leaves and flowers than the grancy graybeard, and it blooms earlier. Its white flowers have a lilac-like appearance; its shrub-type growth habit enhances this image.

Green Ash

Fraxinus pennsylvanica

Zones: 8 and 9 **Size:** Expected mature size 50 feet tall, with a 30-foot spread **Type:** Deciduous	**Light Requirement:**

The green ash is a Louisiana native that grows on sites too damp for many other tree species. Its compound pinnate leaves provide good shade, and its moderately fast growth rate marks it as a suitable choice for landscape use, especially in newly developed landscapes. Trees that bear the one-seeded, winged fruit can cause a minor litter problem, and borers are sometimes a cause for concern. The oval to round crowns of this species commonly attain a height of 50 feet and a spread of around 30 feet; in fertile soils a mature green ash may be one-third larger.

When to Plant

Green ash trees are best planted in the dormant season (November through February in most of the state). More care is required when they are planted at other times. This moderately fast grower is easily started from seed.

Where to Plant

These trees are quite suitable for street or lawn locations, and they make good shade trees. Green ash is suitable for planting in a wide variety of soils, and will tolerate poorly drained sites.

How to Plant

Dig a hole the depth of the rootball and 2 or 3 times its width. Cut bindings on a balled-and-burlapped tree, and roll the burlap to the bottom of the ball. Carefully loosen the root system; if the tree is root-bound, slash through the rootball to break up circular growth patterns. Place the rootball carefully in the hole, and add backfill until the hole is two-thirds full. Next fill the hole with water (adding a root stimulator, if desired); allow the water to soak into the ground until it is completely absorbed. Mix a small amount of slow-release fertilizer into the remaining backfill, and finish filling the hole.

Complete the job by mulching the soil surface around the base of the tree. Water often enough to keep the soil evenly moist, but don't overwater. Use good staking techniques to stabilize the tree for the first year, then remove the stakes.

Care and Maintenance

Promote more rapid growth by fertilizing every February with a general-purpose fertilizer such as 12-12-12; use 1 pound per inch caliper of trunk. Watch for attacks by borers and treat with insecticides such as Dursban or Lindane. Water biweekly if necessary.

Additional Information

Green ash trees make good companion trees for bald cypress trees on high-moisture sites. Male trees may be selected to reduce litter problems, since they do not bear the winged fruits.

Additional Cultivars or Species

F. americana (white ash) has seedless selections, including 'Autumn Applause' and 'Autumn Purple'. There are several other cultivars of this species. Improved selections of the green ash include 'Marshall Seedless' and 'Summit' (both seedless), as well as 'Emerald' and 'Lanceolata'. 'Marshall Seedless' is highly regarded by many horticulturists. *F. velutina,* the Arizona ash, is a related species.

Japanese Maple

Acer palmatum

Zones: 8 and 9
Size: Expected mature size 12 to 20 feet, with a 10- to 15-foot spread
Type: Deciduous

Light Requirement:

Japanese maples are highly ornamental and commonly add a "different" element to the scene. This is why they are so often used as specimen plants—both in small gardens and in extensive landscapes. Some cultivars have dark-red foliage, and the color lasts the entire growing season. Others initially have beautiful red foliage, but it changes to green after a short period. All have gorgeous fall foliage, with colors ranging from red to yellow to orange. The various cultivars also differ tremendously in leaf texture. Most have leaves that are divided into several lobes, each of which has a border of teeth. Japanese maples are well suited to small spaces; they may even be grown in large containers. They make superb accent plants to improve the view from a porch, patio, or terrace.

When to Plant

Favor the dormant period for installation. A month on either side of the November-through-February span will also generally be satisfactory.

Where to Plant

Choose locations that offer day-long partial shade, or where the tree will get only morning sun. Avoid hot, windy sites and heavy-shade situations.

How to Plant

Start with a young, healthy, disease-free plant of good form. Dig a hole slightly deeper than the rootball and twice as wide, so that the plant may continue to grow at the same level as it did in the container. If you purchased a balled-and-burlapped specimen, cut the bindings, and roll the burlap down to the base of the rootball. Enrich the soil from the planting hole with a slow-release fertilizer and a touch of humus, then use it to refill the hole. When the soil is near the top of the rootball, fill the hole to the top with water or a starter solution; allow the liquid to soak completely into the ground. Finish filling the hole with soil. Surround the newly set tree with a mulch, and conclude by watering the zone around the tree.

Care and Maintenance

Since soil moisture is of utmost importance, use a drip irrigation system or a low-profile sprinkler set-up where possible. Check soil moisture often during the hottest months, and every 2 weeks at other times of the year. Trees planted on windy sites may benefit from an anti-desiccant (such as "Wilt-Proof®" or "Cloud Cover®") to retard the drying effects of summer winds. Use a slow-release fertilizer in late winter for the necessary nutrition; do any pruning at that same time. When new leaves expand, prevent disease by spraying with a fungicide of your choice or a material recommended by your county agent. Use an insecticide only when necessary.

Additional Information

Although seedling trees are more vigorous than grafted plants, grafted selections generally offer more intense foliage colors, more diversity in leaf shape, and better form. Do not allow any growth to develop below the graft union of such trees.

Additional Cultivars or Species

The paperbark maple, *A. griseum* (probably better suited to the northern parishes), features cinnamon-colored exfoliating bark and bright-red foliage in the fall. *A. japonicum* 'Aconitifolium', the fern-leaf fullmoon maple, is a shrub-type form with extremely deeply cut leaves and great fall color. Popular cultivars of *A. palmatum* are 'Atropurpureum', 'Bloodgood', 'Burgundy Lace', 'Dissectum', 'Garnet', and 'Ornatum'. Another cultivar of interest is 'Sango kaku', which has yellow fall foliage followed by a display of coral-red branches and twigs.

Lacebark Elm

Ulmus parvifolia

Other Names: Chinese Elm, Evergreen Elm
Zones: 8 and 9
Size: Expected mature size 35 to 45 feet tall, with a 25- to 30-foot spread
Type: Deciduous to semi-evergreen

Light Requirement:

The lacebark elm rates high throughout the state, thanks to its nearly evergreen foliage—and its high resistance to both insects and diseases. Like other elms, its vase-like shape adds a somewhat different form to the average landscape—thereby providing some variety that may not be obtainable from most other tree species. Its wide adaptability to soils and its tolerance to drought add to its care-free qualities. Because it can grow under rather stressful conditions, it is frequently selected to line streets, and for a variety of other uses in urban situations. Adding to its beauty and it uniqueness among elms, the lacebark elm has exfoliating bark that reveals its colorful underbark.

When to Plant

Plant this species in its dormant period, late October to early March. It may be planted at other times if given extra care. Avoid planting in the scorching summer months.

Where to Plant

Plant wherever a small shade tree is needed. Do not plant near or under power lines.

How to Plant

Dig a hole as deep as, and 2 or 3 times wider than, the rootball. Cut bindings on balled-and-burlapped trees, and roll the burlap to the bottom of the ball. Enrich the soil from the planting hole with a slow-release fertilizer, and use it to cover the rootball. Before completely covering the roots with soil, flood the hole with water. Allow the water to soak in, then use the remaining soil to finish filling the hole. Mulch the soil surface around the tree, and water thoroughly. Stake the tree to reduce wind movement; remove any stakes after one year.

Care and Maintenance

Fertilize annually in late winter with a general-purpose fertilizer such as 12-12-12; use approximately 1 pound of fertilizer per inch of trunk diameter after the second year. Spread fertilizer evenly over the soil under the outer two-thirds of branches. Water the tree frequently during hot, dry spells; soak the soil to a depth of at least 4 inches. Do any necessary pruning in late winter. Pests are uncommon, but don't ignore them if they do appear.

Additional Information

This species is somewhat resistant to elm leaf beetles and to Dutch elm disease. Attractive trunk mottling results from the tree's shedding of patches of the exfoliating bark.

Additional Cultivars or Species

'Valley Forge' and 'New Harmony' are new varieties of American elm that look promising in terms of disease resistance. At this time, they are still being tested. 'Brea', 'Sempervirens', 'True Green', and 'Drake' are selections of lacebark elm that are semi-evergreen in Louisiana. 'Drake' is being used extensively in urban Shreveport as a street tree. Some related species are winged elm (*U. alata*), American elm (*U. americana*), cedar elm (*U. crassifolia*), and Siberian elm (*U. pumila*).

Loquat

Eriobotrya japonica

Other Name: Japanese Plum
Zones: 8 and 9
Size: Expected mature size 15 to 20 feet tall, with a 10- to 12-foot spread
Type: Evergreen
Flowers: Small, yellowish-white
Bloom Period: Late fall (fruits borne in late water, early spring)

Light Requirement:

The loquat is a native of China, but grows very well in the lower South. In northern Louisiana, the developing fruit crop is wiped out nine out of ten years because of frosts and freezes—but otherwise the plant is quite hardy. Where landscape design calls for a coarse-textured plant, the loquat is a good choice. In the warmer parts of the state, the loquat fruits dependably. The yellowish, plum-type fruits are approximately one inch wide and are very tasty. If you don't use them, the fruits can be messy under the tree. Plants can be trained as small trees or as shrub-type plants; both forms are easily adaptable to small spaces such as enclosed courtyards. Pest problems occur infrequently. Fire blight is a major disease that can kill a loquat if it is not controlled.

When to Plant

Plant in the dormant season, and up to a month earlier in the fall. Planting at other times carries a higher risk of failure.

Where to Plant

Select full-sun sites wherever possible. Partially shaded locations are a second choice. Avoid sites with poorly drained soils.

How to Plant

Container-grown stock is the most common. The tree should be planted so that it will be growing at the same level as in the container. Dig a hole the same depth as, and much wider than, the rootball. In the unlikely event that you have purchased a balled-and-burlapped plant, be sure to cut the binding, and roll the burlap down to the base of the rootball. Improve soil from the planting hole with a slow-release fertilizer; use it to cover the rootball to a point just below its top. Flood the hole with water or a starter solution. After the water has soaked completely into the ground, use the remaining soil to finish filling the hole. Surround the tree with a heavy mulch and water well. Staking is optional, unless the plant is rather large.

Care and Maintenance

Prune as needed for controlling size and shaping the tree; give preference to the late-winter period and just before new growth begins. You should also fertilize in late winter; use no more than 1 cup of 8-8-8 per 30 square feet of ground surface under the tree. Better still, use a slow-release plant food at that time. Overfertilization promotes succulent growth that is a prime target of the devastating fire blight disease.

Additional Information

A loquat may be left in a very large container for several years. If kept in a greenhouse or atrium during the cold months, it can bear fruit regularly in the northern part of the state. It is also a suitable plant to use as an espalier—but not on a hot wall. In areas of the state where it fruits annually, early removal of excessive fruit will increase the size of those remaining on the tree. The cut foliage is suitable for decorating indoors.

Additional Cultivars or Species

The species, *E. deflexa* (the bronze loquat), pushes out new foliage that has a coppery color. Nice cultivars of *E. japonica* include 'Champagne', 'MacBeth', and 'Thales'.

Oriental Magnolia

Magnolia × soulangiana

Other Names: Saucer Magnolia, Tulip Tree (the often-used latter name is incorrect, but it is descriptive of the flowers)
Zones: 8 and 9
Size: Expected mature size 20 to 25 feet tall, with a 15- to 18-foot spread
Type: Deciduous
Flowers: Pinkish purple with creamy-white centers
Bloom Period: Early spring
Light Requirement:

This magnolia is a hybrid between *M. liliiflora* and *M. denudata*. It is more commonly grown as a multi-trunked tree, but you may occasionally see good-sized single-trunk trees. Its popularity is probably due to its beautiful large flowers, which have pinkish to purple margins fading to creamy-white centers; these appear in masses prior to the unfurling of the leaves. During the winter, the trunks are silvery in color; they bear some resemblance to those of the crape myrtle, but show much less of a sculptured look. The large flower buds present in winter and the nice fragrance of the flowers are two other popular features of this plant. If you can offer only heavy clay soils, choose another type of plant; such conditions will lead to permanent stunting of a magnolia.

When to Plant

Give preference to the dormant season for planting this tree. It may be planted at other times with some degree of success, but avoid the hot summer months.

Where to Plant

Plant in full sun on fertile, porous soils that are well drained and moderately acidic.

How to Plant

Select small specimens, as they transplant more easily. Prepare a hole that will allow the tree to grow at the same level it grew in its container. The hole should be at least twice the width of the rootball. Enrich the soil from the planting hole with a slow-release fertilizer, and use it to cover the rootball almost to its top. Fill the remaining space in the hole with water or a starter solution; allow it to soak completely into the ground. Finish filling the hole, and mulch around the tree with an organic material. Water to wet the soil thoroughly.

Care and Maintenance

Fertilize in late winter with either a slow-release fertilizer or a general-purpose material such as 12-12-12. After establishment, increase annual applications by 1 pound per year of age, up to about 6 or 8 pounds for mature specimens. Should a leaf-spot fungus become severe, make a practice of spraying the foliage as it opens with dependable fungicides that contain chlorothalonil or benomyl . . . or use the product or method of your choice to deal with the problem. Water about every 2 weeks during hot, dry weather.

Additional Information

In the middle or northern sections of the state, you can try to reduce cold damage to opening flowers by locating trees on the south sides of buildings or board fences. Where there is sufficient room, plant a carefully chosen selection of cultivars to stretch the season of bloom.

Additional Cultivars or Species

Species somewhat similar in appearance to the oriental magnolia are the white saucer, *M. denudata*; the tulip (or lily) magnolia, *M. liliiflora*; and the star magnolia, *M. stellata*. There are various cultivars of each of these. Noteworthy cultivars of the Oriental magnolia include 'Alexandrina', 'Rustica rubra', 'Elizabeth', and 'Susan' (which has a lemon smell). Certainly, this is not a complete listing.

Pistachio

Pistacia chinensis

Other Name: Chinese Pistache
Zones: 8 and 9
Size: Expected mature size 40 to 50 feet tall, with a 25- to 30-foot spread
Type: Deciduous

Light Requirement:

Once you have seen the flaming orange-to-red luminous foliage in the fall, you are not likely to rest until you have one of these trees to grace your own landscape. This slow-growing, low-maintenance tree lives a long time, grows in most soil types (acid or alkaline), and is drought resistant. It is just as much at home in the city as it is in the wide-open spaces of vast fields, or landscapes of great size. Gardeners are often disappointed to learn this is not the tree that produces the edible nut, but those that choose to plant it are rarely sorry when it starts showing its striking fall color every year. Early pruning and training to develop a desired form usually create a specimen of great beauty.

When to Plant

Plant this tree in the dormant season (November through February), or a week or two on either side of this period. Greater care is needed when planting at other times of the year, especially during summer heat.

Where to Plant

Choose locations that offer well-drained soil and full sun, but don't hide this beauty. A spot in full view of the house or street will let you and others admire the intensely colored fall foliage.

How to Plant

Dig a hole equal to the depth of the rootball and twice as wide; this will allow the tree to continue growing at the same level, while it offers an easier path for lateral root expansion. Improve soil from the planting hole with a slow-release fertilizer, and use it as backfill. Free the tree of its growing container or any burlap that is binding its roots. Position the tree in the hole and steady it while placing backfill around the rootball. When the soil has covered most of the roots, add water or a starter solution. Let the liquid soak completely into the ground, then finish filling the hole with the remaining soil. Place a good organic mulch around the tree, and use stakes to provide the necessary anchorage. Conclude with a good watering.

Care and Maintenance

Fertilize annually in late winter with a general-purpose fertilizer (such as 12-12-12) to accelerate the naturally slow growth. Use 1 pound for each inch of trunk diameter; spread evenly under the branches. As the tree increases in size and age, expand the area covered to beyond the branch tips. Prune and train the tree from a young age to develop a desirable form. Pruning is best done in late winter. Water sparingly—and only during periods of high heat stress—to avoid problems with verticillium wilt.

Additional Information

This species is the main understock for the edible pistachio, *P. vera,* which is not cold hardy in our region.

Additional Cultivars or Species

The Texas pistachio, *P. texana,* is a smaller tree (or shrub) with many of the same fine qualities of the Chinese pistache. *P. atlantica* is almost evergreen and worthy of planting.

Redbud

Cercis canadensis

Other Name: Eastern Redbud
Zones: 8 and 9
Size: Expected mature size 25 to 30 feet tall, with a 15- to 20-foot spread
Type: Deciduous
Flowers: Magenta
Bloom Period: Early spring

Light Requirement:

The redbud is a valued tree in the northern parishes, as the Annual Redbud Festival in Vivian, Louisiana, attests. Its magenta flowers (which also decorate the trunk and larger limbs) help usher in the spring season. In the fall, the tree's attractive heart-shaped leaves turn yellow—adding their touch of beauty to the landscape. It grows well with few problems throughout the northern region, but it is not highly rated in southern Louisiana because of an uncommonly large number of problems.

When to Plant

Plant this species anytime during the dormant season (November through February, give or take a few weeks), so that it will be well established before the heat stress of summer arrives.

Where to Plant

Since this species looks more comfortable and at home in a natural setting, favor it by placing it with other trees at the perimeter of your landscape. Avoid low, poorly drained sites.

How to Plant

Dig a hole of about the same depth as the rootball, and at least twice its width; this will encourage rapid, lateral root spread. Improve soil from the planting hole with a slow-release fertilizer and just a touch of organic material, and use it as backfill. Position the plant in the hole, and fill in around the roots with backfill. With the tree partially anchored, add water or a starter solution to the hole to "melt" the soil around the roots. When the liquid has drained into the soil, completely fill the hole with the remaining soil. Mulch around the tree, stake it (only until it is firmly established), and water the area well.

Care and Maintenance

Fertilize after bloom with a general-purpose fertilizer such as 8-8-8. Use only 1 pound or less per inch of trunk diameter, and spread the material evenly under the branches. Natural rain usually makes extra watering unnecessary. In northern Louisiana, however, irrigation may be necessary in the late summer and fall months (this is typically a dry, hot period in that region). Since the more humid portions of the state are conducive to greater pest problems for redbuds, the frequent use of fungicides and insecticides may be required to preserve the health of these trees. Use chemicals or methods of your choice—or consult your county agent, or other local expert, for up-to-date information on the subject of pest control.

Additional Information

Early training and proper pruning of young trees helps develop a more attractive, better-shaped crown.

Additional Cultivars or Species

'Avondale', a nice variety of the *C. chinensis* species, has deep-purple flowers. 'Oklahoma', a variety of *C. reniformis*, has dark-red flowers and thick foliage—a Southwestern mimic of the Eastern redbud. Selections of *C. canadensis* that are noteworthy include 'Alba' (white flowers), 'Flame' (double pink flowers), 'Forest Pansy' (purple leaves), 'Rubye Atkinson' (clear pink flowers), and 'Silver Cloud' (white, variegated foliage).

Shumard Oak

Quercus shumardii

Other Name: Shumard Red Oak
Zones: 8 and 9
Size: Expected mature size 60 to 70 feet tall, with a 40- to 50-foot spread
Type: Deciduous

Light Requirement:

Shumard oaks have a very good reputation in Louisiana. They are often recommended by nurserymen and horticulturists. Their leaves tend to be a bit more lustrous than many of the other oaks, and are consistently red in the fall (although some authors say they can also be yellow). They grow to large sizes rather quickly when "pushed" by annual fertilization. These trees are clearly an asset to private landscapes. They give proper size and scale to two-story and larger homes. For smaller homes, they work well as background trees, or for framing. Their strong wood resists wind damage when severe storms come through; their well-anchored roots guard against blow-over. Their abundant crop of acorns attracts wildlife; unused acorns can, however, cause a litter problem.

When to Plant

The dormant season (November through February) is best for transplanting this species. A month on either side of these dates is usually also satisfactory. Steer clear of the hot summer months unless you are prepared to give extra care.

Where to Plant

Full sun is always best when you are planting an oak tree. Consider the mature size of a Shumard oak when selecting a planting site.

How to Plant

While acorns can be easily germinated around the edges of undisturbed compost piles (or started in deep containers of good potting soil), gardeners tend to favor purchasing container-grown nursery stock. Dig a hole the same depth as, and much wider than, the rootball, so that the roots can spread more easily into the surrounding soil. Position the tree in the hole so that it will be growing at the same level it grew previously. If the tree was balled and burlapped, cut bindings or remove nails, then roll the burlap down to the base of the ball. Improve the soil from the planting hole with a slow-release fertilizer, and use it for backfill. When the hole is two-thirds full, fill it to the top with water or a starter solution; let the water soak completely into the ground. Fill the remaining space above the roots with backfill. Cover the ground around the tree with a mulch, and water well. Specimens of good size should be properly staked, but the stakes should be removed after the first year.

Care and Maintenance

If no significant rain falls, soak the soil under the tree's crown to a depth of 4 inches every 3 to 4 weeks during the summer heat. Fertilize in late winter with a general-purpose material such as 12-12-12 at the rate of 1 pound per inch of trunk diameter; spread the fertilizer evenly under the outer parts of the branches. As pests are seldom a major problem, treat on an "as needed" basis, according to advice from local experts. Lindane and Dursban are good insecticides to use on tree trunks for a variety of borers.

Additional Information

For greatest aesthetic appeal, plant these trees a good distance apart (based on expected mature size), so that they can develop natural, well-balanced crowns.

Additional Cultivars or Species

The scarlet oak, *Q. coccinea*, lacks the natural beauty of the Shumard oak but can be planted for variety of form.

Silver Bell

Halesia diptera

Other Name: Two-Winged Silver Bell
Zones: 8 and 9
Size: Expected mature size 25 to 30 feet tall, with a 20- to 25-foot spread
Type: Deciduous
Flowers: White, bell-shaped
Bloom Period: Spring

Light Requirement:

The silver bell is a native tree with several nice attributes. Although it prefers slightly acidic soil, it can be grown in many places where dogwoods will not survive; it is considered a suitable substitute for that popular species. It is a nice choice for relatively small spaces such as courtyards, small patios, and terraces. Those who have it in their landscape spend little time on pest control. About the only problem it has is a foliage fungus that occasionally appears in warm, wet weather. This tree's delicate, bell-shaped flowers hang along its branches, just as the foliage unfurls in spring—you will be impressed when you look up through the branches of a mature tree in full bloom. The two-winged fruit that follows the blossoms commands far less attention, but in the fall, the yellow leaves make a very nice display.

When to Plant

The cool dormant season (November through February) is the best time to plant this native species. Expect little trouble, however, if you plant shortly before (or just after) this period. A summer planting requires far more care to succeed.

Where to Plant

Plant near a cluster of other trees for a more naturalistic look, but don't hesitate to use this tree by itself. It can serve as a source of both shade and flowers around patios, terraces, or in enclosed courtyards.

How to Plant

Some authorities say this species is hard to transplant; others say it transplants rather easily. For best results, handle the young tree carefully to minimize injury to both the roots and the crown. Plant at the same level the tree was growing previously. By making the hole much larger than the mass of roots, the surrounding soil can be enriched with small amounts of organic materials and a little slow-release fertilizer—both of which will favor rapid spread of lateral roots. After removing container or burlap from the roots, place the tree in the hole and cover most of the rootball with improved soil. Add water or a starter solution to the hole to "melt" the soil around the roots; allow the liquid to drain completely into the ground. Finish filling the hole with the remaining soil. Mulch the tree, stake if necessary, and water.

Care and Maintenance

Little care is required after the tree is well established. To keep the tree vigorous and healthy, however, spread a little fertilizer under the branches in late winter. Materials like 8-8-8 or 12-12-12 are suitable. Use them at the rate of 1 pound per inch of trunk diameter. Don't worry about pests unless you see a problem. In the absence of sufficient rain, water every 2 to 3 weeks, especially during summer heat stress. When you do water, wet the soil to a depth of at least 4 inches.

Additional Information

When these trees are in bloom, hummingbirds will find them.

Additional Cultivars or Species

The Carolina silver bell, *H. carolina* (*H. tetraptera*), is a similar tree, but has four-winged fruit. Generally, Louisiana is not a suitable climate for this species. *H. monticola* is a northern Florida native that would probably do well in Louisiana. A variety of *H. diptera*, 'Magniflora' (also a native of Florida), is reported to have extra-large flowers.

Southern Live Oak

Quercus virginiana

Other Name: Live Oak
Zones: 8 and 9
Size: Expected mature size 50 to 60 feet tall, with an 80- to 90-foot spread
Type: Evergreen

Light Requirement:

The live oak is very popular statewide, but because of the occasional severe winters in the more northern parishes, it is really better adapted to the bottom part of the state. Nevertheless, very large, healthy, undamaged trees are not uncommon across the top of the state. Huge specimens with historical significance may be found throughout southern Louisiana—including the Evangeline Oak, the Seven Sisters Oak, and stately trees at such well-known plantations as "Rosedown." This oak's potential size requires careful selection of a planting site, so that it will have plenty of room to develop without creating problems for structures, pedestrians, vehicular traffic, and utility service lines. Gardeners living near coastal waters will be glad to know the live oak can handle salt spray. Although live oaks have a reputation for growing very slowly, their growth rate can be accelerated substantially by proper and regular fertilization, by supplying water at critical times, and by appropriate pruning.

When to Plant

The dormant season (November through February) is best, but a month on either side is satisfactory. Plan for extra care when planting at other times.

Where to Plant

Choose moist, fertile soil where there is plenty of space and full sun.

How to Plant

Dig a hole that is deep enough to allow the specimen to continue growing at the same level, but is much wider than the rootball (to encourage root spread). Improve the soil from the planting hole with a slow-release fertilizer, and use as backfill. Cut bindings or remove nails from balled-and-burlapped trees, and roll the burlap to the bottom of the rootball just after putting the tree in the hole. Position the rootball in the hole, and partly cover it with backfill to anchor the tree. Add water to "melt" the soil around the roots, and finish filling the hole with soil. Mulch tree, stake (if necessary), and water the area around the tree.

Care and Maintenance

Do any pruning in late winter; fertilize at the same time. Use a general-purpose fertilizer such as 12-12-12; apply it evenly under the tree's branches at a rate of 2 pounds per inch of trunk diameter. Water regularly to promote sustained growth; give emphasis to summer watering, when stress is greatest. To fight pests, use products with which you are comfortable, or consult with a local expert for specific advice.

Additional Information

If you are not familiar with old live oaks, visit areas where some of the historical specimens are located. Get a feel for their mature size and growth habits. Such an experience may help you decide if you want one of these potential giants, and where to plant one on your own property, if you do.

Additional Cultivars or Species

The Texas live oak, *Q. virginiana* 'Fusiformis', has a branch structure that is different from that of the species. The laurel oak, *Q. laurifolia,* is semi-deciduous, but its foliage bears a resemblance to that of the live oak. Its smaller mature size and rapid rate of growth make it better suited for cramped situations. Although obviously not a native, the Japanese evergreen oak, *Q. glauca,* has a much smaller crown than the live oak, and its branch structure is vastly different. It also has a lot of good qualities that make it worthy of planting, especially where space is limited. Unfortunately, this species may be difficult to find.

Southern Magnolia

Magnolia grandiflora

Other Name: Bullbay
Zones: 8 and 9
Size: Expected mature size 40 to 50 feet tall, with a 25- to 30-foot spread
Type: Evergreen
Flowers: White
Bloom Period: Spring to midsummer

Light Requirement:

Among evergreen trees, the southern magnolia is practically the monarch of the South. Its enormous white flowers stand out in bold relief against the dark green of the big leathery leaves, making it a tree of outstanding character. Perhaps this is why its flower was designated the State Flower of Louisiana; Mississippi chose the southern magnolia as its State Tree. Its nice, pyramidal form is often destroyed by homeowners who remove lower branches for mowing purposes. Unfortunately, they discover later that few plants are a match for this tree's highly competitive roots, and they wind up with frustration and a display of ugly roots. Without the lower branches to conceal the litter of the huge leaves, gardeners must perform yet another job. Although natural growth is relatively slow, late-winter applications of fertilizer can speed up the process. Several insects and diseases afflict this tree; they must be controlled to preserve its beauty. The tree does not take kindly to having any part of its root system disturbed, so avoid any major garden work near where it is planted. 'Little Gem' is a superior dwarf cultivar that is suitable for small spaces.

When to Plant

It is very important to install this tree between November and February. The further that you stray from this time, the greater the risk of losing the tree.

Where to Plant

Select a full-sun location for maximum bloom. Avoid heavy, compacted soils and wet sites.

How to Plant

Buy a plant of no more than 2- inch caliper. Dig a hole that is much wider than the rootball, and of such depth that the tree can be planted at the same level it was growing in the nursery. Cut bindings on balled-and-burlapped plants, and roll the burlap to the base of the ball. After positioning the plant, nearly cover the rootball with soil that has been enriched with a slow-release fertilizer and a small amount of organic material. Next, fill the hole to the top with water or a starter solution and allow it to soak completely into the ground. Finish filling the hole with the remaining soil. Apply an organic mulch around the tree and stake if necessary (this is optional for smaller trees). Thoroughly wet the soil surrounding the tree.

Care and Maintenance

Fertilize in late winter with a fertilizer such as 12-12-12; use it at the rate of 1 pound per inch of trunk diameter, and scatter evenly over the soil under the tree's branches. Confine any pruning to the period immediately after flowering. By consulting with your county agent, you can get the most up-to-date advice about handling insect and disease problems. Water as often as necessary to keep soil reasonably moist, especially during the summer months.

Additional Information

Foliage and cones of this species are widely used for decorations. The tree's ability to tolerate salt means that it can be used in coastal areas. Flowering occurs sooner on many of the new cultivars.

Additional Cultivars or Species

The sweet bay magnolia (*M. virginiana*) is a similar, but smaller, tree. Hybrids between these two species have resulted in 'Freeman' and 'Maryland' cultivars that possess greater cold hardiness (this is relatively unimportant in Louisiana). Some noteworthy cultivars of *M. grandiflora* are 'Little Gem' (the dwarf), 'Majestic Beauty', and 'Samuel Sommer'. Many other cultivars exist.

Swamp Red Maple

Acer rubrum 'Drummondii'

Other Name: Drummond Red Maple
Zones: 8 and 9
Size: Expected mature size 40 to 50 feet tall, with a 30- to 35-foot spread
Type: Deciduous
Flowers: Red; red fruits
Bloom Period: Early spring

Light Requirement:

The swamp red maple is a species native to the state. The greatest wild population is concentrated in southern Louisiana. Its ability to grow under both wet and dry conditions make it a frequent choice for landscaping. Its striking red flowers and early-spring fruits are most attractive, while the various reds, yellows, and oranges of the fall foliage give this species a second season of color. While the leaves show considerable variation, all are more deeply lobed than the red maple found in the cooler climate of the eastern United States. The swamp red maple is rated very highly in the New Orleans area; it also performs well in other regions. Perhaps its greatest shortcoming is its weak wood, which is subject to damage from high winds.

When to Plant

It is best to transplant this tree in the dormant season (late October to early March). More care is required if planting outside of this time period. Avoid planting during the hottest summer months.

Where to Plant

Choose full-sun locations if possible. If these are not available, sites in partial shade are satisfactory.

How to Plant

Select a young, vigorous plant to minimize transplant shock. Dig a hole slightly deeper than the rootball and twice as wide, so that the plant may continue to grow at the same level as it did in the container. If you purchase a balled-and-burlapped plant, cut the bindings, and roll the burlap down to the base of the rootball before filling the hole. Improve the soil from the planting hole with a slow-release fertilizer, and use it for backfill. After nearly covering the rootball with this soil, fill the hole to the top with water or a starter solution; allow the water to soak completely into the ground. Use the remaining soil to fill the space above the rootball. Mulch the ground surface around the tree and water thoroughly. Staking is optional for small specimens.

Care and Maintenance

In late winter each year, use a general-purpose fertilizer (such as 12-12-12) at the rate of 1 pound per inch of trunk diameter; spread it evenly over the outer parts of the root system. Mature trees need fertilization only once every 3 years. A permanent mulch over the shallow roots is beneficial to the tree but may not be aesthetically appealing. Pests are not usually a major concern with this species. Water as needed during dry periods, especially summer. This may be as often as every 2 to 3 weeks, depending upon soil type and other environmental factors.

Additional Information

Female trees have the bright-red, winged fruits that are twice the size of *A. rubrum*; these appear before the foliage in the late-winter/early-spring period. The fruit will sometimes stay on the tree for a month.

Additional Cultivars or Species

'Autumn Flame' and 'October Glory' are two cultivars of the red maple that do well in Louisiana.

Sweet Gum

Liquidambar styraciflua

Other Name: American Sweet Gum
Zones: 8 and 9
Size: Expected mature size 40 to 50 feet tall, with a 20- to 25-foot spread
Type: Deciduous

Light Requirement:

The sweet gum is a pioneer species prevalent throughout the state. Despite its good qualities, it is largely unappreciated by much of the populace; it is often referred to as a "trash tree." For a long period of its early life—a couple of dozen or more years—it has a shapely, elongated, pyramidal form which is quite attractive. The fall foliage is a rainbow of colors, from dark shades of purple to orange and yellow. On the downside, sweet gum has at least three major drawbacks. One is the abundant production of its fruit, commonly called sweet gum balls. If you are bare-footed, these prickly balls will be painful to walk on. They are a nuisance that must be removed from under the tree. Second, older trees are noted for their network of protruding surface roots, which makes lawn care more difficult. Finally, the tree is very sensitive to air pollution, making it a poor candidate for city use. But even if the sweet gum has only limited suitability as a landscape tree, it should be valued for the color it lends to rural areas in the fall.

When to Plant

Plant when trees are dormant (November through February). Planting at other seasons is possible, but these trees must receive more care if they are to survive. Avoid planting during the hot summer months.

Where to Plant

Plant in full sun or partial shade, preferably near the edge of the landscape or a short distance beyond any formal landscape.

How to Plant

Plant in a prepared hole at the same depth that the tree was growing in the container. Cut bindings on balled-and-burlapped trees, and roll the burlap to the bottom of the ball. Place the tree in the hole, and backfill with improved soil to cover the rootball. Quickly fill the hole to the top with water, allowing it to soak completely into the ground. Finish filling the hole with soil; mulch the ground surface around the newly set tree. Water the tree zone thoroughly.

Care and Maintenance

This tough tree requires little care, but it may need some extra water every 3 or 4 weeks during dry, hot weather. Remove fallen gum balls from under trees (most varieties) every year.

Additional Information

There is at least one variety of this tree that does not produce fruits: 'Rotundiloba'. Florel is a product which claims to eliminate fruit-set if you spray it on the tree at flowering.

Additional Cultivars or Species

Two related species, *L. formosana* and *L. orientalis*, may not be available in the state. Desirable cultivars of *L. styraciflua* include 'Autumn Gold', 'Burgundy', 'Festival', 'Moraine', 'Palo Alto', 'Rotundiloba', and 'Variegata'.

Taiwan Flowering Cherry

Prunus campanulata

Other Names: Flowering Cherry, Bell-Flowered Cherry
Zones: 8 and 9
Size: Expected mature size 20 to 25 feet tall, with a 12- to 15-foot spread
Type: Deciduous
Flowers: Bluish pink, bell-shaped; black or purple cherries
Bloom Period: Early spring

Light Requirement:

The Taiwan flowering cherry, especially the selection 'Okame', is rapidly developing one of the best track records of all the ornamental cherries in Louisiana. It has performed well in the New Orleans area, where it has received a high rating from horticulturists. It is also spectacular in Riverfront Park at Shreveport in the spring. In this northern location it blooms at about the same time the redbuds do. Despite the fact that it is an early bloomer, it has escaped any major cold damage to its showy blossoms during the time it has occupied the park site. Damage from late freezes is always a possibility, however. Its bluish pink, bell-shaped flowers hang in abundance throughout the branches; the flowers are followed by very small black or purple cherries that are attractive to birds.

When to Plant

It is best to plant this tree when it is dormant; late October to early March is the preferred period throughout the state. More care is required when it is planted at other times.

Where to Plant

Plant anywhere there is full sun and well-drained soil. It may succeed at the edges of plant masses where there is light shade.

How to Plant

Select well-drained areas or plant on a constructed mound. Dig a hole the same depth as the rootball, and 2 or 3 times as wide. Cut bindings on balled-and-burlapped trees, and roll the burlap to the bottom of the ball. Carefully loosen the root system; if the tree is root-bound, slash through the rootball to break up circular growth patterns. Mix a small amount of slow-release fertilizer with soil from the planting hole; use no organic additives. Replace the improved soil until three-fourths of the rootball is covered; then flood the hole with water or a starter solution. After the water has soaked into the ground, finish filling the hole with the backfill. Surround the plant with a shallow mulch, and water thoroughly. Staking is optional. You may plant seed in the top inch of soil; seedlings around mature plants are easily moved in late winter.

Care and Maintenance

Routinely check trees for the presence of insects. Treat as necessary. Scales and borers can be especially bad; tent caterpillars can also be a problem. Fertilize in late winter with a garden-variety fertilizer such as 12-12-12; use sparingly at first, and *never* exceed 6 pounds on mature trees. Spread fertilizer evenly under the outer half of limbs. Drip irrigation is the best way to apply water to established trees; plan for 1 inch of water every 10 to 14 days in hot weather.

Additional Information

Few flowering cherries do as well as this one in the deep South. Although it has been difficult to find in the trade in northern Louisiana, the 'Okame' cultivar should be the number-one choice.

Additional Cultivars or Species

The 'Okame' cultivar of *P. campanulata* may well be the best available. Other ornamental cherries (such as 'Kwanzan') have been planted in Louisiana—but their short life spans and their susceptibility to pests make them poor candidates for your landscape.

Vitex

Vitex agnus-castus

Other Names: Chaste Tree, Lilac Chaste Tree, Monk's Pepper
Zones: 8 and 9
Size: Expected mature size 10 to 15 feet tall, with an 8- to 12-foot spread
Type: Deciduous
Flowers: Blue, pink, and white
Bloom Period: Early summer

Light Requirement:

The vitex is common in older gardens, but for the last decade or so it seems to have gotten lost. When it blooms in early summer, it is commonly the center of attention, as most trees have completed their bloom cycle by then. The spike flowers appear at the tips of the twigs and branches, where they are displayed beautifully against the gray background of the foliage. There are some pink and some white varieties as well as the more common blue. If you are looking for a low-maintenance tree, you may have found one in the vitex. Few problems plague this species in the upper end of the state; in the more humid climate of southern Louisiana, however, there may be some moderate scale insect and disease problems. Other than steering clear of heavily shaded and poorly drained soil, you can plant a vitex about anywhere you wish. In fact, dry, open sites where the plant receives some environmental stress tend to make the tree bloom more profusely. Should temperatures bottom out during a very severe winter in north Louisiana, it is possible for the tree to freeze back to the ground—but mature trees that were in existence when the Red River froze over in 1983 are still doing well.

When to Plant

Give preference to the dormant season, or a few weeks on either end of it. Plants installed at other times of the year require more care. Avoid summer plantings.

Where to Plant

Full sun and relatively dry soils seem to trigger the best performance, so choose planting sites accordingly. With proper pruning to give it good form, the vitex can also be a very suitable specimen plant during the growing season; plant it where it is highly visible.

How to Plant

Position tree in a hole of about the same depth as the rootball, but at least twice as wide; the greater width encourages more rapid lateral root development. Enrich soil from the planting hole with a slow-release fertilizer—and perhaps a couple of shovels of an organic matter; use as backfill. After partly covering the roots with the soil, add water or a starter solution, and let the liquid soak in. Finish filling the hole with soil, and mulch around the tree. Staking is an optional practice, but it is recommended for larger specimens. Finish the planting process with a final watering.

Care and Maintenance

Vitex is relatively free of pests in the state's less humid areas. Where insects and diseases do damage, they must be controlled. Dormant and superior oils are non-toxic, and if applied correctly, will do a good job of killing scales. Diseases may be prevented or reduced with timely applications of fungicides. Use broad-spectrum fungicides, or seek advice from a local expert. Fertilize in late winter with an all-purpose material such as 12-12-12; spread the fertilizer evenly under the branches at the rate of 1 pound per inch of trunk diameter. Extra water is seldom needed, but watch trees for wilting during summer's torrid temperatures—especially in the dryer parts of the state.

Additional Information

The vitex is a native of southern Europe and western Asia. Butterflies may visit its flowers.

Additional Cultivars or Species

V. negundo has less-attractive flowers. Varieties of *V. agnus-castus* include: 'Alba' and 'Silver Spire' (both with white flowers); 'Rosea' (pink flowers); and 'Latifolia' (blue flowers and larger leaves).

Willow Oak

Quercus phellos

Other Name: Incorrectly called "Pin Oak" in some regions of the state (it is not the true pin oak) **Zones:** 8 and 9 **Size:** Expected mature size 70 to 80 feet tall, with a 40- to 50-foot spread **Type:** Deciduous	**Light Requirement:**

Willow oaks have an abundance of good qualities; they should be used much more extensively as shade trees all over the state. This species was chosen to line New Orleans' famous Canal Street in the business district, where it has performed rather well. It gets its name from its narrow, willow-like leaves, which produce much less litter than most of the oaks. Although deciduous, it sometimes acts like a semi-evergreen in Louisiana during mild winters; it nearly always holds its leaves well into the cool season. Low branches are commonly removed to accommodate pedestrian and vehicular traffic, but this in no way detracts from the tree's attractive form. The principal pests are spider mites and galling insects, both of which can be effectively controlled. This species may have a tendency to be chlorotic in alkaline soil. Since the willow oak is not as well known as many of the other oaks, demand for it is lower, and it is less likely to be in a nursery's inventory.

When to Plant

The dormant season (November through February) is the ideal planting time, but a month before or after this period often proves satisfactory. More care is needed when planting at other times.

Where to Plant

Plant in full sun for best form and performance. This tree is quite suitable for street sites and landscapes.

How to Plant

Dig a hole that is deep enough to allow the specimen to continue growing at the same level, but is much wider than the rootball (to encourage lateral root spread). Improve the soil from the planting hole with a slow-release fertilizer, and use as backfill. Cut bindings or remove nails from balled-and-burlapped trees, and roll the burlap to the bottom of the rootball (just after putting the tree in the hole). Position the rootball in the hole, and partly cover it with backfill to anchor the tree. Add water to "melt" the soil around the roots, and finish filling the hole with soil. Mulch the tree, and stake it securely if it is large enough to need it. Water the area around the tree.

Care and Maintenance

In late winter, use a general-purpose fertilizer (such as 12-12-12) at the rate of 1 pound per inch of trunk diameter; spread evenly under the outer parts of the branches. (Some gardeners double this amount.) Wet the soil to a depth of 4 inches during extended dry spells—particularly during summer heat stress. Frequency of watering will depend upon soil type, immediate environment, and severity of the weather. Perform major pruning tasks in late winter; incidental pruning may be done well into the growing season. Use products or methods of your choice to handle pest problems, or consult with a local expert for advice.

Additional Information

After one year, remove the support stakes used at planting time. Smaller trees can be treated with Orthene 75S, Lindane, or Malathion at bud-break to control galling insects. Be sure to follow label directions.

Additional Cultivars or Species

The true pin oak, *Q. palustris*, produces a similar canopy, but has much larger, lobed leaves which it holds most of the winter. It is considered by some to be one of the most beautiful of the oaks. There are more than 600 species of oaks.

CHAPTER ELEVEN

Tropicals

TROPICALS ARE PLANTS THAT ARE NATIVE to the tropical areas of the world where winters are warm. They have evolved little ability to experience temperatures below freezing without injury or even death. Winters in Louisiana are generally mild, but freezing temperatures occur regularly enough that tropicals are usually damaged and often killed during the winter. Even New Orleans gardeners know that they are not gardening in the tropics and that the use of tropical plants involves a certain amount of risk. What is it, then, that makes us want to grow tropicals? Perhaps it is that our winters may be mild-temperate, but our summers are definitely hot, humid, and rainy. As we retreat into our air-conditioned homes during the unbearable months of July and August, it can be tremendously gratifying to watch tropicals which flourish in the hot weather and wet soils as they revel in our gardens.

Another reason for the popularity of tropical plants is their incredible beauty. They often have large leaves that create a lush look in the landscape. Many tropicals are grown for their exotic flowers and have extended bloom periods that stretch through the summer months. They keep on flowering no matter how hot it gets and tropicals produce some of our most fragrant garden flowers.

Protecting Plants from Freeze Injury

One of the major cultural concerns when growing tropicals is how to protect them in the winter. Nighttime temperatures that make a quick dip into the low 30s or upper 20s generally pose little threat other than damage to the foliage. Temperatures in the low 20s or teens can cause major injury or even death, especially if below-freezing temperatures last for a long time.

Mulches can help protect plants growing in the ground. Use a loose, dry material such as pine straw or leaves. Mulches are best used to protect below-ground parts and crowns, or they may be used to completely cover low-growing plants to a depth of at least four inches. Leave plants completely covered for no more than three or four days.

If the weather has been dry, thoroughly watering plants in the landscape before a freeze may also reduce the chances of damage caused by strong dry winds which often accompany cold weather.

If they are not too large, individual plants can be protected by covering them with various-sized cardboard or polystyrene boxes. Larger plants can be protected by creating a simple structure and covering it with cloth fabric, tarps, or plastic. It need be nothing more elaborate than three stakes driven into the ground, sticking up slightly taller than the plant. The cover should extend to the ground and be sealed with soil, stones, or bricks to trap the warmth stored in the earth. Plastic covers should be vented or removed on warm, sunny days. For prolonged freezes with extreme cold in the teens provide a heat source under the covering.

To protect those tropical plants growing in containers and hanging baskets from winter weather, plan on moving them into buildings where the temperature will stay above freezing. If this is not possible, group all container plants in a protected area like the inside corner of a covered patio, and cover them with plastic. If plants are kept inside for extended periods, make sure they receive as much light as possible.

After the freeze is over, check the water needs of plants in containers and in the ground. Unless you are keeping them inside for the rest of the winter, move container plants back to their spots outside. Remove or vent plastic covers to prevent excessive heat buildup if the day is sunny. Pull back mulch that completely covered low plants.

Damaged growth on non-woody plants such as bird-of-paradise or ginger should be pruned away, and dead leaves on all plants may be removed. Delay hard pruning of woody plants until new growth begins in the spring. Don't be too hasty to dig up and remove plants that appear to be completely dead—they may eventually resprout in April or May.

We are fortunate to be able to grow a wide variety of tropicals as enrichment plantings in our landscapes. With careful selection, many will survive all but the most severe winters.

Angel's Trumpet

Brugmansia arborea

Other Name: *Datura arborea*
Zones: 8 and 9
Size: 8 feet tall, 5 feet wide
Type: Evergreen, but may be killed to ground in winter
Flowers: Large trumpets of white
Bloom Period: Summer

Light Requirement:

The large white flowers of angel's trumpet give it its name: the flaring funnel-shaped flowers hang down from the branches as if they were trumpets directed at earth from the heavens above. Native to northwestern South America, angel's trumpet can grow to be 6 feet tall in a single season. If the winter is mild and does not kill back the plant, it will grow to be eight to ten feet tall the following summer. The sweet lemony fragrance produced by the flowers at dusk is almost intoxicating. This is a wonderful plant to have by a patio or outdoor sitting area where the fragrance can be appreciated while enjoying the relative cool of a summer evening.

When to Plant

Container-grown plants can be planted in April (south Louisiana) or May (north Louisiana) through August. Earlier planting is preferred so the plant will have a chance to become well established before winter. Cuttings taken in summer root easily; they can be planted into the garden when they have developed a strong root system or kept in a container and planted out the next year at a larger size.

Where to Plant

Angel's trumpets bloom best and produce stronger trunks in locations that receive 6 to 8 hours of direct sun. These plants grow large, so allow them ample room. They are effective when planted at the back of a bed or used as a specimen plant.

How to Plant

Enrich the soil by digging in generous amounts of compost, rotted manure, or peat moss and a sprinkling of general-purpose fertilizer.

Plant at the same level it was growing in its container. Water-in thoroughly and mulch to conserve soil moisture and prevent weeds.

Care and Maintenance

Water during hot, dry weather, especially those plants that are newly planted and just getting established. Fertilize with your favorite granular, slow-release, or liquid fertilizer according to label directions. The type of fertilizer you choose is not of crucial importance, but fertilizing will indeed stimulate more vigorous and faster growth. In November, pile at least one foot of pine straw around the base for protection. If the plant is small enough, you may choose to cover it during freezes to preserve the top growth. With the protection of a thick mulch, the base should resprout in spring, even if freezes in the teens occur.

Additional Information

The complete hardiness of this plant may be questionable in the northern part of the state, but planting it is worth a try. With protection, the chances of its surviving an average winter are excellent. Angel's trumpet will bloom if grown in a large container; this method of culture allows the gardener to move the plant into a protected location for the winter or on those nights freezing temperatures are predicted to occur.

Additional Cultivars or Species

Brugmansia × *candida* produces white, yellow, or pink flowers that hang straight down facing the ground. *B.* × *insignis* produces white or salmon flowers. *B. versicolor* produces white flowers that turn apricot-peach with age. All are wonderfully fragrant.

Bird-of-Paradise

Strelitzia reginae

Zone: 9
Size: 4 to 5 feet tall with an equal spread
Type: Evergreen, but subject to freeze damage in winter
Flowers: Orange with a blue tongue
Bloom Period: Summer to fall

Light Requirement:

One of the most exotic-looking tropicals, bird-of-paradise is popular as far north as Baton Rouge. Where winters are colder in the central and northern parts of the state, growing this plant in the ground is a bit of a challenge. Bird-of-paradise plants have survived temperatures as low as 11 degrees Fahrenheit and extended periods below freezing in New Orleans with protection. Nonetheless, growing the plants in containers that can be brought in for the winter is wiser up north. The paddle-shaped leaves are 12 to 18 inches long, bluish green, and borne on stems two to three feet long. The plant has an upright, mounding growth habit. Its coarse leaves and architectural shape make it a noticeable focal point or specimen plant in the landscape. The dramatic flowers are produced on tall stems, usually above the foliage. Their shape is striking—a fan of orange-and-blue flowers rising out of a boat-shaped sheath.

When to Plant

Plant bird-of-paradise in late spring (after danger of frost has passed) through mid- to late summer. Earlier planting is best, as it gives the plants a better chance to become established before winter.

Where to Plant

Choose sunny locations on the south side of a house or another structure to protect plants from north winds in winter. Good drainage is important.

How to Plant

Prepare the spot for planting by digging in generous amounts of organic matter such as compost or fine pine bark. Plant it at the same level it was growing in the pot or slightly above. The crown may rot if planted too deep. If the plant is pot-bound, loosen the root system before planting. Water-in and mulch. When planting in a container, avoid using an overly large one; slight underpotting encourages bloom. Use a good well-drained potting mix.

Care and Maintenance

Bird-of-paradise plants require little care other than grooming and protection during hard freezes. Trim off unattractive leaves and faded flowers as needed. In winter, pile pine straw around the base, and cover the plant with plastic or fabric if nighttime temperatures are predicted to go below 28 degrees Fahrenheit. Make sure the covering extends to the ground, and remove it when temperatures go back above freezing. Prune freeze-damaged growth as it occurs. Fertilize in early summer, but be moderate. Excessive fertilizer stimulates foliage growth and means less flowering. Bird-of paradise plants are quite drought tolerant and rarely need to be watered when planted in the ground. Water containerized plants when the soil begins to dry. An occasional problem with white scale can be easily controlled with oil sprays.

Additional Information

If plants are frozen to the ground, cut them back and pile a thick mulch of pine straw over the crowns. Pull back the pine straw in spring when the weather is warm and settled. The plants will often come back up from the roots. Be patient, as they may not resprout until late April or May. The flowers are beautiful and long-lasting when cut.

Additional Cultivars or Species

Strelitzia nicolai, the giant bird-of-paradise, is too tender to plant in the ground even in New Orleans, although during mild winters, plants in the ground have grown large and bloomed there. This plant, with its large banana-like leaves, produces enormous white-and-blue flowers of typical shape.

Common Banana

Musa × paradisiaca

Zones: 8 and 9
Size: 15 feet tall, 8 feet wide
Type: Evergreen, but subject to winter injury
Flowers: Unusual pendulous spike with clusters of small flowers and large, dark-purple bracts
Bloom Period: After 2 or 3 years in early to midsummer

Light Requirement:

Yes, we can have bananas—we can grow these massive tropical plants throughout the state. Only in the warm coastal areas can we expect production, however, and then only occasionally. The banana is not a true tree. Since none of its parts ever become woody, it is considered a giant herbaceous plant. The true stem of the banana plant grows horizontally underground. The shoots that we think of as "trees" grow up from this underground stem. What is thought of as the "trunk" is actually the bases of the leaves tightly wrapped together, and is botanically called the pseudostem (false stem). Like most plants, the flower stalk of the banana originates from the stem, not from the leaves. This means that it starts at ground level, and must grow up through the pseudostem to emerge from the top among the leaves. A banana shoot must survive two or three years before the flower stalk will emerge and bloom.

When to Plant

Plant trees from containers or transplant clumps in April or May.

Where to Plant

Bananas are large plants and require plenty of room. This needs to be taken into consideration before you include them in your landscape. Locate banana plantings well away from property lines, as their ability to spread may cause problems for neighbors who do not want them in their yard. Bananas do well in full sun to part shade. They are not particular about soil or drainage and are widely adaptable.

How to Plant

Little or no soil preparation is necessary. The incorporation of organic matter and a little fertilizer into the area of planting will encourage quick establishment and vigorous growth (although lack of vigor in bananas is rarely a problem).

Care and Maintenance

Do not allow bananas to grow beyond their allotted space. Dig out any shoots in unwanted areas promptly. If you want to encourage fruit production, cut down banana trees only if they have truly been frozen to the ground. Otherwise, just trim off cold-damaged foliage.

Additional Information

Bananas require at least 2 summers, with a mild winter (temperatures staying in the mid- to upper twenties) in between, to successfully produce fruit. Fruits usually begin to appear in May or June and are produced on a long, pendulous stalk in clusters of five called hands. A number of hands form on each stalk, and all together are called a bunch. Once the bunch is set, no more bananas form, although the flowering stalk will continue to bloom and lengthen. The fruit begin to ripen in October through early December; they vary in quality. Harvest the bunch in the green stage and ripen indoors if threatened by freezing temperatures. Otherwise, let them turn yellow on the tree.

Additional Cultivars or Species

Although specific cultivars of bananas are rarely available at local nurseries, mail-order specialty companies are beginning to offer a wide selection of good-quality edible types. *Musa ornata*, the rose banana, is an ornamental species even hardier than its larger relative (to Zone 7). It is smaller growing and produces showy lavender-pink bracts and yellow flowers on erect stems. The small pink bananas produced are not edible.

Firespike

Odontonema strictum

Other Name: Cardinal Spear
Zones: 8 and 9
Size: 6 feet
Type: Evergreen, but subject to freeze damage in winter
Flowers: Terminal spikes of intense scarlet-red
Bloom Period: Midsummer to fall

Light Requirement:

At six feet tall, firespike has an imposing presence and makes a wonderful background plant for the garden. Its medium-coarse texture is created by shiny, six-inch-long leaves that are a rich green color and have slightly wavy margins. The flower spikes occurring at the tips of the branches are indeed fiery red, and they enliven shady areas where the firespike is planted. Growing about a foot long, they produce loosely spaced, one-inch, thin, tubular, dark-red flowers along their length. Despite their intense color, they are not overwhelming and have an overall graceful appearance. The flowers are irresistible to hummingbirds, and many gardeners plant firespike for that reason.

When to Plant

Transplanted or container-grown plants should be planted in April (south Louisiana) or May (north Louisiana) through August. If you plant earlier in the season, it will give the plant more time to establish itself before going through the winter. Transplanting should be done early when the weather is warm but not yet intensely hot.

Where to Plant

Plant in shady to partly sunny spots where the cardinal-red flowers can brighten up their surroundings. Firespike does not seem to be picky about soil type or drainage. Beds under trees are especially good as the canopy provides some protection from cold.

How to Plant

Careful bed preparation is not crucial if firespike is planted into average garden soil. Incorporating organic matter into the area along with a light sprinkling of general-purpose fertilizer will generally benefit the plant and encourage it to grow more vigorously. Set plants into the ground at the same level they were growing at the nursery. Water-in and mulch.

Care and Maintenance

Firespike can be kept smaller and bushier if you cut it back occasionally, especially in early to midsummer. Mild winters in coastal Louisiana will not kill back the plants, though average winters in the northern part of the state will often kill firespike to the ground. But don't worry. Mulch over the roots with 12 inches or more of pine straw in late November; if the winter kills them to the ground, cut the plants back and they will reliably resprout in the spring, even in the north.

Additional Information

Firespike is a dramatic plant for shady areas. It looks great with ferns, gingers, white sasanquas (*Camellia sasanqua*), and spider plants (*Chlorophytum comosum* 'Variegatum'). The flowers are long-lasting in fresh-flower arrangements.

Additional Cultivars or Species

A variegated form has been offered, but there is some debate on whether it is *Odontonema strictum*.

Fountain Plant

Russelia equisetiformis

Other Names: Coral Plant, Firecracker Fern
Zones: 8 and 9
Size: 3 to 4 feet tall with an equal spread
Type: Evergreen, but subject to winter injury
Flowers: Brilliant coral-red
Bloom Period: Summer to fall

Light Requirement:

It is easy to see how the common name of fountain plant arose. It looks like a fountain of green spray emerging from the ground with sparkling red droplets at the ends of its branches. The texture of this plant is incredibly fine, almost fern-like, yet it is tough as nails. In the mild climate of New Orleans, fountain plant has colonized crevasses in brick walls at the Botanical Garden in City Park. The color of the flowers almost glows, and it is set off beautifully by the filigree of light-green stems. The tiny leaves are not noticeable. Temperatures in the low twenties or teens will freeze fountain plant to the ground, yet even with no protection, it has been known to resprout from its roots after temperatures as low as 11 degrees Fahrenheit.

When to Plant

Plant in the late spring or early summer, although it may be successfully planted into the garden all summer. Transplant young seedlings that may appear around established plants in late spring.

Where to Plant

Fountain plant will thrive in full sun but will also bloom well with some shade. Planting in deep shade will result in sparse flowering. In north Louisiana where it will freeze back most winters, the plant will generally grow about 2 feet by 2 feet. In coastal areas with milder winters, fountain plant can grow twice as large as that. Plan accordingly for the space it will need.

How to Plant

Plant into a well-prepared bed enriched by digging in a 2-inch layer of compost, peat moss, or rotted manure and a sprinkling of general-purpose fertilizer. Set plants into the ground at the same level they were growing in their containers.

Care and Maintenance

This plant is virtually care-free. It has no insect or disease problems and is drought tolerant. Fertilize in early and midsummer with light applications of a general-purpose fertilizer (15-5-10, or 8-8-8 if soil phosphorus is low). Cover the plant when temperatures below the upper 20s are predicted. Cut back freeze damage if it occurs, and mulch heavily to protect the roots.

Additional Information

Fountain plant is outstanding in a container where its trailing branches can dangle gracefully over the sides. In a container, the plant is more vulnerable to the cold and should be brought in on nights when freezing temperatures are predicted. Fountain plant roots easily from 4-inch stem cuttings.

Additional Cultivars or Species

There are no selected cultivars or other species of *Russelia* in common cultivation.

Mexican Heather

Cuphea hyssopifolia

Other Names: Cuphea, Hawaiian Heather
Zones: 8 and 9
Size: 12 inches
Type: Evergreen, but may freeze back in winter
Flowers: Tiny; purple, lavender, or white
Bloom Period: Spring to late fall

Light Requirement:

In a chapter full of flamboyant, colorful plants, Mexican heather is quiet, unassuming, and utterly charming. This low-growing shrubby plant has small 1/4- to 1/2-inch bright-green leaves and is constantly covered with tiny flowers from spring to late fall. If cold weather didn't arrive, this native of Mexico would never stop blooming. Its texture is fine, and its flowers, though small, can virtually cover the dense, mounding shrub. The flowers are generally a pinkish-purple, but can also be pale lavender or white. Generally reliable at surviving winters in the southern part of the state, Mexican heather will also return from its roots in north Louisiana if the winter is not too severe.

When to Plant

Plant in spring after danger of frost is past, and through the summer.

Where to Plant

Locations that receive morning sun and some shade in the afternoon are ideal, but Mexican heather will grow in full sun if kept well watered. Plants will bloom fairly well in all but the densest shade. Avoid poorly drained areas which tend to cause the plants to rot.

How to Plant

Adaptable to a variety of soil conditions, Mexican heather will nonetheless appreciate good bed preparation. Dig in a 2-inch layer of organic matter and a light sprinkling of general-purpose fertilizer before planting. Plant at the same level the plants were growing in their pots and water-in. Mulch the bed to conserve soil moisture and prevent weeds.

Care and Maintenance

Water plants occasionally during hot, dry weather. Mexican heather can be sheared back as needed to keep the plants shapely and full. Mulch thickly during winter cold to protect the roots. Plants can be covered during sub-freezing weather to minimize damage to the top growth.

Additional Information

Many gardeners in Louisiana grow Mexican heather as an annual and pull it up when winter browns back the top growth. New plants are readily available and inexpensive to buy in spring. Mexican heather is excellent in containers.

Additional Cultivars or Species

The plants called Hawaiian heather generally grow more vigorously and have larger leaves than the standard types. There is a dwarf form that seems to be less reliable and more prone to rot.

Night-Blooming Jessamine

Cestrum nocturnum

Zones: 8 and 9
Size: 6 to 10 feet
Type: Evergreen, but subject to winter injury
Flowers: Clusters of small tubular flowers
Bloom Period: Late summer

Light Requirement:

The evening fragrance of night-blooming jessamine immediately transports one to the tropics. No self-respecting temperate-climate plant would dream of producing a perfume so sensual! You could wander around the garden at dusk for some time before you found the source—the clusters of small, greenish white, tubular flowers are as easy to overlook as the fragrance is obvious. The scent can be overpowering for some gardeners and is definitely not for the faint-of-heart, but it somehow seems just right on the sultry evening air of the Deep South.

When to Plant

Container-grown plants can be planted after the weather is warm and settled. Transplant seedlings that appear in the garden in late spring or summer.

Where to Plant

Night-blooming jessamine is a vigorous grower and sends out arching branches. Plant it to the back of beds or borders or in out-of-the-way corners. It is especially effective in enclosed courtyards where the fragrance will be intensified, and by patios and other outdoor sitting areas.

How to Plant

Plant in any good garden soil that isn't soggy. Night-blooming jessamine needs no special soil preparation to thrive. If your soil is rather poor, dig in generous amounts of organic matter and a light application of general-purpose fertilizer before planting. Set the plant into the ground at the same level it was growing. Water-in and mulch. Seedlings under 2 feet tall transplant easily.

Care and Maintenance

Mulch thickly around the base in early winter to protect the roots. The plant will freeze to the ground in winter in north Louisiana, but it should resprout reliably from well-mulched roots in late spring and rapidly regain its original size. In New Orleans, many gardeners cut back the plant in spring to control its size even if winter's cold caused little damage.

Additional Information

After the flowering, night-blooming jessamine produces clusters of attractive snow-white fruit that persist well into December if there are no freezes. Seedlings are rather common in landscapes with fruiting plants.

Additional Cultivars or Species

C. elegans produces showy clusters of rosy-purple flowers with no fragrance in fall and winter. *C. diurnum*, the day-blooming jessamine, bears clusters of creamy white flowers that are not nearly as fragrant as the night-blooming species.

Split-Leaf Philodendron

Philodendron selloum

Zone: 9
Size: 5 to 6 feet tall, larger with age in mild-winter areas
Type: Evergreen, but subject to freeze injury
Flowers: Large white spathes seldom seen, particularly in the northern part of its range
Light Requirement:

This plant is almost indispensable if you want to create a tropical-style landscape, as long as you have the room for it. Its overall effect is massive. With deeply lobed leaves up to three feet across on three- to four-foot-long petioles, a split-leaf philodendron can easily dominate the part of the garden where it is planted. Stemless when younger, with age and mild winters a trunk-like structure forms and holds the leaves well up off the ground. Common in landscapes in the southern part of the state, split-leaf philodendron is too tender to be completely reliable in north Louisiana—but in a protected location and with a little help, it has a chance of surviving all but the worst winters.

When to Plant

Plant in spring when the weather is warm and settled, and through the summer. Planting early in the season allows the plant to become better established before going through its first winter in the ground, and that may help it to survive.

Where to Plant

Although split-leaf philodendrons will grow in nearly full sun, the foliage will be darker green and growth will be more lush in partially shaded locations. They will also thrive in complete shade.

How to Plant

Plant in a well-prepared area enriched with organic matter at the same level the plant was growing at the nursery, though depth of planting is not critical. Water-in and mulch.

Care and Maintenance

Protect the crown and lower stems of the plants in the winter with a deep mulch at the base. You can reduce cold injury to the foliage if the plant is covered with cloth or plastic on nights when temperatures are predicted to go below the upper twenties. Remove freeze-injured leaves as damage occurs and cut the plant to the ground if damage is severe. It will resprout from its base in the spring. Water during hot, dry weather, particularly during the first year after planting. Fertilize with a general-purpose fertilizer in summer.

Additional Information

The split-leaf philodendron is an excellent houseplant. It stays smaller indoors and grows well in a brightly lit window.

Additional Cultivars or Species

The cultivar 'Hope' suckers freely at the base. Other philodendron species are of questionable hardiness in Louisiana.

Thryallis

Galphimia glauca

Zone: 9
Size: 4 to 6 feet
Type: Evergreen, but subject to winter injury
Flowers: Bright yellow
Bloom Period: Produced abundantly summer into fall

Light Requirement:

Few shrubs flower as profusely or over such an extended period as thryallis. Clusters of cheerful, small yellow flowers cover the bush continuously from June to early winter. The oval two-inch leaves are rich green with a slightly bluish cast, and are attractive in their own right. Although recommended hardy only in Zone 9, thryallis has returned from its roots after 11-degree temperatures with only a mulch for protection. This wonderful shrub has never been given a proper common name. Thryallis is the old genus name it bore before it was changed to *Galphimia*.

When to Plant

Wait to plant thryallis until after danger of frost is past, in April or May. Containerized shrubs can be planted anytime during the summer, even when in bloom.

Where to Plant

The shrubs will be more compact and heavier flowering when planted in full sun, but plants also grow well and bloom quite nicely in part shade. Choose a well-drained location. Thryallis can be used in the back or middle of beds and borders.

How to Plant

A well-prepared bed enriched with organic matter such as compost, peat moss, or fine pine bark will encourage establishment and vigorous growth. Add a light sprinkling of general-purpose fertilizer when you incorporate the organic matter. Set plants into the ground at the same level that they were growing in their container. Water-in and mulch.

Care and Maintenance

Little care is needed during the summer. Just sit back and enjoy the show. Thryallis plants are not susceptible to insects or diseases. Water during hot, dry weather and fertilize once or twice with a general-purpose fertilizer according to label directions. Mulch thickly around the base at the beginning of winter to protect the roots. You may also cover the plant if temperatures below the mid-twenties are predicted, but even if the top freezes, the plant will reliably resprout from the roots if mulched. Wait until spring and prune it back after it has resprouted so you can more clearly see just how far back to cut.

Additional Information

The bright-yellow flowers of thryallis work beautifully in a warm color scheme with oranges, peach, and warm reds. It also looks great with blues and purples and combines well with various perennial salvias, stokesia, and Russian sage (*Perovskia atriplicifolia*). Thryallis is excellent in containers and may actually be more satisfactory grown this way and protected from severe cold in north Louisiana.

Additional Cultivars or Species

There are no cultivars or other species of *Galphimia* in common cultivation.

Yesterday-Today-and-Tomorrow

Brunfelsia australis

Other Name: Brunfelsia
Zone: 9
Size: 5 feet
Type: Evergreen, but susceptible to freeze injury
Flowers: Violet-blue fading to white with age
Bloom Period: Late spring to early summer

Light Requirement:

Brunfelsia's hardiness in the ground is questionable if it is planted much farther north than New Orleans, and it is one of the more tender plants in this chapter, but it would have been hard to leave out such a lovely shrub. Still, some intrepid gardeners in Baton Rouge or Lafayette might have success with a sheltered location and winter protection. Besides, who could resist the chance of growing a plant with a name like yesterday-today-and-tomorrow? This charming but unwieldy name comes from the flower's changeable color. Opening rich violet-blue, the flowers fade with time to pale lavender and finally white. All three colors appear on the plant at the same time. The flowers produce a light, sweet fragrance and are at their peak in April and May, with an occasional second flowering in fall. This upright-growing shrub produces attractive, slightly glossy green leaves of medium texture.

When to Plant

Plants are usually purchased in full bloom at nurseries in late spring, and that's a good time to plant them into the garden.

Where to Plant

Brunfelsias do best in locations that receive some shade during the day, but avoid deep shade. Planting close to a house or under a tree will afford some protection in the winter. Make sure the spot drains well.

How to Plant

Prepare the spot for planting by digging in generous amounts of organic matter such as compost or fine pine bark and a light application of general-purpose fertilizer such as 15-5-10. Plant at the same level it was growing in the pot or slightly above. The crown may rot if planted too deep. If the plant is pot-bound, loosen the root system before planting. Water-in and mulch. When planting in containers, avoid using an overly large pot since slight underpotting encourages bloom. Use a good well-drained potting mix.

Care and Maintenance

Fertilize established plants in March with about 1/4 cup of 15-5-10 (8-8-8 if your soil is low in phosphorus). Water during hot, dry periods, especially newly planted bushes. Cold damage will be reduced if the plants are thoroughly covered when temperatures below the upper twenties are predicted, and mulch thickly around the base (at least a foot) with pine straw to protect the crown. Temperatures in the teens will usually kill the tops back even if covered, but with the protection of a heavy mulch, the base of the plant will usually resprout.

Additional Information

Use yesterday-today-and-tomorrow as a specimen plant or accent. Large plantings where permanent shrubs are needed are questionable because of lack of hardiness. The fragrance is especially nice in courtyards where it is intensified by the enclosure, and courtyard plantings are more protected.

Additional Cultivars or Species

According to *Hortus III*, most of the available cultivars belong to *Brunfelsia pauciflora*. They include 'Eximia', with slightly larger flowers; 'Floribunda', a rather dwarf, free-flowering selection; and 'Macrantha', with very large flowers.

CHAPTER TWELVE

Turfgrasses

IT HAS BEEN SAID THAT AN ATTRACTIVE LAWN is to a landscape what a canvas is to a work of art. This analogy only goes so far. While a painting is a static, relatively unchanging entity, a lawn is a dynamic collection of turfgrass plants, ever changing and subject to the pressures of the environment that surrounds and acts upon it.

The climate in Louisiana varies from slightly temperate in the northern tier of parishes to distinctly subtropical for the larger part of the state. This simply means that all Louisiana gardeners must depend on warm-season turfgrasses for their permanent lawns, using only one or two cool-season grasses to obtain a green lawn in the winter months. The long growing season, which ranges from eight to ten months depending on where you live in the state, provides sincere gardeners with lots of reasons to be outdoors. There always seems to be grass to cut, leaves to rake, insect and disease problems to handle, fertilizer to apply, irrigation water to add, and grooming to perform in order to meet standards of the community or perhaps your own high standards. But fear not! If there is severe competition for your time from family, organizations, or business, there are both professional lawn service companies and enterprising individuals to whom you can turn.

The number of turfgrasses is fairly limited. The most popular grass seems to be St. Augustinegrass because of its dark, rich, green color, its luxurious look, and the fact that it will grow satisfactorily on several different soil types. Second in popularity and definitely closing the gap is centipedegrass. It is well suited to the many poor soil areas in the state (even seeming to grow better on them than on extremely fertile soils) and has fewer pest problems than most other turfs. Bermudagrass ranks a solid third. Both carpetgrass and zoysiagrasses are still far back in the pack even though each has some desirable qualities. The ryegrasses—both annual and perennial species—cannot withstand the torrid heat of Louisiana's long summers and can therefore be considered only for temporary covers during the cooler months of the year or for use as an overseed grass to camouflage the dull brown colors of dormant warm-season turfs.

Warm-season turfgrasses spread by means of horizontal runners (stolons) that hug the ground or by underground stems called rhizomes. Their management, therefore, differs from that of the well-known Kentucky bluegrass of much cooler climates. Although the zoysiagrasses and the very fine-textured Bermudas present their best appearance when cut with a reel mower, the other species give a well-manicured look when cut with a rotary mower, provided the mower blades are kept sharp.

Both thatch and soil compaction are common problems that can keep lawns from giving their best performance. The first of these is fairly obvious to even the casual observer and can be addressed by a process known as de-thatching. A special machine made for this job will take care of a thatch problem nicely; cheap attachments for ordinary rotary mowers can damage the lawn when used improperly. Some of the turf species used in Louisiana have bad thatching problems, particularly the zoysias when they are planted in full sun. The new breed of mulching mowers is helping to reduce thatching since the ground-up clippings they produce rapidly decompose at the base of the turf. Soil compaction is a much less obvious problem than thatching, but it can be just as serious. Certainly it is worse in some types of soils than in others, but for any soil, loss of porosity means less soil air and thus less oxygen for the turf plants. Oxygen is just as essential for plant survival and development as is water, and it too enters a plant primarily through the root system. In some areas of the state, professional aerator machines can be rented, or you can pay lawn service companies to do this job for you. Late spring and summer are the best times for aerating lawns.

Establishing a Lawn

The appearance of a soil can be quite deceptive. Whether establishing a new lawn or renovating an old one, always collect a representative soil sample first and have it tested. In Louisiana, this can be easily accomplished by taking your pint sample to the nearest Louisiana Cooperative Extension Service office where you will be assisted in preparing your sample for sending to the LSU Soil

Testing Lab. The cost is minimal (less than $5.00 per sample) and the results will be in your mailbox in approximately three weeks. If you are unable to wait that long, there are private labs all over the country that will test your soil for you in much less time, but don't expect them to match the price. Here is a suggested step-by-step approach to "building" a lawn:

1. Use soil analysis information to determine the materials to use for soil improvement.
2. Remove any stones, litter, or other debris, including nails and miscellaneous materials that may have accumulated during new home construction.
3. When the soil will work well, loosen it to a 4- to 6-inch depth, preferably with a tiller for small areas or a tractor-pulled disc or tiller for large areas.
4. Evenly broadcast the soil-improving materials (recommended fertilizers, lime, or organic substances) over the entire lawn surface and then incorporate them using the machinery on hand.
5. Walk on the prepared ground as little as possible to avoid making indentations in its soft surface, and keep other people and animals off the prepared ground.
6. Use the planting method of your choice. If using seed, broadcast one half evenly in a north-south direction, the remaining half in an east-west direction. Cover most of the seed to a shallow depth by using light strokes with a leaf rake.

   If using sod, lay the pieces of sod tightly together, space plugs at recommended distances for the species of grass planted, and partially cover sprigs with soil or organic material. Dragging a heavy roller over newly sprigged ground has some advantages. Regardless of the planting method, finish the job with a slow but thorough watering. Solid sodding is the most expensive method, but it will give an "instant" lawn.
7. Keep the new turf reasonably moist for several weeks until it is well established.

8. In some situations, it is wise to kill the existing vegetation with a non-selective herbicide such as Round-up® (glyphosate) several days before seedbed preparation.

Basic Lawn Maintenance

The level of lawn maintenance varies greatly with individuals. Some gardeners are perfectionists who desire a picture-perfect expanse of grass, while others are satisfied just to have something green covering the bare soil around their homes. Reasonably well-kept lawns receive annual applications of fertilizer, are cut on a regular basis (usually weekly), are watered during hot weather, and receive help from their owners in fighting weeds, disease, and insect pests. There are many details that must be attended to when discussing the best practices in lawn care. Louisiana Cooperative Extension publication 2293, *Louisiana Lawn Maintenance,* is a very helpful guide. This publication is updated periodically to provide the user with the latest information on the subject.

Choosing a Turfgrass: Cool-Season Grasses

Cool-season grasses are used as winter covers for bare soil or as overseeds for permanent warm-season turf lawns. **Annual ryegrass** or mixtures of annual and **perennial ryegrass** are widely used in the state for both these purposes. **Turf-type fescues** have generally not proven very dependable in Louisiana.

Choosing a Turfgrass: Warm-Season Grasses

The **warm-season turfgrasses** offer a range of textures, shade tolerance, and pest resistance, and all can be grown successfully throughout the state. Some may be propagated by vegetative means only, while others may also be seeded. Most species are adapted to a variety of soil types, but **centipedegrass** seems particularly suited to poor, extremely acid soils. The **Bermudas** and the **zoysias** are tops for wear and tear, while **St. Augustine** and centipede are sensitive to heavy use. The characteristics of the various grasses should enter into the decision-making process, and you must also carefully evaluate your site, its soils, the presence (or potential presence) of heavy shade, and how the lawn area will be used before deciding which turf species will best fit your needs.

Bermudagrass

Cynodon spp. and hybrids

Other Names: Common Bermuda, Wiregrass, Couchgrass
Zones: 8 and 9
Texture: Fine
Climate: Thrives in heat
Wear Resistance: Good

Light Requirement:

Bermudagrass is a good choice where full-sun conditions prevail. Its dark-green color, fine texture, drought resistance, and wearability make it ideal for shade-free landscapes. When cut with a reel mower it can lend a touch of beauty and an air of formality to a home. The hybrid types are cut at a half-inch height which gives them good density and quality that is almost like a golf green. The common types are clipped at a one-inch height and also show good density. Due to their aggressive runners and rhizomes, they can all too quickly become a pest in flower beds and other non-turf areas of the landscape. Grass-specific herbicides can aid in their control.

When to Plant

Spring is the preferred planting time. Begin as early as late March in southern Louisiana and as late as early June in northern Louisiana. Some success may be possible as late as 2 months before the first frost.

Where to Plant

For best results, plant only in full sun.

How to Plant

Prepare a good seedbed and enrich it according to soil-test guidelines. Soak the seedbed. After it has dried sufficiently, sow seed of hulled common Bermuda at a rate of 1 to 1$^1/_2$ pounds of seed per 1000 square feet of lawn. Double this rate for unhulled seed. Separate the seeds in 2 equal parts, broadcasting half the seed in a north/south direction and the other half in an east/west direction. Rake in lightly with a leaf rake, and roll or cultipack. Complete the job with a slow, thorough watering. When starting with vegetative

parts, prepare the seedbed as directed above. Lay sod pieces tightly together or put plugs on 12- to 15-inch centers. Another technique is to scatter sprigs (stolons) over the surface, partially covering them with a bit of soil or other suitable materials and then compressing them into the seedbed with a heavy roller. Around 5 bushels of stolons will be needed for each 1000 square feet of lawn. Finish by watering to wet the soil to at least a 4-inch depth. Whether starting from seed or vegetative pieces, keep the newly installed lawn moist until turf plants are well established.

Care and Maintenance

Apply approved preemergence herbicides in late fall (to reduce winter weed populations) and again in late winter (to reduce spring/summer weed populations). Use a cleanup postemergence herbicide before the onset of hot weather to help control perennial weeds and those not killed by the other herbicides. Fertilize with a 3:1:2 ratio fertilizer in mid-spring, midsummer, and early September. Slow-release types are best but cost more; do not use these types for the fall application. If no label instructions are given, use 10 to 20 pounds of the regular fertilizers per 1000 square feet of lawn except for the last application, which should be only 5 pounds. If not using a slow-release fertilizer in spring, ammonium nitrate (34-0-0) may be used at spaced intervals in the summer, using no more than 3 pounds per 1000 square feet of lawn. Apply all fertilizers to a dry turf only and water-in immediately to avoid turf burn. The proper cutting height for common types is $\frac{3}{4}$ to $1\frac{1}{2}$ inches; for hybrids, $\frac{1}{2}$ to 1 inch.

Additional Information

Use a reel mower for best appearance. De-thatch as needed.

Additional Cultivars or Species

Common types are Jackpot, Sonesta, Sundevil, Guymon. Hybrids are Tifway 419 and Tifgreen 328.

Carpet Grass

Axonopus compressus

Zones: 8 and 9	**Light Requirement:**
Texture: Coarse	
Climate: Cold sensitive	
Wear Resistance: Moderate	

Carpet grass is a native of our state, but it does not make a high-quality lawn. Its heavy seedhead production demands frequent mowing with a rotary mower for best appearance. The medium-dense sod wears only moderately well, even if properly fertilized and watered. With its sensitivity to cold, it is best suited to southern Louisiana where other conditions for its best performance are also prevalent. Establishment is usually by seed.

When to Plant

Spring planting when soil temperatures are 70 degrees Fahrenheit or higher is best. Early to midsummer is okay.

Where to Plant

Plant in full sun, but lightly shaded areas will be tolerated.

How to Plant

Clear the area of perennial weed species with appropriate non-selective herbicides. After a few days, prepare a good seedbed and enrich it according to soil-test information. Several hours before planting, soak the seedbed with plenty of water. When it is dry enough to walk on, plant seed or vegetative parts. Divide the seed in half and sow the first half in an east/west direction, the other half in a north/south direction. One to $1^1/_2$ pounds of seed is needed for each 1000 square feet of lawn. Use a leaf rake to mix the seed with surface soil, and firm the seed in the soil with a heavy roller or cultipack. Water slowly and lightly to prevent washing. Keep the seeded area moist until the plants are well established. For vegetative establishment, prepare for planting as described for the seed method. Space plugs on 12- to 15-inch centers or place pieces of sod tightly together.

Care and Maintenance

Use a 3:1:2 ratio fertilizer in mid-spring, midsummer, and early September. Slow-release types are superior—but do not use a slow-release type for the September feeding! Follow label directions for all applications. Apply regular fertilizers at a rate of 10 to 15 pounds per 1000 square feet. Two pounds of ammonium nitrate per 1000 square feet may be used as a substitute for the midsummer feeding if used at spaced intervals during the summer months. Use only 5 pounds of regular fertilizer per 1000 square feet of turf in the fall. Apply all dry fertilizers only to a dry turf and then water immediately to avoid turf burn. The proper cutting height for carpet grass is $1^1/_2$ to 2 inches.

Additional Information

Because of the this grass's ugly seedheads, frequent mowing with a sharp-bladed rotary mower is necessary for an acceptable lawn appearance.

Additional Cultivars or Species

Authors are unaware of any.

Centipedegrass

Eremochloa ophiuroides

Zones: 8 and 9
Texture: Medium
Climate: Warm season
Wear Resistance: Moderate to poor

Light Requirement:

While its yellow-green color may keep many gardeners from choosing centipedegrass, this species of warm-season turf is rapidly gaining wide acceptance due to it relatively few pest problems, its need for less fertilizer, its adaptability to moderate shade, and its good performance on poor, very acid soils. Mowing has to be done less often due to its slower growth . . . but few complain about that. Centipedegrass is not a good choice for high-use areas, but flower beds that it surrounds will be reasonably safe from encroachment.

When to Plant

Late spring through early summer is the best time to establish centipedegrass.

Where to Plant

Plant centipedegrass in full sun or in light to moderate shade.

How to Plant

Use non-selective herbicides for perennial and other weeds occupying the area. After a few days, prepare a good seedbed and enrich according to soil-test information. Soak the new seedbed with water. After sufficient drying, distribute the seed evenly over the bed surface and mix it with surface soil with a leaf rake. One fourth to 1/3 pound of seed is required for each 1000 square feet. Water slowly to prevent washing. Germination may be sporadic and uncertain on soils that crust. Centipede is most commonly established by sod, plugs, or sprigs. Prepare a good seedbed as described for seeding and place sod pieces tightly together, alternating ends and middles. To plug, place plugs on 6- to 10-inch centers for faster coverage (use slightly greater spacing for economic considerations). If sprigging, distribute sprigs evenly over the bed area, partially cover with a small amount of soil or other suitable material, and firm the sprigs into the soil with a heavy roller or cultipack. Then water thoroughly. Keep the grass moist until the plants are well established.

Care and Maintenance

Use a 3:1:2 fertilizer in mid-spring, midsummer, and early September. A slow-release product is generally superior but costs more. Do not use a slow-release type for the fall feeding! Regular fertilizers are applied at a rate of about 6 to 8 pounds per 1000 square feet, except in the fall when the rate is cut in half. Ammonium nitrate may be substituted in the summer months at spaced intervals, at a rate of 2 pounds per 1000 square feet. Apply all dry fertilizers to a dry turf and water heavily immediately afterwards to avoid turf burn. Rotary mowers give a well-groomed appearance. The recommended cutting height is $1\frac{1}{2}$ to 2 inches.

Additional Information

Pest problems are relatively few in number, but be sure to identify them if any should occur and then treat for control. Do not overfertilize! Some authorities suggest using no more than one pound of actual nitrogen per 1000 square feet per growing season.

Additional Cultivars or Species

Two cultivars are 'AU Centennial' (a dwarf selection) and 'Oaklawn'.

Ryegrass

Lolium multiflorum

Other Names: Annual, Common, Italian
Zones: 8 and 9
Texture: Medium
Climate: Cool season only
Wear Resistance: Moderate

Light Requirement:

The ryegrasses are used in Louisiana to cover bare-soil areas in the cooler parts of the year and for overseeding warm-season permanent turfs to camouflage their brown-to-tan dormant foliage while providing a carpet of green for the winter scene. Although not noted for cold hardiness, they are rarely damaged by Louisiana winters. Unlike the warm-season turfs, they do not produce either stolons (runners) or rhizomes. This means they must be started from seed—but germination is almost certain and the seed is fairly cheap. Mixtures of annual and perennial types may give better appearance and wear but may not be worth the extra cost.

When to Plant

Plant or overseed in October or November, depending on where you live in the state. The later date may be best for southern areas.

Where to Plant

Ryegrass does best in full sun but may be planted in lightly shaded areas.

How to Plant

Prepare a good seedbed and enrich according to soil-test information. This will benefit both the ryegrass and the warm-season species that will replace it the following spring. Wet the soil; when it is sufficiently dry, distribute the ryegrass seed evenly over the surface. Use about 8 to 10 pounds per 1000 square feet and scratch the seed into the soil surface with a leaf rake. To prevent washing and to encourage rapid germination, finish by watering slowly but thoroughly. To overseed, cut the permanent turf much closer than normal. Collect the clippings unless you are using a mulching mower. Distribute the seed evenly over the existing turf at a rate of 10 to 15 pounds of seed per 1000 square feet. Water heavily to hasten germination.

Care and Maintenance

Cut as needed to maintain an approximate 2-inch height and to thicken the grass through a process known as "tillering." In order to favor good color, adequate growth, and reasonable winter hardiness, use at most one pound of nitrogen per application (for example, 2 to 3 pounds of ammonium nitrate for each 1000 square feet of lawn). Make the first application around the end of November in northern Louisiana and in mid-December in southern Louisiana. Follow these with a second and final application 7 weeks later.

Additional Information

A single application of a slow-release high-nitrogen fertilizer may be applied around the end of November in lieu of any other fertilization. Keep mower blades sharp to avoid brown tips at the ends of the grass leaves.

Additional Cultivars or Species

There are many varieties of ryegrass, but since ryegrass is used only as a temporary grass in Louisiana, buying expensive cultivars is a waste of money. We recommend using high-quality seed. Another type is turf-type perennial ryegrass, *L. perenne*.

St. Augustinegrass

Stenotaphrum secundatum

Zones: 8 and 9
Texture: Coarse
Climate: Cold sensitive
Wear Resistance: Moderate

Light Requirement:

Even with its many problems and the fact that it is not generally established by seed, St. Augustine is usually the first choice of Louisiana gardeners. Its rich look, its vigor, and its ability to grow well in sun and moderate shade all contribute to its popularity. Its cushiony feel is that of a soft carpet. Tolerance of salt spray makes it one of the few turfs suitable for coastal areas.

When to Plant

Plant in the spring when soil temperatures reach 70 degrees Fahrenheit. Summer plantings are less desirable.

Where to Plant

Plant in full sun or moderate shade. Avoid high-traffic areas when practical.

How to Plant

Eradicate existing vegetation with appropriate non-selective herbicides. After a few days, prepare a seedbed and enrich following soil-test guidelines. Water thoroughly, then let it dry until you can walk on it. Solid sodding is expensive but will result in an "instant" lawn. Lay sod pieces tightly together and alternate ends and middles. Small plugs are spaced from 1 to $1^1/_2$ feet apart; large 4-inch plugs are spaced one foot apart. The root part of the plugs should not protrude above the soil line. Sprigs should each have a few roots. Place the sprigs in parallel shallow trenches spaced 10 to 20 inches apart. Individual sprigs should be upright with roots completely covered with soil. The closer the sprigs, the faster the coverage. Water the area thoroughly when finished and keep it moist until the plants are well established. Thereafter, irrigate as necessary to maintain soil moisture.

Care and Maintenance

Use a 3:1:2 ratio fertilizer in mid-spring, midsummer, and early September. A slow-release plant food is a good choice, but don't use this type for the fall feeding. If using regular fertilizers, you may want to use a high-nitrogen product for the summer application. Such materials are best applied in small doses at 4- to 6-week intervals, but don't exceed 5 pounds of actual nitrogen per 1000 square feet per year. Apply dry fertilizers to dry turf only and then water heavily to avoid turf burn. Weekly mowings are normally required and the grass should be cut at a 2- to 3-inch height. Mulching mowers eliminate the need to collect clippings. De-thatching may be necessary on occasion, and periodic aeration is a rewarding practice that promotes good, healthy turf. Help prevent diseases with timely spring and fall applications of recommended fungicides; control insects on an "as needed" basis. Use appropriate herbicides in late fall, early spring, and late spring for weed problems. Brown patch is the most common disease, while chinch bugs are the worst insect pest. Seek advice from your county agent on these pest problems.

Additional Information

Virus-infected turf must be replaced. Varieties with the greatest cold tolerance should be chosen for northern Louisiana. St. Augustine is somewhat invasive of flower beds and other non-turf areas.

Additional Cultivars or Species

'Floratine' may be the oldest variety still available; it is somewhat susceptible to disease. 'Floratam' should not be used north of New Orleans. 'Seville' is finer textured and has virus resistance and chinch bug tolerance, but it is less cold hardy than some others. 'Raleigh' has cold tolerance and virus resistance. 'Delmar' is better than 'Raleigh' and has greater shade tolerance. 'Floralawn' has superior disease and insect resistance, coarse foliage, and reddish stolons. Seeded St. Augustine cultivars are relatively new.

Zoysiagrass

Zoysia spps.

Zones: 8 and 9
Texture: Fine to medium-fine
Climate: Heat and cold tolerant
Wear Resistance: Good

Light Requirement:

Zoysia's tendency to thatch badly in full sun, the slow growth of several varieties, and its limited availability in some parts of Louisiana may have diminished its popularity. The absence of seeded varieties in the past may also have been a contributing factor to the fewer plantings of this turf. Now gardeners are discovering the newer zoysias, some of which can be established from seed and some which are capable of single-season coverage. Their toughness to wear, competitiveness against weeds, and ability to grow in some degree of shade should expand their use.

When to Plant

Zoysia is best planted in the spring after soil temperatures reach 70 degrees Fahrenheit. Summer plantings require more care.

Where to Plant

Zoysia is best planted in light- to moderate-shade areas. It grows well in full sun, but thatches badly, especially in southern Louisiana.

How to Plant

First eliminate perennial weeds with appropriate herbicides. After a few days, prepare a seedbed following soil-test guidelines. Soak the seedbed and then let it dry until it is workable. When planting seeded varieties, broadcast the seed evenly over the bed and scratch it into the surface with a leaf rake. Water thoroughly (but slowly to prevent washing). Maintain soil moisture with timely irrigation. Establish non-seeded varieties by sprigs, stolons, or sod. Plugs may be used, but this method is not recommended. After seedbed preparation, place sod pieces tightly together, alternating ends and middles. This produces an "instant" (though expensive) lawn. Place sprigs (small pieces with roots) in shallow trenches in an upright position, with most of each sprig embedded in the soil. Spreading chopped stolons (runners) over the loose seedbed is a good way to start zoysia. Ten bushels of stolons will be needed for each 1000 square feet. Press stolons into the loose earth with a heavy roller or cultipack. Then cover them with 1/4 inch of sand or 1/2 inch of a mulch such as peat moss, rotted sawdust, or shredded bagasse. Re-roll to ensure soil-stolon contact. Wet the area thoroughly and maintain an even moisture supply by timely irrigations.

Care and Maintenance

Use a 3:1:2 ratio fertilizer in mid-spring, midsummer, and early fall. Slow-release fertilizers are ideal but expensive, and they should not be used for the fall application. Ten pounds of fertilizer per 1000 square feet of turf should be sufficient for spring and summer feedings; 5 pounds is suggested for the fall. Whatever you choose, don't exceed 4 pounds of actual nitrogen per 1000 square feet per year. Apply fertilizers to a dry turf and water heavily to avoid turf burn. Failure to de-thatch once or twice annually in sun areas can necessitate turf replacement after just a few years, especially in southern areas. Cut to maintain a height of one inch. Help prevent diseases with timely treatments of appropriate fungicides in the spring and fall seasons, and control insects as necessary. Your county agent can advise you on these matters.

Additional Information

Zoysia makes one of the highest-quality lawns. The greatest beauty is achieved with a reel mower. Watch for more introductions of seeded cultivars.

Additional Cultivars or Species

'Meyer Z52' (japonica), though coarse-textured, is highly advertised. 'Emerald' is frequently used in southern Louisiana and has a desirable fine texture. 'Matrella' is similar to 'Emerald' but more shade tolerant. 'El Toro' resembles 'Meyer' but can give complete coverage in one season, and it seems better able to handle stress. 'Zenith' is a new seeded cultivar, but the seeds are expensive.

CHAPTER THIRTEEN

Wildflowers

WILDFLOWERS CAN COLOR A LANDSCAPE like a painter colors a canvas. To our delight, they come in a seemingly endless variety of colors, shapes, and sizes, and the flowers of many species are enhanced with foliage of interesting textures and colors. Some send up a blossom on the end of a leafless stalk and are so dazzling that they grab our attention the instant we see them. Some that are very attractive lack any hint of fragrance, while others are endowed with a perfume-like essence.

Although Louisiana is blessed with a broad array of wildflowers, it's only been in recent years that substantial efforts have been made to get them established along primary roadways where they can be showcased to the passing public. Perhaps it was the beauty of the bluebonnets and the Indian paintbrushes along Texas interstates that finally triggered the move to get Louisiana wildflowers out where they could be seen and enjoyed. Whatever the reason, citizens' groups and civic organizations across the state are now promoting wildflower plantings in an attempt to beautify their cities and the corridors which run through them as well as the long stretches of rural highways that link these metropolises. I believe there are active bodies in each of the major cities working on wildflower projects; I personally work with a wildflower committee in Shreveport Green to achieve better coverage of barren or unattractive areas within the urban setting.

Even though gardeners receive much pleasure from the beauty of roadside wildflowers, many want to have them a bit closer to home, perhaps in the backyard or just across the fence from the formally landscaped area. They really don't require much space, and once established, can take care of themselves with only a little care from their owners. For the record, a wildflower is a plant which is native where it is found and thrives there because it is so well suited to the soils and climate of that region. It typically grows and prospers without cultivation or interference by humans. There are some exceptions to this general description. Some wildflower species may not have originated in a particular place, but they were introduced in some way and continued to grow and spread just like one of the true natives. The "naturalization" of such species often increases the variety of plants and is considered desirable as long as the new kids on the block do not become overly invasive and crowd out any existing species.

Inexperienced gardeners may think that it doesn't take much to establish a planting of wildflowers, but nothing could be further from the truth. It takes a lot of work and planning to get wildflowers started and into a cycle whereby they can perpetuate themselves from year to year. Most gardeners work with mixtures rather than single species, although there are some advantages to either approach. Mixtures are usually customized for a particular area or region and should be used primarily in or close to that geographical space. It is strongly suggested that these mixtures, or seeds of specific flowers, be ordered from reputable seed firms, for collecting seed from the wild carries both legal and physical risks. Physical risks? Yes, in Louisiana, the places where the wildflowers grow may also be where the snakes lie.

Establishing wildflowers usually means starting with an unused space. The first step is to free it of any vegetation that would compete with the plants you're trying to establish. This may be done mechanically or with the right kind of herbicides . . . or both. The idea is to kill both the green plants that are seen and to sprout and kill as many of the seeds in the top layer of soil as possible. A soil test will reveal whether or not fertilizer or other amendments should be mixed into the soil, but only a minimum amount of soil improvement should be done because wildflowers are usually better competitors on poor soil of low fertility. Seed are generally sparsely broadcast over a thin layer of disturbed soil in March and early April or, even better, in October and early November. Special seed treatments or a regular supply of moisture in the absence of rain may be needed to get the seed sprouted and to help root penetration of the soil. Both annual and perennial species are included in most mixtures. Until your wildflowers are well established, you may have to give them some help fighting competing vegetation.

Beebalm

Monarda fistulosa

Other Names: Oswego Tea, Horsemint
Zones: 8 and 9
Size: 2 feet tall
Type: Perennial
Flowers: White with light-pink or purple centers
Bloom Period: Summer

Light Requirement:

This species of beebalm is native east of the Rockies; it is not as showy as some of the forms that have been adapted for garden use. The *M. fistulosa* has light-purple to light-pink flowers in tight whorled clusters surrounded by near-white bracts with flowers located at the tips of the stems. This "wild-type" beebalm does not attract hummingbirds and butterflies to the extent that the garden varieties with red flowers do. Although fertilization is not suggested for wildflower plantings, beebalm will respond to generous additions of organic matter to the soils that it occupies. With ample soil organic matter and plenty of water, the clumps of this plant spread rather rapidly, forming dense mats of fibrous roots. When soils are too fertile, the plant can become invasive and crowd out other plants.

When to Plant

Beebalm is probably best started from divisions or transplants in March or April and from seed in October or early November. Seed may be sown in the spring months and divisions may be set out in the fall. With care, this species may be planted almost anytime.

Where to Plant

Plant in sun or partial shade, but if you have a choice, select sunny areas. If planted where soils have a relatively high content of organic matter, performance tends to be somewhat better as long as soil fertility level is only average.

How to Plant

First eradicate existing vegetation with appropriate chemicals and/or by tilling the soil to a shallow depth several times to germinate and subsequently kill unwanted "weed" seed. Next incorporate generous quantities of organic materials into the topsoil. Peat moss (if it can be afforded), compost, and weed-free grain straw or hay are all suitable amendments. Mix seed at a ratio of 1:1 or 1:2 (by volume) with coarse sand and scatter sparsely over moistened soil. Use 1.2 ounces of seed per 1000 square feet of space. Lightly rake it into the soil surface and then press with a heavy roller or, for large areas, use a cultipacker. Keep soil moist for 4 to 6 weeks. When planting divisions or transplants, set at a shallow depth and space plants 10 to 24 inches apart.

Care and Maintenance

Assist established plantings by removing stubborn perennial plants of competing species by either pulling them up on a regular schedule or by smearing them with an appropriate systemic herbicide such as Roundup®. Water to supplement natural rain whenever plants show signs of drought stress, but wet the soil, not the plants, if that can be conveniently done. Thin out overly thick plantings to prevent the crowded conditions that create a favorable environment for diseases such as powdery mildew or rust. Spray plants with broad-spectrum fungicides to curb the spread of diseases when they appear. A well-timed mowing after seed have matured and raking off the litter will give a better appearance to the area.

Additional Information

Beebalm is not regarded as a long-life plant in Louisiana, but will perpetuate itself via seeds, much like an annual, if planting is properly handled. Removing spent flowers regularly extends the period of bloom. *M. fistulosa* plants have been quite long-lived (8 years) at the Botanical Garden in New Orleans. *M. didyma* does tend to be short-lived.

Additional Cultivars or Species

M. didyma is a similar species that has been more fully developed for garden use. Its 'Cambridge Scarlet' is an old variety that has remained popular. Newer varieties are 'Croftway Pink', 'Adam', 'Blue Stocking', and 'Mahogany'. 'Violet Queen' and 'Marshall's Delight' (pink) are mildew-resistant varieties. *M. citriodora* is another species recommended for wildflower use in Louisiana.

Black-Eyed Susan

Rudbeckia hirta

Other Name: Gloriosa Daisy
Zones: 8 and 9
Size: $1^1/_2$ to 3 feet tall
Flowers: Yellow with black center
Bloom Period: Summer

Light Requirement:

Black-eyed Susan, a tough native of the region that includes Louisiana, is probably one of the most recognized of all the wildflowers. It is a perennial that grows on almost every type of soil except very wet soil. It actually seems to thrive on dry, infertile soils, where it is a strong competitor for other species of plants. Typically growing to a three-foot height, its yellow-petaled, almost daisy-like blossoms are a joy to see whether massed in colonies of thousands or scattered in small groups among other plant species. The black-eyed Susan is classed as either a short-life perennial or a biennial, but since it commonly produces flowers the first summer after a spring planting, for all practical purposes it can be considered an annual. Not only does this species attract butterflies, it also furnishes a good supply of seed for birds. There are good reasons to include the black-eyed Susan in your wildflower plantings!

When to Plant

Plant seed in March, early April, October, and early November, or set out good-sized transplants any time during the growing season.

Where to Plant

The most important location considerations are a well-drained soil and full sun, but try to select areas of high visibility as well.

How to Plant

Eradicate competing species where the plants are to be established; this may be done either mechanically or chemically. When it has been determined that such a goal has been met, mix the seed with coarse sand at a 1:1 or a 1:2 ratio and broadcast over the prepared soil. Use 0.8 ounces of seed per 1000 square feet of space. Rake the seed into the soil so that they will be covered with earth to no more than 1/4-inch depth. Then tamp or use a heavy roller to assure good soil-to-seed contact. Moisten the soil and keep damp until plants become established. Fall-planted seed may not germinate until the following spring. Should you want to start with established plants, you may be able to find some at local nurseries. Plants may be set out any time during the growing season, but establishing them before the arrival of severe heat stress has its advantages.

Care and Maintenance

Once established, very little care is required. Reduce the numbers of competing plant species by occasionally pulling up invaders or by smearing them with systemic herbicides. Mow after seed have matured to disburse the seed over the ground; remove excessive clippings.

Additional Information

Black-eyed Susan, particularly some of the improved cultivars, makes good cut flowers. Cutting some of the earliest-appearing blooms may encourage a second, late-season blossom cycle.

Additional Cultivars or Species

Some excellent cultivars of *R. hirta* are 'Goldilocks', 'Marmalade', 'Pinwheel', and 'Sputnik'. *R. maxima, R. amplexicaulis,* and *R. fulgida* are related species.

Blazing Star

Liatris spp.

Other Name: Gayfeather
Zones: 8 and 9
Size: 1 to 5 feet tall
Flowers: Purple or white
Bloom Period: Summer, fall

Light Requirement:

This interesting perennial grows from thick, fleshy rootstocks which send up long stems in the summer or fall months, depending upon the species. The stems are clothed in short, narrow leaves. Above the leaves are small, fluffy flowers of purple (mostly) or white, crowded together in a plume-type structure at the top of the plant. An unusual characteristic of this plant is that the flowers of most of its species open from top to bottom, the opposite of most plants. These plants are survivors—they are able to withstand cold winters, the severe heat stress of Louisiana summers, poor soils, and extended periods of low rainfall. The grass-like foliage of the liatris is unexpected, but it serves the needs of the plant quite well. If larger flower spikes are desired, just raise the fertility level with a little fertilizer and floral spikes will increase in size. Be prepared to provide extra support with stakes, as the plants may become top-heavy with their bigger blossoms. While valued for the most part as a wildflower, the liatris produces a "line" type flower that is frequently used in fresh floral arrangements. This may be reason enough to include it in any of your wildflower plantings.

When to Plant

Plant seed in March, April, October, or November, but give preference to the fall months. Plants may be set out when they are available during the growing season, but the more stressful the environmental conditions, the greater the amount of care will be required.

Where to Plant

For best results, plant in full sun on a fertile, well-drained soil.

How to Plant

Mechanically or chemically eliminate competing species wherever plants are to be established. To reduce the number of embedded seed brought to the surface, disturb the soil only to a shallow depth. Plant liatris seed at the recommended times and mix them with coarse sand at a 1:1 or 1:2 ratio before broadcasting over the prepared soil. This will help prevent getting the plants too crowded. Rake the seed into the top surface of the soil, tamp lightly or roll with a heavy roller to improve seed-to-soil contact, and keep the area moist for 4 to 6 weeks. If fall-planted seed don't germinate within several days, look for them to come up the next spring. Use just under 5 ounces of seed per 1000 square feet of space.

Care and Maintenance

If planting showed a significant lack of vigor the previous year and foliage color left much to be desired, consider a very light application of an all-purpose fertilizer in late winter. A commonly available fertilizer such as 8-8-8 may be used at the rate of 2 to 3 pounds per 1000 square feet of space. One-quarter to 1/3 of a pound per 100 square feet would be a comparable amount. Neither insects nor diseases are common problems. If necessary, remove competing plants. Mow the planting in fall after seeds have matured. Rake and discard cut stems if they are excessive.

Additional Information

Several improved varieties of this flower are used in large quantities in the florist business.

Additional Cultivars or Species

L. ligulistylis features darker, reddish-purple flowers, and *L. microcephala* is practically a miniature at a foot in height. *L. scariosa* has flowers that open all at the same time. *L. spicata* appears to be the most preferred species and seemingly has undergone more development. Cultivars of this species listed in the trade include 'Floristan White' and 'Alba' (both white) along with 'Floristan Purple' and 'Kobold'.

Butterfly Weed

Asclepias tuberosa

Zones: 8 and 9
Size: $1^1/_2$ to 3 feet tall
Flowers: Orange
Bloom Period: Mid- to late summer

Light Requirement:

Previously regarded as no more than a common weed, and not fully appreciated for its beauty, the butterfly weed has gained more respect in recent years. This plant's brightly colored orange flowers seldom fail to grab our attention when they begin appearing along our roads and in our fields during mid- to late summer and into the fall. Because this perennial can endure hot, dry, infertile soils, its competitors are often few in number and it may have the stage all to itself. As this is a plant that doesn't mind alkaline soils, you will find it in alkaline soils throughout Louisiana, but generally only in colonies of limited size. The name "butterfly weed" did not happen by accident—this plant's flowers always attract great numbers of butterflies. The butterflies don't have exclusive rights to it, however; bees also visit it often when it's in bloom. It is a member of the milkweed family, but it doesn't leak milky fluid when it is broken or cut. It does have one characteristic in common with them: it's extremely poisonous.

When to Plant

Collect seed in late summer after they have matured and put in sealed containers in your refrigerator until spring. Plant in March. Root cuttings may also be planted at this time.

Where to Plant

Choose full-sun locations where the soil is sandy and infertile.

How to Plant

Till the area to be planted to a shallow depth, water to encourage sprouting of embedded seed, then re-till to destroy the seedlings which appear. After mixing with sand to help avoid too thick a stand (although in practice this is rarely a problem), rake the soil level and distribute the butterfly weed's seed as evenly as possible over the surface. Use about 10 ounces of seed for each 1000 square feet of space. Next, rake the seed into the soil surface and tamp lightly or roll with a heavy roller to improve seed-to-soil contact. Keep the area moist for several days to favor germination of the seed. Place root cuttings at a shallow depth.

Care and Maintenance

Little care is required. If competing plants crowd the butterfly weed, remove them by pulling or smearing with a systemic herbicide. Use markers to identify location of dormant butterfly weed plants so that resting plants will not be disturbed or destroyed. Do not use insecticides, even if it appears they might be needed.

Additional Information

The butterfly weed is a host for various butterflies and seems to be a special favorite of the monarch butterfly.

Additional Cultivars or Species

Related species are *A. asperula, A. syriaca,* and *A. incarnata*. A white selection of this last species named 'Ice Ballet' is reported in the literature.

California Poppy

Eschscholzia californica

Zones: 8 and 9
Size: Less than 1 foot to 2 feet tall
Flowers: Variety, including orange and yellow
Bloom Period: Summer

Light Requirement:

The California poppy is the State Flower of California, but it is adapted to climatic conditions all over the United States, including Louisiana. The plant features multiple branching and blue-green leaves that are somewhat lacy in appearance. It is estimated that there are over fifty different, distinguishable flower colors, but the list of named varieties is not that long. Flowers of wild plants are usually either orange or yellow in color; garden varieties may be of several other colors, but upon re-seeding, they tend to revert back to the color of the wild species. In our mild climate, the California poppy may bloom most of the summer, but the foliage turns a straw color once blooming is over. Spaces to be planted with this perennial should be well prepared in advance of direct-seeding. It might be interesting to try growing this wildflower just to see how well you can get it to perform in the conditions you have to offer.

When to Plant

Plant in October and early November.

Where to Plant

Plantings in our state must be located in full sun on well-drained soils in order to succeed.

How to Plant

The first step is to mechanically or chemically eliminate competing species. Till the soil to a shallow depth to encourage sprouting of any seed present in the top layer, water to further encourage the germination, then re-till at no greater depth to kill any seedlings that respond. Rake the soil level, removing any litter, debris, or extraneous material. Mix seed with sand to aid in better distribution and broadcast over the prepared area. Use about $3^1/_2$ ounces of seed for each 1000 square feet of space. Rake lightly to mix seed with surface soil, then gently tamp or roll with a heavy roller to assure good seed-to-soil contact. Keep the area moist for several days, but don't expect any action before the following spring.

Care and Maintenance

Once the planting is well established, your major task is to help keep down invading species that are native to the region. Pull up these pioneer species or smear them with a systemic herbicide.

Additional Information

The flowers of this species close at night, and sometimes even on overcast days. Various birds find the seeds delectable. Once established, California poppies re-seed freely.

Additional Cultivars or Species

'Cherry Ripe', 'Milky White', and 'Purple-Violet' are just three garden forms of many—but it's probably better to select the species from the beginning. The garden forms easily revert to the wild types that are predominately orange and yellow.

Cardinal Flower

Lobelia cardinalis

Zones: 8 and 9
Size: 2 to 4 feet tall
Flowers: Deep red, small
Bloom Period: Summer

Light Requirement:

While not necessarily uncommon, the cardinal flower is far from abundant in Louisiana. Its best performance is on rather fertile soils that contain substantial amounts of organic matter and remain cool and moist during the growing season. Due to these preferences, it's no surprise to find that its neighbors are frequently various types of ferns. Indeed, cardinal flower might be thought of as a bog plant. While partial shade is where this perennial does best, it doesn't reject sites in deeper shade. The flowers are borne on a tall stalk and are loosely clustered along the terminal end for a distance of a foot or more. They are of a deep red color, and each is from 1 to $1^1/_2$ inches in length. Since they resemble a honeysuckle flower in form and a red salvia in color, they attract both hummingbirds and butterflies. Self-seeding is the main method by which this plant multiplies, but small plants that develop from the joints of mature stems bent over and partly covered with soil (a form of layering) may be transplanted with reasonable success. Moving established plants is difficult and failures are frequent. If you have suitable growing conditions and have access to a cardinal flower, plant one and give it the proper care. You just may find you have a treasure in plant form.

When to Plant

Plant seed in October; plant seedlings and small plants when they are of sufficient size.

Where to Plant

You must choose a moderate-shade location, and the site must have a constantly moist, organically rich soil.

How to Plant

Prepare a loose seedbed and distribute seed evenly over its surface, in October or early November. Plant only small areas. Rake seed lightly into the soil surface and tamp them lightly for good seed-to-soil contact. Keep the soil moist at all times. Move seedlings located near the mother plant, or layered plants, to new sites when they are of sufficient size (but not when they're in flower). Plant at the same depth they were growing on the original site, and mulch around them to prevent the soil from drying. Maintain a good moisture level in the soil, just as for seed. If you are able to purchase plants from a retail nursery or garden center, handle them in the same way.

Care and Maintenance

Little care is needed except to maintain an adequate level of moisture in the soil, to keep a light mulch around the plant, and to eliminate any other plants that attempt to crowd this flower too much. Weak stems may need some support and will benefit from a convenient stake to which they can be tied. Trace amounts of a slow-release fertilizer of fairly low analysis may be used on a trial basis to encourage better performance.

Additional Information

The cardinal flower makes a nice show when located near bodies of water such as a creek bank or a shaded pond or bayou. Swamp edges are also good places . . . but how many people live at the edge of a swamp?

Additional Cultivars or Species

L. erinus is an annual commonly used for edging purposes. *L. gerardii* is a perennial, a hybrid with *L. cardinalis* as one of its parents. Some cultivars of this species are 'Vedrariensis' (royal purple flowers), 'Rosea' (rose pink flowers), and 'Ruby Slippers' (dark-red flowers). *L. syphilitica* is a perennial with blue flowers. Cultivars of *L. cardinalis* that may be of interest are 'Pink Flamingo' (orange-red flowers) and 'Angel Song' (salmon). Additional hybrids that are reported to have larger plants and flowers are 'Queen Victoria' and 'St. Elmo's Fire'.

Coral Bean

Erythrina herbacea

Other Names: Mamou, Cherokee Bean
Zones: 8 and 9
Size: 6 feet tall and 4 feet wide
Flowers: Bright red
Bloom Period: Summer and fall into frost

Light Requirement:

The coral bean is one of only two shrub species in a genus comprised mostly of trees. It is a native of the state and may be found as a single specimen or in small colonies of plants, but seldom in abundance. While its best performance is on sandy soils of average-or-above fertility, coral bean will grow and survive on poor soils even during periods of climatic stress. A plant may have a solitary stem, or it may have several stems that rise from a fleshy, tuberous root-type structure. Since most plants in Louisiana (except perhaps in the southernmost areas) freeze back to the ground during the winter, the plant generally attains a height of only about three feet, with a spread of four to five feet. When not the victim of freezes, the coral bean can grow to be eight to ten feet high and almost as wide. The beauty of this perennial species lies not only in its bright red flowers, but also in the very hard, shiny red beans that are exposed when the legume-like pod opens. The mature beans cling tightly to the dark-brown mature pod which makes a very nice contrasting background color. Fruit (pod) production is usually very skimpy if the plants are growing in much shade. The coral bean is regarded as pest-free, but not surprisingly, the red flowers get the attention of passing hummingbirds. The flowers often bloom during summer and fall and may last until frost.

When to Plant

Plan to plant seed or parts of divided clumps in October or the first part of November. Do not expect to see any plants before the next growing season.

Where to Plant

Plants will do best when planted in a fertile but light-textured sandy soil that's well drained. Seek out sites that offer full sun, or locate plantings at the edges of woodland-type areas that are bathed with a dappled light that comes through tall, high-branched trees.

How to Plant

Before planting coral bean, clear the area of existing plant species using either mechanical or chemical methods, and till the soil to a 4- to 6-inch depth. Mix a small amount of a slow-release fertilizer of relatively low analysis into the top part of the disturbed soil, then either set out rooted parts of divided clumps or plant the seed. Set out the pieces of clump about 2 feet apart at about the same depth they were originally growing; place the seed 6 inches to a foot apart in 1- to 2-inch-deep holes. Water the planting space thoroughly, and cover with a light mulch of available organic materials. Keep the area moist until natural rainfall takes over.

Care and Maintenance

As is true of most wildflowers, little care is required. Help reduce competition by pulling up invading weeds from time to time—and just a very little slow-release fertilizer in late spring may be of benefit.

Additional Information

"Pretty but deadly" is an accurate way to describe the colorful beans of the coral bean plant. *These beans are extremely poisonous!* The dried pods with beans attached are occasionally used in dried floral designs.

Additional Cultivars or Species

The Tambookie thorn, *E. acanthocarpa,* is the only other plant in the genus that has structural similarities, but it grows at higher latitudes where temperatures are much cooler. It is not suitable for planting in Louisiana.

Coreopsis

Coreopsis tinctoria

Other Names: Annual Coreopsis, Calliopsis, Plains Coreopsis
Zones: 8 and 9
Size: 1 1/2 to 3 feet tall
Flowers: Yellow, maroon, and orange
Bloom Period: Late spring

Light Requirement:

The annual coreopsis is a common roadside resident of Louisiana, but it also finds a home on private properties throughout the state. It may be seen giving its golden-yellow color to large expanses, or it can be a bright component of mixed wildflower plantings that are confined to small areas or pocket gardens. Its late-spring bloom often borders on the realm of the spectacular as thousands of plants bloom simultaneously in large patches that border some of Louisiana's interstates. And this plant's flowers are not always yellow; the annual coreopsis can boast of flower colors that include bronze, maroon, orange, and even a reddish hue. Banding on the petals is a characteristic that is common to all the flowers, and purplish-brown centers bind the colorful ray petals together. Sandy soils of various types are well suited for growing this annual species of coreopsis, but it will grow on many kinds of soil if there is good drainage. Full sun is necessary. In cooler regions north of Louisiana, the annual coreopsis blooms for much of the growing season, but our hot and humid climate generally confines its major bloom to the mid- and late-spring months. You may mow the plants down to regain a more aesthetic appearance to the spaces they occupy; coreopsis re-seeds itself easily when seed are allowed to mature on the plant before the plants are mown.

When to Plant

Plant seed in the months of October or November so they'll be ready to come up and perform the following spring.

Where to Plant

Select a sunny, well-drained site, preferably one where the flowers can be conveniently viewed when they are at their peak of bloom.

How to Plant

Prepare the soil loosely with a tiller to a 3- to 5-inch depth, then water to encourage sprouting of any weed seed that is present. Re-till after new seedlings appear, and level the soil with a garden rake to create a smooth surface free of clods and other non-soil items. Broadcast the seed (mixed with an equal volume of sand) evenly over the seedbed to help get good plant distribution, and then lightly rake the soil to incorporate seed into the very top layer. The suggested rate of seeding is just under 1 ounce per 1000 square feet. Tamp or press with a heavy roller to ensure good seed-to-soil contact, and finish with a gentle soaking that won't wash the seed to the surface. A moderately thin mulching with an organic material is advisable to keep pounding winter rains from eroding the planted surface.

Care and Maintenance

Once established, this very hardy species should be able to stand most adversities of the weather. It may be possible to slightly extend the period of bloom by keeping the spent flowers removed on a regular basis. Invading perennials of other kinds of plants may be removed or chemically destroyed by smearing individual plants with appropriate systemic herbicides. (Just don't spray.) Reducing the competition by such actions will favor the coreopsis.

Additional Information

There are both dwarf varieties and varieties with double flowers.

Additional Cultivars or Species

C. lanceolata is the most commonly used garden species. One of the hybrid cultivars that may have *C. tinctoria* as a parent is 'Mardi Gras', which has large variegated blossoms. All of the coreopsis but *C. tinctoria* are perennial.

Evening Primrose

Oenothera speciosa

Other Names: Buttercup, Mexican Evening Primrose
Zones: 8 and 9
Size: Approximately 1 foot tall
Flowers: Pinkish to white
Bloom Period: Spring to summer

Light Requirement:

One of the first places you may notice these plants blooming every year is close to the pavement of the roads you travel, often in the gravel of the road shoulders. Did you ever wonder why they were thriving in such a stressful place? It's because they are one of a few plants that can withstand thin, compacted soils that are alkaline from the materials of road construction and where water is often limited. While the plant can grow under stressful conditions, it may also be found in more favorable environments. But wherever evening primrose is found, you'll appreciate the thin pinkish-to-white blossoms that open in the evening and allow their fragrance to waft out onto the breezes to beckon some insects in for the sweet nectar . . . which they pay for by pollinating the flower. Individual flowers are open only for one day but are replaced by flowers from new buds that open to succeed them. The earliest blossoms are around $2^1/_2$ inches across when the flowers begin blooming in the spring, but their size is noticeably reduced when they encounter the greater stress of early summer. Colonies of several to several hundred plants are far more common than are single specimens.

When to Plant

Plant the evening primrose in the fall, preferably during October and into early November.

Where to Plant

Choose a site that can offer a full day of sun and a well-drained sandy soil, preferably one that's slightly alkaline.

How to Plant

Till the soil to a 3- or 4-inch depth a few weeks before planting time, and moisten to sprout any seeds it contains. After seedlings emerge, re-till to destroy them, but don't go deeper than the original tilling depth. Rake to level the surface and to remove clods and other non-soil items. When smooth, scatter seed evenly over the soil at the rate of 2 ounces per 1000 square feet and barely cover them with soil by raking lightly. Tamp or roll to improve seed-to-soil contact, then water gently so that the seed don't get washed out of the soil. Cover the area with a moderately thin mulch to help prevent winter erosion. Plants should appear in the spring months of the following year.

Care and Maintenance

Evening primrose plants should be able to grow and spread without any help after they are established. If other species intrude and threaten the planting, pull them out and/or smear a systemic herbicide such as Roundup® over their foliage. There will be insects, but just ignore them. Mow plants in late June or early July after the seed have matured.

Additional Information

If full-sun sites are not available, evening primroses will grow in very light shade, but they probably won't bloom quite as well. The Mexican primrose, unlike many other *Oenothera* species, blooms during the day rather than in the evening.

Additional Cultivars or Species

'Alba' has white flowers; 'Woodside White' has white flowers that change to pink as they age. 'Siskiyou' has light-pink blossoms; it seems to be a bit more vigorous and have a longer flowering period than the species.

Indian Blanket

Gaillardia pulchella

Other Names: Blanket Flower, Firewheel	**Light Requirement:**
Zones: 8 and 9	
Size: $1^1/_2$ to 2 feet tall	
Flowers: Gold, red, yellow, and white	
Bloom Period: Summer	

Here is an almost care-free wildflower that will reward those who get it started with masses of color. A native of the southern plains, it goes on with its business of coloring the earth in spite of heat or drought or other adverse elements that take a toll on less hardy species. The flower heads average about two inches in diameter and dazzle the eye with their various hues of yellow and gold and red. One variety of Indian blanket has no ray petals, so the flower has a ball-shaped appearance; other varieties have blossoms that are nearly white in color.

When to Plant

Plant in the spring after the frost-free date, when the soil has absorbed enough of the sun's energy to begin to feel warm to the touch.

Where to Plant

Plant this colorful annual wherever you need some quick and dependable color; it's hard to go wrong with this flower. Just give it plenty of sun.

How to Plant

There's no need to make a big fuss about planting this flower. Simply till up a patch of soil, rake it level, and scatter the seed over the surface. A suggested amount is about 4 ounces of seed to each 1000 square feet of soil surface. After sowing, rake again (lightly) to mix the seed into the top of the loose soil. Press the soil over the seed with a tamping board, a roller, or whatever you have that will do the job with the least effort. Water the planted space gently but thoroughly, and wait for the seedlings to emerge.

Care and Maintenance

Little care is required by this plant. If other plant species begin to move in and crowd the planting (as might happen on a relatively fertile soil that is supplied with adequate moisture), reduce the competition by eliminating the intruders from time to time.

Additional Information

Once a few plants become established, wind dispersal of the seed will increase their population. These plants produce suitable cut flowers. The Indian blanket is the State Flower of Oklahoma.

Additional Cultivars or Species

G. aristata and *G. grandiflora* are perennial species of this flower and contain several desirable cultivars that should be considered for garden use. 'Gaiety' and 'Lollipop' are well-known strains of the Indian Blanket. 'Lorenziana' (the one with no flower petals), 'Red Plume', and 'Yellow Sun' are recognized varieties of *G. pulchella*.

Purple Coneflower

Echinacea purpurea

Other Names: Prairie Coneflower; *Rudbeckia purpurea*
Zones: 8 and 9
Size: 1½ to 2 feet tall
Flowers: Purplish petals, orange cone
Bloom Period: Summer into fall

Light Requirement:

The purple coneflower is distinguished by its prominent brownish-orange cone and the drooping rosy-purple ray petals that surround its base. Like so many wildflower species, it requires a well-drained soil. It grows best where the soil is neutral or a bit on the alkaline side. Purple coneflower is reported to grow as tall as four to five feet in parts of its native range, but expect a shorter plant in Louisiana, probably from one and one-half to two feet. In time it will develop a large clump which may be divided as a source of plants. Purple coneflower produces an abundance of seed which are relished by birds, especially finches. Uneaten seed are, of course, an important means by which the plant propagates itself. When Louisiana summers get into high gear, so does the purple coneflower, which presents its attractive blossoms at the tips of its stiff stems for all to enjoy. Not one to give up easily, the perennial puts out sporadic blooms well into the fall season; occasionally, there are a few left to greet the first frost.

When to Plant

Divide and plant "clump" plants in October or early November. Seeds may also be planted during this time period. Plants purchased from retail firms are often available at other times and may be planted soon after purchase if given the necessary care.

Where to Plant

Plant in full sun on well-drained soils. After it's well established, don't worry about watering; it's very much accustomed to arid conditions.

How to Plant

First reduce competition from other plants by eliminating them by either mechanical or chemical means. Well-entrenched perennial species may require the use of systemic herbicides. Set the clump division plants or the purchased plants 2 or 3 feet apart (at the same depth they were previously growing) in ground that has been disturbed about 3 inches deep. Keep the soil moist until the plants seem to be making it on their own, then gradually wean them from the bountiful supply of moisture and let natural rainfall take over. If all goes well, flowers should appear the following summer. Prepare for seeding in the same manner, then distribute the seed over the soil surface at a rate of about 5 ounces per 1000 square feet of area to be planted. Mix seed with sand at a 1:1 ratio to help avoid crowding of the seedlings. Tamp the planted surface lightly after a gentle raking to incorporate the seeds into the soil. Finish the task with a slow but thorough watering. Don't be concerned if no seedlings appear; you'll probably not see them until the next growing season. Remember, with wildflowers, patience is the word.

Care and Maintenance

Since the purple coneflower handles adverse climatic conditions with apparent ease, little care is needed. Watch for invading plants of other kinds and eliminate them as necessary to reduce competition. It is also suggested that spent flowers be removed from time to time, as this practice will extend the period of flowering.

Additional Information

Flowering plants are an excellent source of good-quality cut flowers for floral designs. Medicines are made from components of this species.

Additional Cultivars or Species

Both 'Magnus' and 'Bright Star' are selections that have ray petals that are rosy red and rosy pink, respectively, instead of the typical purple color. 'White Swan' and 'White Lustre' are two white-petaled cultivars. *E. pallida* is a similar species with pale purple flowers.

SOURCES

Bibliography

American Rose Society, The. *1997 Handbook for Selecting Roses*. Shreveport, Louisiana. 1997.

Bailey, L. H. and E. Z. *Hortus Third*. New York: Macmillan Publishing Co., Inc. 1978. Third Printing.

Dirr, Michael A. *Manual of Woody Landscape Plants-Their Identification, Ornamental Characteristics, Culture, Propagation and Uses*. Champaign, Illinois: Stipes Publishing Co. Revised, 1990. Fourth Edition.

Doughty, Severn C. *Identifying and Growing Palms in the New Orleans Area*. Orleans Extension Publication. 1992.

Hill, Madalene and Gwen Barclay with Jean Hardy. *Southern Herb Growing*. Fredericksburg, Texas: Shearer Publishing. 1987.

McNair, James K. *All About Roses*. San Francisco, California: Ortho Books, Chevron Chemical Company. 1976.

Odenwald, Neil and James Turner. *Identification, Selection and Use of Southern Plants for Landscape Design*. Baton Rouge, Louisiana: Claitor's Publishing Division. 1996. Third Edition.

Ogden, Scott. *Garden Bulbs for the South*. Dallas, Texas: Taylor Publishing Company. 1994.

Phillips, Roger and Martyn Rix. *Roses*. New York: Random House. 1988.

Seidenberg, Charlotte. *The New Orleans Garden*. Jackson, Mississippi: University Press of Mississippi. 1993.

Still, Steven M. *Manual of Herbaceous Ornamental Plants*. Champaign, Illinois: Stipes Publishing Co. 1994.

Sunset National Garden Book. Menlo Park, California: Sunset Books, Inc. 1997.

Welch, William C. *Perennial Garden Color*. Dallas, Texas: Taylor Publishing. 1989.

Welch, William C. and Greg Grant. *The Southern Heirloom Garden*. Dallas, Texas: Taylor Publishing. 1995.

Wilson, Jim. *South Carolina Gardener's Guide*. Franklin, Tennessee: Cool Springs Press, Inc. 1997.

Louisiana's Gardens

LOUISIANA HOLDS SPECIAL PLEASURES for visitors who enjoy spectacular gardens—hilly and swampy, urban and rural, traditional and modern. From the spring blaze of azaleas at plantations, parks and public gardens to the miles of roadside wildflowers planted by citizens' groups in many parts of the state, flower watching becomes a big part of almost any outdoor activity. Below is a listing of some of these gardens. Call in advance to obtain calendars of gardening events along with standard hours of operation.

Avery Island

Jungle Gardens and Bird City
Highway 329 Avery Island
318/369-6243

Baton Rouge

Burden Research Plantation
I-10 at Essen Lane
504/763-3990

Cohn Arboretum
12206 Foster Road
504/775-1006

Louisiana State University Hilltop Arboretum
11855 Highland Road
504/767-6916

State Capitol Grounds
State Capitol Drive at Third Street
504/342-3717

Windrush Gardens/Rural Life Museum
4600 Essen Lane
504/765-7437

Bourg

Le Jardin Sur Le Bayou Bed and Breakfast and Gardens
256 Lower Country Drive
504/594-2722

Burnside

Houmas House Plantation and Gardens
40136 Highway 942
504/473-7841

Donaldsonville

Donaldsonville Elementary School Nature Trail
38210 Highway 30
504/474-2720

Gibson

Wildlife Gardens
5306 N. Bayou Black Drive
504/575-3676

Greenwood

American Rose Center
8677 Jefferson-Paige Road
318/938-5402

Hammond

Zenmurray Gardens
LA Highway 442
504/878-9777

Jefferson Island

Rip Van Winkle Gardens
5505 Rip Van Winkle Road
318/365-3332

Sources

Lafitte
Victoria Inn and Gardens
Highway 45, Box 545B
504/689-4757

Many
Hodges Gardens
Highway 171
318/586-3523

Monroe
Elsong Gardens
2006 Riverside Drive
318/387-5281

Louisiana Purchase Gardens and Zoo
Highway 165 and Standifer Road
318/329-2400

Morgan City
Original Swamp Gardens
725 Myrtle Street
504/384-3343

Natchitoches
Briarwood
Highway 9
318/576-3523

New Orleans
Heymann Conservatory at Audubon Park
St. Charles Avenue/Magazine Street
504/891-2419

Longue Vue House and Gardens
7 Bamboo Road
504/488-5488

Ruston
Rock Corner Garden of Prayer
Louisiana Highway 83, north of Ruston
318/255-2031

Louisiana Tech Arboretum
Tech Farm Road/Louisiana Tech University
318/257-2879

St Francisville
Afton Villa Gardens
US Highway 61
504/635-6773

Audubon State Commemorative Area
South of St. Francisville via US 61 and LA 965
888/677-2838 • 504/635-3739

Rosedown Plantation and Gardens
12501 Highway 10
504/635-3332

Shreveport
Barnwell Art and Garden Center
501 Clyde Fant Parkway
318/673-7703

Old Covered Bridge Garden
6905 Greenwood Road
318/635-6296

Ville Platte
Louisiana State Arboretum
4213 Chicot Park Road (LA Highway 3042)
888/677-6100 • 318/363-6289

Courtesy of the Louisiana Office of Tourism.

INDEX

Index

Index

Index

Index

Index

Index

Index

ABOUT THE AUTHORS

DAN GILL is a horticultural agent for Orleans Parish: a position he has held with the LSU Agricultural Center/Extension Service for nearly twenty years. Best known to New Orleans area listeners as the popular radio host of The WSMB Garden Show, Gill is featured weekly in gardening segments on The Channel 4 Morning Show. Readers of the *Times-Picayune* have long benefitted from Gill's weekly column, The Weekend Gardener.

Gill received the bachelor and master degrees in horticultural from Louisiana State University. The author has been recognized for horticultural achievement by numerous groups including The Louisiana Garden Club Federation, The Metro-area Horticulture Foundation and the Friends of City Park.

Gill gardens in the historic New Orleans neighborhood of Algiers Point. His enthusiastically planted gardens reflect the style and architecture of his nineteenth-century Victorian home.

JOE WHITE serves as the LSU area agent in horticulture for several northwestern Louisiana parishes. White has been with the Louisiana Agricultural Center/Extension Service for twenty-five years.

A popular columnist, White's weekly garden columns have run in the *Shreveport Times* since 1972. His gardening information has also been featured regularly on Shreveport radio stations during that same time, and many persons have benefitted from ıe numerous short courses on various plant topics he has taught on three local 3hreveport) college campuses.

/hite holds three degrees in horticulture including the Ph.D. from Louisiana tate University. The author serves as editor of the R.S. Barnwell Memorial arden and Art Center newsletter and helps coordinate the horticultural segient of the Center's educational program.

'hite has been honored for his gardening accomplishments and service by umerous organizations. He was the 1980 recipient of the Floyd S. Edmiston ward of Excellence in Extensions Programs.

/hite lives in Shreveport where he and his wife and daughter carefully tend ıeir acre garden.